D1161274

Ceramic Art in Finland

Ceramic Art in Finland

A contemporary tradition

Edited by Åsa Hellman

Thames & Hudson

First published in the United Kingdom in 2004 by
Thames & Hudson Ltd, 181A High Holborn,
London WC1V 7QX

www.thamesandhudson.com

First published in 2004 in hardcover in the United States of America by
Thames & Hudson Inc., 500 Fifth Avenue
New York, New York 10110

thamesandhudsonusa.com

© 2004 Authors and Otava Publishing Company Ltd

Original title: Taidekeramiikka Suomessa

Translations from Finnish by Malcolm Hicks
Pages 19–48, 58–64, 256–260, 272 and captions 65–249
Translations from Swedish by Eva Malkki
Pages 49–57, 65–249 and 261–271

Photographer: Johnny Korkman
Picture Editors: Hannele Nyman and Åsa Hellman

British Library Cataloguing-in-Publication Data
A catalogue record for this book is available from the British Library

Library of Congress Catalog Card Number 2004102108

ISBN 0-500-51187-X

Printed and bound in Finland

Contents

Jatta Lavi

Soile Paasonen

Foreword

Alfred William Finch's signature.
Porvoon museum. Photo: Jan Lindroth/
Porvoo museum.

A. W. Finch, seen by many as the father of Finnish ceramics, supposedly said: 'Woman is Man in Finland.' In actual fact, most ceramic artists in Finland are women. Initially only well-to-do family girls were taught the art of ceramics. Those who wished to pursue a career in this field had to abandon thoughts of married life and sacrifice the social status associated with marriage. They had to make their choices, i.e. opt not to belong, quite early in life.

Critics assumed a condescending tone when reviewing work by women artists; they were simply ladies playing the game of art. Sigrid af Forselles (1860–1935), sculptor and ceramic artist, no doubt led an exciting life in younger years but died alone in Florence with hardly any recognition of her contribution to art. Her contemporary Sigrid Granfelt (1868–1942) was a ceramist and highly educated painter of animals. She received negative reviews and soon abandoned fine arts in favour of ceramics and textiles. Many competent ceramists did not have the heart to pursue careers in the field.

Today, at the beginning of the twenty-first century, things have changed. Women have babies, complete their university degrees and manage successful ceramics studios, all at the same time. There has been a change for the better although it still is challenging to survive financially as a ceramist for men and women alike. Artefacts imported from countries where labour is cheaper, make most crafts economically unviable in industrially developed, expensive countries. Today's ceramists are also forced to make clear choices between a vast range of materials and techniques. Some get lost in endless experimentation, unable to focus on a personal style or genre. It is still a question of choice.

I wish to express my profound thanks to everyone who has contributed to this book: first and foremost my co-authors Airi Hortling, Harri Kalha, Marjut Kumela, Esa Laaksonen, Hannele Nyman and Jennifer Opie. Quite apart from their specific roles, each has given invaluable advice and support. Photographer Johnny Korkman's sensitive approach to every object and Hannele Nyman's keen attention to the photographic content are highly appreciated. With her international publishing experience, Solveig Williams has been instrumental in bringing about the English language edition of this book.

The facts in this volume are based on several years of intensive research in museum archives, private collections and among the shelves of antique dealers. Tedious hours were occasionally rewarded with amazing discoveries of signed pieces that revealed significant, long since forgotten names and fascinating personalities.

8

Special thanks are due to writer Carl-Fredrik Sandelin and scenographer Antti Laakkonen who made significant contributions by collecting archival information. Other individuals, companies and organizations who have supported the publication financially and otherwise are separately and specifically acknowledged on page 251.

In Finland, works of ceramic art have always been of a lower rank than paintings or glassware, to pick something in the field of applied arts. Countless books have been published about Finnish sculptors, painters and architects but there are few on ceramic artists. Many ceramists who were once celebrated and culturally significant are now largely forgotten. This is particularly true of artists who were not connected to Arabia, the all-important corporation within the Finnish ceramics industry.

The aim of this book is to provide a record of ceramic artists in Finland and to give them their rightful place in Finnish art history. This should strengthen personal and professional identities. This book is equally directed toward professionals, ceramics enthusiasts and collectors who, until now, have had no work of reference in this field. To serve all has at times been problematic. As in all works of this type and magnitude, the desire to be comprehensive at some point collides with the need to be concise, and as a consequence there are talented artists who could not be included. I ask for their understanding.

This volume encompasses ceramic art engendered from individuals' desire to create. Some sculptors and traditional country potters are included, mainly to illustrate that the boundaries between art and craft, between sculpture and functional ware are forever fluid.

Åsa Hellman

JENNIFER HAWKINS OPIE

Some favourite pots and potters;
tracing a course through Finnish ceramics

This light-blue dish of diameter 43 cm stands out from A. W. Finch's other works produced at Iris. Its clear, stylized pattern seems to have gained its inspiration from spruces or lichens and is very Finnish, in contrast to the Central European Art Nouveau style that he normally favoured. Porvoo Museum.
Photo: Jan Lindroth/Porvoo Museum.

Finnish ceramics have never been produced in isolation. From around 1890, the interchanges of personalities and cultural influences have been as varied and as influential as in any other country. This makes tracing their course by means of a few key pots and potters a challenging and salutary experience. The artist-makers are as fascinating as the works themselves. Understanding the human costs, the sacrifices of comfort, company and country, has proved to be as rewarding a means of appreciating the ceramic works as understanding the technical and aesthetic achievements.

Alfred William Finch

In 1883 Anglo-Belgian Alfred William (Willy) Finch became a founder-member of Les Vingts, a progressive, international group of painters which held annual exhibitions in Brussels under the direction of art critic Octave Maus. Through this group and its successor, La Libre Esthetique, Finch met Anna Boch who invited him to her family pottery of Boch Frères at Saint-Vaast in the area of Hainaut, southwest Belgium. Finch's senior by only six years, Boch

used ceramics as an alternative canvas on which to paint landscapes, plants and other subjects in an eighteenth-century manner. In contrast, Finch was to prove himself very much part of the new world of Art Nouveau.

Far from decorating ready-made pots, he learned the skills of throwing and making and the chemistry of slips and glazes for himself. He worked at the pottery for about three years from 1890, and the earliest surviving example of

his ceramics was made around the end of this period.[1] It is an earthenware vase, richly lead-glazed in greens and browns, with painted slip decoration. It is traditional in concept and technique, like the plain and decorated folk ware that had been made across Europe throughout the nineteenth century and for several hundred years before that. The difference is that Finch's pot is by his own hand — that of the self-conscious artist searching for a new form of art. Nevertheless, although we may find in its painted decoration some echo of the contemporary fashion for Art Nouveau, in comparison with his later ceramic work it is clear that his real engagement with the style occurred only after his arrival in Finland.

Finch moved from Belgium to Finland in 1897, at the invitation of the Swedish count Louis Sparre. By then Finch had exhibited his ceramic work on a number of occasions, and his knowledge of the material, his enthusiasm and his increasing skill were clearly appreciated by Sparre. Nevertheless, the conversations that persuaded him to make this move must have been interesting. Finch had not been to Finland before. Had he any idea of the landscape, the weather, the people? Did he anticipate that he was to stay there for the rest of his life? Was he content to be invited not as a maker or painter but as a designer and factory director? Porvoo occupied a key position on the route between Helsinki and St Petersburg, but in moving there Finch and his wife surely had to embrace a very different world from that of metropolitan Brussels.

In 1897 Sparre's idealistic commitment to his company, AB Iris, would have been infectious, and his friend Axel Gallén (Akseli Gallen-Kallela) was equally enthusiastic. Like William Morris before him, Sparre was committed to designs which were both artistic and practical, made of quality materials by skilled craftsmanship. Commerciality was not part of his plan, but of course it proved to be essential, and elusive: the enterprise lasted a mere five years. But in that time, Sparre opened a shop in Helsinki where AB Iris's own production was sold as well as fabrics and wallpapers from the London shop Liberty.[2] AB Iris designed interiors for clients in St Petersburg and supplied La Maison Moderne, the avant-garde shop established by Julius Meier-Graefe in Paris. Finch, who by 1897 had taken up potting as passionately as he had painting, was offered the opportunity to set up an entirely new and ambitious ceramics production.

The range of ceramics made by AB Iris was surprisingly large, from tableware and tiles to planters and lighting. The company's ceramics catalogue was issued in four languages (Swedish, Finnish, German and French). In general, Finch's designs for decoration were a succinct synthesis of the ubiquitous, sinuous line instantly recognizable across Europe as Art Nouveau, and local Finnish materials and techniques. Under his direction and that of foreman Gustaf Sjöblom, who was hired in 1899, this line was rendered with simple brush-strokes in slip, or cut through the limited palette of green and blue slips to the local red clay. This type of ware was common at the time: the ceramics of Theodor Hermann Schmuz-Baudiss in Germany are among the most comparable to those of Finch, as was his career. After earlier success as a painter, Schmuz-Baudiss abandoned this for ceramics in the 1890s and eventually became art director at the imperial porcelain factory in Berlin. But in the 1890s his ceramics, like Finch's, were of local red earthenware, in simple forms with incised and slip-painted decoration. Elsewhere in Germany, Elizabeth Schmidt-Pecht, working near Lake Konstanz, made ceramics with slip-decoration or incised ornament which she also showed at the World's Fair in Paris in 1900. Similarly semi-rustic wares were made with the art market in mind by C. H. Brannam in Somerset, England. Like the Porvoo ceramics, all these are of local red earthenware, in a generally recognizable Art Nouveau style. But there is one dish by Finch for AB Iris which springs out for its 'Finnishness' and surely here is the evidence that he had absorbed the cultural lessons of his new homeland.

This dish is quite unlike any Iris ceramics advertised in the factory's catalogue of standard production. No other ceramic designed by Finch of this type is known. For display rather than use, it has a sophisticated, elegant summary of a plant-like pattern around the rim which probably derives from either spruce or lichen, a well-established motif in Finnish textile patterning. Axel Gallén used a similar motif on the textile furnishings for the Iris Room in the Paris Pavilion and it seems very possible that the two men discussed this design. Although the motif is not unique in Finch's work, the dish has far more crisply incised decoration than the standard wares and an unusually pale blue colouring.[3] On its base it is marked in incised script A. W. F. (for Finch) IRIS FINLAND, and it has the impressed monogram of LMM for La Maison Moderne. It is undated but otherwise these are the standard markings for Iris production. It is thought to have been in the possession of Edvard Rindell, a Latin teacher at the local boys' school in Porvoo, whose house was built around 1900 and largely furnished by Louis Sparre.

Was this dish made by an independent pottery rather than AB Iris's own? At the time there was only one other local pottery, C. E. Green, but no connection between this and Iris has been researched. With its La Maison Moderne backstamp, could it have been made as a prototype for the Paris shop? If so, and

the dish was sent to Paris, did it generate any interest? Was a whole firing or more of these sold in Paris; are there others now in France, or even further afield, that have not been recognized? Or was the supply of Iris ceramics to Paris discontinued before the company's final demise in 1902? We know that La Maison Moderne took far less of the production than anticipated and much of it remained in Finland. Was this remarkable dish made too late to save the company? Did it remain in Porvoo to be offered as part of Sparre's furnishing of Rindell's house?[4] Did Rindell recognize its quality and buy it direct? Finch, the cosmopolitan European, came to ceramics with a highly sophisticated understanding of what could be achieved. With this dish he reached a summit. It is unique, and an enigma; a crisp, smart, confident design incised and fired with a skill and panache unmatched by any other known ceramic designed or made by Finch.

Maija Grotell

After the closure of Iris, Finch became the first head teacher of a new ceramics course at the Central School of Industrial Art (now the University of Art and Design Helsinki) attached to the Atheneum gallery. Privately, he painted and continued with his own ceramics in Helsinki. In 1979 he was described as 'one of Europe's finest pioneer artist-potters' in a biographical note on Maija Grotell, one of his last postgraduate students.[5] Grotell was herself a pioneer, taking this commitment to America and,

in her turn, infusing it into a generation of American makers with her own brand of instinctive dedication.

After graduating in painting, design and sculpture, Grotell was in the group of students under Finch who specialized in the study of the technique and artistry of ceramics — with no hope of earning a living outside of factory production. Later, teaching would supply the means, but in the 1920s there was only one teaching post and that was occupied by Finch, followed by Grotell's contemporary Elsa Elenius. There were no other ceramic courses. The possibility of setting up a studio-workshop, as the financially independent Bernard Leach did in England in 1920, did not occur in Finland until much later. Presumably both the economic and political situation of those decades militated against it. So Maija Grotell followed the emigrant route and moved to America in 1927, aged twenty-eight. After nearly ten years of further study and teaching and the award of a silver medal at the Paris International Exposition in 1937, she was finally invited to join Cranbrook by her fellow Finn, Eliel Saarinen, in 1938. By then she had enormous practical experience and was a mature artist.

Established in 1904 as a group of private art schools, Cranbrook Academy of Art was developed in the 1920s into a community where practising artists could live, work and teach in a stimulating and sympathetic environment. The Academy was headed by Finnish architect Eliel Saarinen, who designed

furnishings and a group of buildings set in superb garden grounds. Saarinens, enlisted the artists, and on her arrival Grotell joined an all-Scandinavian faculty composed of Eliel and Loja Saarinen, weaver Marianne Strengell and Swedish sculptor Carl Milles.

Many of Grotell's ceramics meet the predictable Cranbrook aesthetic. They are classics of Modernism. The forms are monumentally simple vehicles for Grotell's superb and well-fitting glazes. Her belief in ceramic as a serious medium for artistic expression and in the celebration of clay handled with skill and total control was part of her inheritance from Finch. She was an independent artist and, in the making of non-functional, unique works as an expression of her own artistry, she knew she was engaged in the highest of the ceramic arts. Her sense of moral superiority was unshakeable. But from her earliest years, she had also picked up an interest in surface decoration other than the classic glazes. There is a two-handled bowl of 1924 in the Design Museum in Helsinki with painted decoration of a milkmaid, with a yoke and two buckets, flanked either side by tulips. And she was still making pots with this type of painted decoration at Cranbrook.

During the 1940s, this unexpectedly folksy style was overtaken by other pots with curiously expensive decoration of raised motifs of repeated spiky zigzag patterning highlighted with platinum. These sit uneasily in a world which now values her classic, glazed wares most of all. But it is worth remembering that Cranbrook was always an extremely smart, expensive environment, with the Saarinens' bespoke furnishings setting the pace, using the most elegant of Art Deco styling.

With the skill that underpins her mastery of the art, Grotell was able to synthesize these apparently conflicting concepts. One of the best examples of this is a globular vase, known as *Opalescent Sphere*, now in the American Museum of Arts & Design in New York.[6] Made in 1953, it is covered with a streaked slip glaze, overlaying a randomly repeated, sometimes overlapping patterning of raised slip motifs. At first these motifs and their execution seem to form part of a continuum with the abstract repeated patterning which was by then one of Grotell's trademarks. But

they also suggest a snowy landscape and branched shapes. Maybe they are antlers? Perhaps fir trees? Even without firm evidence, it is easy to imagine Grotell, the emigrant-immigrant, recalling Finnish memories. A comment included in the tender little book, *Maija Grotell: Works Which Grow From Belief*, says that 'she liked sitting in Battery Park (New York), looking towards the Narrows, thinking about Finland and the same water touching both shores'.[7] Grotell's influence on her students shines through the affectionate interviews with her in this book by the American potters Jeff Schlanger and Toshiko Takaezu.

From Finch to Grotell, the mythologizing of clay had been set in motion. The essential steps had been taken in elevating the status of the potter from artisan to artist, from artist to hero.

Grotell was succeeded at Cranbrook by Richard DeVore in 1966. Ten years before that, a revolution had begun in American ceramics. Although it resulted in a very different output and apparently stemmed from a radically different view of clay, it was based on several key beliefs which Grotell would have recognized. Abstract Expressionist ceramist Peter Voulkos was, in many senses, the hero of this revolution, which included Rudy Autio, who later spent time at Arabia. Voulkos was a painter, sculptor and printmaker, but his remarkable achievement was in using clay as an equal, if not more appropriate medium for the very physical action-charged engagement that Abstract Expressionism

demanded.[8] The ties binding American ceramics to European heritage were finally being challenged. Grotell represented this link in the most tangible way, but in the meticulous approach by DeVore a continuing thread remained, even as the link was being breached by Voulkos and his circle.

Kyllikki Salmenhaara

In Finland, the Scandinavian ideals of restraint, balance and good design still held, and never more so than in the work of Kyllikki Salmenhaara. Even where she introduced a gritty, local clay, or splashed glazes in an apparently haphazard way, the result is in elegant taste, supremely balanced and utterly desirable. More directly than any of her predecessors, Salmenhaara is credited with establishing the Arabia 'house style'. She perfected the celebrated grey-brown grog-enriched body known as chamotte, revelling in the rough, uncompromising character of clay mixed with burnt and crushed porcelain or stoneware. It rapidly became an Arabia trademark, and its success has been a liberating opportunity for those working within the factory's art studio, and a challenge to find an alternative for those outside. Salmenhaara explored form with unerring honesty, setting herself demanding problems of balance, strength and lightness which she solved with an impeccable combination of daring and control. She used glazes and oxides apparently randomly and yet with sure precision. She radicalized the practice of ceramic art and making in Finland, giving it a national purpose, a highly recognizable identity and confidence on the international stage. She has since become a mythic figure in her home country.

Nevertheless, although so closely identified with Finland, Salmenhaara was very much an international artist. It is easy to make close comparisons between her work and that of ceramic art, design and making abroad. Salmenhaara spent a formative period in England during the 1930s when a lively debate was under way on ceramics, on usefulness and art, on commerciality and the Japanese *mingei undō* folk craft movement, the concept of which was introduced to British ceramics by Bernard Leach. The works of Leach himself, as well as those of William Staite Murray and R. J. Washington, are predecessors to Salmenhaara's own sense of form and texture. Britain-based Lucie Rie and Hans Coper were her contemporaries in the 1950s.

In 1946 newly graduated Salmenhaara spent a year on the Danish island of Bornholm, at Saxbo, the ceramics studio run by chemist Nathalie Krebs and ceramist Eva Staehr-Nielsen. Returning to Helsinki, Salmenhaara took up a place at Arabia in 1947. Following her formative lessons at Bornholm, she continued her experiments with the relative chemistry of clay, glaze and firing, spurning the easy option of relying on the factory to supply materials and technology. In a 1955 review of her ceramics in a British journal, she was described

as 'at the moment perhaps the foremost name in Finnish ceramics…her art…has full universality. Salmenhaara represents the purely ceramic creation, the mass, form and glaze making a complete whole just as her different pieces together show unusual homogeneity and quality of production.'[9]

In 1956 Salmenhaara travelled to America, where she met Marguerite Wildenhain, whose Bauhaus training had given her a highly developed sense of form and an ethical stand on craft, utility and affordability.[10] In her view all ceramic making, from useful wares to the most extreme of artworks, deserved the same attention to detail and the same commitment to material. Salmen-

haara clearly learned from this encounter. Despite a lifelong antipathy to industrial manufacture, she was required to design for Arabia production. On her return she offered some tableware (only a cup was accepted), a rare foray into that world, which was perhaps eased by Wildenhain's influence.[11] Where the two were in immediate agreement was on the absolute necessity of understanding the material and its properties. All else flowed from that understanding; without it the ceramic was impersonal and worthless.

In 1959 and 1960 the American Richard Fairbanks was resident at Arabia on a Fulbright Scholarship. Handsome, enthusiastic and entirely caught

up by Salmenhaara's dynamic artistry, Fairbanks responded to her personality and she to his. Their work developed, and he learned a great deal from her; indeed in the very first year of Fairbanks's residence the similarities were striking. They maintained a lifelong closeness through occasional visits but especially through dozens of touching and affectionate letters, now published by Fairbanks's widow.[12] There are also diary entries for the year Fairbanks spent at Arabia, describing the exchange of gifts and the many Finnish meals cooked by Salmenhaara for him.

Perhaps it needed an American to observe, as Fairbanks did, that the trip to the USA in 1956 may have generated Salmenhaara's late 1950s' sense of landscape and colour.[13] The imperative to manage form and balance had always been there, but the introduction of shimmering blues and greens is the clearest indication that something fundamental had happened. Although she never allowed control to slip, what was new was her willingness to engage with sculptural qualities, to manage colours which were no longer confined to the rusts, browns and greys of Finnish landscapes, and to allow – even welcome – the accidental, whether it be a splash of colour or an erupting oxide.

In her letters to Fairbanks after his return to the USA, Salmenhaara is revealed as highly strung, sometimes difficult and lonely, alluding to the many small rivalries and jealousies that were bound to emerge in the small working unit that was Arabia's art department.[14] Salmenhaara's career at Arabia came to an abrupt end early in 1960, while Fairbanks was still there, when her right hand was catastrophically damaged by a rusty blade left in the clay she was using. For more than a year she was unable to throw.[15] Although she recovered enough to continue her own work, her hand was permanently damaged and the anguish of a thwarted artist almost certainly led to considerable bitterness.

After this traumatic year, Salmenhaara left Arabia, travelled to Taiwan, and took up teaching. From 1963, taking over from Elsa Elenius, she spent nearly twenty years at what was by then the Institute of Applied Arts, at the Atheneum. In 1985, four years after her early death from cancer, a former student, Henrik Gröhn, wrote an illuminating letter in her memory recalling her resentment of influences other than her own: 'your wish to lead us forth to your truths by following your "prescriptions" exclusively'.[16]

Difficult, demanding, uncompromising are all characteristics ascribed to Salmenhaara. They underpin the clear evidence that she commanded enormous respect from those who knew her. Her ceramics now speak for her in the most powerful way, confirming how valuable these stubborn characteristics proved to be. But it is also clear that affection for her proved as durable.

Because her life's work was so immense and so varied, and each phase became a major landmark in the development of Finnish ceramics, it is unreasonable to pick on any one type. How could you choose an early bottle over the *Windings or Letters* of the late 1970s? Perhaps the most surprising are the *Flying Saucers*. Sudden breaths of wind, almost weightless, about to take off, they sit within the production of the late 1950s like an unexpected, uncharacteristic aside. Questions hover. Do they work? How far was she prepared to go in risking the tiniest foot beneath the most outstretched saucer? Were they more to her than demonstrations of miraculous throwing? Mere exercises? Surely not. At one time she placed an amaryllis given to her by Fairbanks in a Flying Saucer.[17] But for others they sent a different, less practical message. A second student wrote: 'At some stage those Flying Saucers turned into mere moods. I noticed that they were not so important as objects as they were perhaps as transmitters of spirit, of ideas.'[18] Perhaps this is the highest praise that any artist could wish for.

Raija Tuumi

Salmenhaara herself carefully rationed praise to anyone, but it is claimed that she regarded one younger colleague as a serious artist, even a threat: Raija Tuumi, eight years her junior. Unlike Salmenhaara, Tuumi spent the major part of her career at Arabia, after completing the ceramics course at the institute. She joined the company in 1950, only three years after Salmenhaara, and much of her earlier work must have

been done almost within view of the older woman. It is clear that they remained on good terms despite Salmenhaara's verdict on Tuumi's potential as a rival. In 1962 she remarked in a letter to Fairbanks that Tuumi was one of the few to have written to her in Taiwan.[19]

Although Tuumi represented the country and the company in many exhibitions abroad, she has never been accorded the mythical status that Salmenhaara achieved. Perhaps, like architects and designers who for decades benefited from – and struggled against – the brilliant sun of Alvar Aalto's celebrity, ceramists have been overshadowed by Salmenhaara's powerful presence. Nevertheless, Tuumi can be seen to have followed a distinctive and personal route which has undoubtedly emerged in its own right. Benefiting from the developments in clay mixtures and glaze technology, and having learned to develop her own, Tuumi explored formal options which were extremely individual. The most distinctive of these was her use of perforation. A forerunner of this might be distantly construed as the Chinese-style rice-grain porcelain perfected at the factory in the 1940s by Friedl Kjellberg. Pierced porcelain without the connecting skin of glaze was also a Chinese skill, copied extensively in European porcelain factories in the eighteenth and nineteenth centuries. The transposition of this delicate art to rough stoneware turned it into a far more muscular technique, clearly analogous to prehistoric wares. In addition, stone-

ware implies a basic functionality which is apparently denied by the perforations. This denial raises some interesting thoughts about the disturbing qualities of a technique which still contradicts so many of our established expectations, despite its ancient lineage. Perhaps we could learn from the rich tradition of African ceramics where piercing and encrusting of ceramic forms are known to have had symbolic meaning. Tuumi's other trademark of small, curled handles also recalls ancient predecessors – some of the earliest made pots. She recognizes no overt influence, apart from acknowledging possible subconscious memories of school museum visits, but she is relaxed about this interpretation, which has been made so frequently.[20]

Tuumi was the subject of a retrospective exhibition held at the Arabia Gallery in 2002, the first she had been awarded. The perforated pots are those

which commanded the greatest attention and of these several had enormous presence not least because of their size. The huge bowl of 1973 is a monumental work with undisguised throwing lines – evidence of formidably strong hands at work. Its generous capacity is inviting and yet this essentially useful shape, with all of its references to the vessel, to utility and capacity, is somehow undone by the perforations. Tuumi used a single-sized, circular tool and the holes are carefully and regularly punched. Around its flared sides are draped swooping panels of these holes almost like a circle of dancers. Seen on a bright afternoon, with the sun shining through the perforations to create a play of light and shadow on the nearby wall, it was full of movement.[21]

Birger Kaipiainen

The all-powerful presence of the Arabia art department as identified by Salmenhaara's ethos has cast a long shadow. But even at the time there was an alternative to her clay-dominant practice. Decoration had not been forsaken: Birger Kaipiainen was there to promote its place in both the art and the factory's multiple production. An individualist, with no discernible followers since, Kaipiainen was a Finnish phenomenon. At the start of his career he was regarded as Finland's answer to Sweden's Stig Lindberg and Denmark's Bjørn Wiinblad – a trio of artists each with a passion for decoration and colour.

Kaipiainen brought to Arabia wit, extravagance and theatricality, probably seen as frivolous in the extreme by some of his contemporaries. Salmenhaara certainly had this view: 'Only once been in B's room. He isn't really any potter, he is a painter, who does pots which he sees around him. Too bad!'[22] But, joining the company in 1937, by the time of his death in 1988 he had produced one of the most successful designs for the factory's production. 'Paradise' (*Paratiisi*) was first introduced in 1968. Withdrawn for fourteen years, it was reintroduced by public demand, a remarkable demonstration of affection for so personal and in many ways so quirky a design. It has been in continuous production since 1988. But most of Kaipiainen's work consisted of unique sculptures, dishes and plaques. The earliest were decorated with pale, delicately drawn and coloured scenes of knights and maidens and other romantic and mysterious subjects. During the late 1950s, his colours darkened and became far richer, more opulent. He introduced purple, blue, orange, crimson and iridescence. His drawing too developed a far stronger linear quality, with stylized and often repeated motifs of birds, giant flowers, fruit and berries. And it was this that led to Paradise. In the collection of the Arabia Museum there is a grand oval, unique dish – a favourite shape for painting – of 1962, and in the decoration several of the main elements of Paradise are already fully formed. The scraped and firmly drawn surface and relatively subdued colouring all underwrite Kaipiainen's long experience and

sound training in ornamental painting and in ceramics.

Kaipiainen was exceptional in several ways. In 1926, when he was just eleven, he was accepted as a trainee student at the Central School; he became a full-time student in 1933. He was an exact contemporary of Salmenhaara although he had been at the Arabia factory for ten years before she arrived. He spent a year at Richard Ginori in Milan, Italy, and four years at Rörstrand in Sweden; unlike most of his contemporaries he did no teaching. Instead he was content to work from 8.30 a.m. to 4.30 p.m. each day in his top-floor studio at Arabia until his death in 1988. His work was shown in many exhibitions in Helsinki and Stockholm, and also in France and the United States but it remains something of a mystery, especially as it does not conform at all to the commonly held perception of ideal Scandinavian restraint, balance and good design. He immersed himself in the social round in Helsinki, especially the ballet at Helsinki's Finnish National Opera. As is easily apparent, he was thoroughly versed in art from Byzantium and Renaissance Italy to the fantastic paintings of Marc Chagall and 1930s Surrealism. At Arabia, his studio took on some aspects of his art as he surrounded himself with an accumulation of hanging stuffs. In his last years he was fleetingly glimpsed through this fantasy jungle, a fragile, aristocratic creature it seemed, but an omnivorous one.

Like many artists, Kaipiainen re-

lied on the assistance of skilled helpers, firstly Karl-Heinz Schultz-Köln, then Paul Enwalds and Terho Reijonen. Reijonen's first job was to make the millions of ceramic beads which were the fabric of Kaipiainen's sculptural work, but he graduated to become the indispensable assistant, painting, assembling – and making coffee. There are photographs of Kaipiainen at work, neatly dressed, often in a Marimekko shirt, surrounded by the paraphernalia which was his stock-in-trade – watches, clock faces, wire and mirrored glass. Self-sufficient, he marshalled his ideas, the tools he needed, and his inspirational surroundings and produced a stream of extraordinary works which are truly unique. There were no like contemporaries; there are no followers. It is this that now makes it more difficult to assess Kaipiainen than almost any other ceramist. Indeed it might be easier to dismiss him as a mere decorator. But he certainly attracted admirers. In 1960 he was awarded a Grand Prix in Milan. In 1962 the 'Finlandia' exhibition came to London after its initial showing in Vienna. It was held at the V&A Museum and was reviewed extensively: 'No-one who visited the last Milan Triennale can forget the delightful giant bird made up of metal, beads and old watch faces. This fantastic fowl will be on show…'[23] Birds feature frequently throughout Kaipiainen's work: three-dimensional and flat, mirrored or beaded or drawn on a dish. The most magical example is a grey-white beaded panel with that same

Birger Kaipiainen is known best for his highly
colourful, theatrical works. One of his favourite themes
was birds. His wall relief *Kuovi sateessa*
(Curlew in the Rain) shows his long-beaked friend
stepping out from behind a shimmering curtain of
rain. The colours are unusually restrained, but the
construction of the picture out of thousands of beads
is typical of Kaipiainen. The work belongs to collector
Kyösti Kakkonen (seen in the picture). On the table
are items by Kyllikki Salmenhaara. Photo: Kari-Kuva.

unmistakable long-beaked bird step-ping forward in front of a shimmering curtain of rain. Kaipiainen's work is the product of an imagination untroubled by meeting any criteria but its own. Now, when we recognize that ceramics can be put to the service of art in any guise the artist chooses, Kaipiainen has an unas-sailable place in the pantheon. He was simply before his time.

Today, Arabia's influence is no longer overwhelming. The ceramists who are there are still among the strong-est of Finland's artists working in clay. They are by no means the only strong ones, but the powerful creativity which emanates from each studio as you enter

is unmistakable and not encountered elsewhere. The security of working with-in a factory environment must develop a certain confidence. Yet this protection comes with a heavy heritage. Outside Arabia, the daily pressure of survival engenders a different sort of art.

Johanna Rytkölä

Johanna Rytkölä is an independent stu-dio potter working in Vantaa, on the outskirts of Helsinki. One of many suc-cessful individual Finnish ceramists, she plays with three-dimensionality in a highly stylish, decorative manner. Underlying her work is a strong aesthet-ic which recalls much from the past. It

is impossible to look at her work with-out recalling design elements from the 1950s and distinctive motifs from the 1920s and 1930s. There are reminders of the fluid, flat, amorphous shapes be-loved of Hans Arp and of Picasso before him. In addition to this play on the line-ar decorative form, Rytkölä has a high-ly developed sense of colour – and the technique to create and control this in her work. The mix of colour and strong linear outlines is transformed by her in-to positive, joyful, standing sculptures. With names like *On the Way to Paradise* or *The Waves Rocking Me*, they are irresisti-ble. She herself says of her work: 'Mem-ories, fantasies, fact and fiction entwine and merge with one another. My works could be compared to poems, stories and fairy tales.'[24] But, seductive though the forms and colours are, there is more to these sculptures. Rytkölä is a member of Hot Line, a group of six women art-ists all working in clay. In the catalogue to an exhibition of their work, historian Susanna Lehtonen comments: 'Johan-na Rytkölä's works are all about move-ment. It seems that their forms and col-ours have been created in a natural and simple fashion, without forcing, but it is the movement that is the essence of the massive sculptures. Each sculpture has its own movement; brisk, aggres-sive, rhythmic, paralysed.'[25] This move-ment is something that Rytkölä has in-vestigated further with monumental works which recall nothing so much as giant bones, jointed, about to take one menacing, shaky step forward. Singly,

Johanna Rytkölä plays with three-dimensionality and has a well-developed sense of colour. Above all, her works have movement and rhythm. This free-standing form, *Aallot mua keinuttaa* (The Waves Rocking Me, 1997), is a motif that has escaped from its architectural context and has begun to live a life of its own. Photo: Johanna Rytkölä.

the interlocking bones are each related to the individual works. Assembled into a skeletal construction, they become a far more imposing sculpture, threatening the viewer by its very size and apparent fragility. Rytkölä is part of a growing group of ceramists who each began their artistic odyssey at the University of Art and Design Helsinki (a course started all those decades before by A. W. Finch), who look beyond the clay for inspiration in their use of graphics, photography, colour and a sense of design, and yet are deeply engaged in the craft of making. In this engagement they are all determined to make ceramics as valid a material as any other for the creative process.

A journey such as this, through over one hundred years of Finnish ceramics, is a lesson in Finnish history, economic change and the determination of the dedicated artist. The few artists highlighted here represent some pinnacles of art, design, skill and craft, but there are many others. The luxury of choice is balanced by the downside of omission. This is repaired elsewhere in this book.

MARJUT KUMELA

A potter's paradise:
the Arabia Art Department, 1932–2002

Arabia grew into one of the largest potteries in Europe in the 1930s, and at the same time gained the necessary technical equipment and expertise for producing high-quality artistic works. The managing director at the time, Carl Gustaf Herlitz, looked favourably on the work of his artists as a counterbalance to the contemporary rationalization and standardization of mass production in the factory. Photo: Arabia Museum.

International pioneers
A small but enthusiastic group of ceramic artists had emerged in Finland in the 1920s, trained by A. W. Finch, but their working opportunities were extremely limited. Setting up a workshop of one's own required large-scale investments, and potential customers on the domestic market were few and far between. The ceramics and porcelain markets in Finland at that time were dominated by the Arabia Company, which as a result of extensions and technical improvements had one of the most modern factories to be found anywhere in Europe.

On the other hand, Arabia had a number of artists working for it on a regular basis: Thure Öberg from Sweden, Greta-Lisa Jäderholm-Snellman, who had studied in France, the Austrian Friedl Holzer (later Kjellberg) and from time to time the Swede Tyra Lundgren, and it was through them that the factory maintained direct contact with contemporary international trends — the Art Nouveau style, the Modernism of the Wiener Werkstätte and Art Deco, with its touch of Classicism. Gradually efforts were made to place the work of these artists on a more organized footing, and in 1929 Tyra Lundgren was invited to act as coordinator of artistic production for both Arabia itself and the Turku Porcelain Works and Lidköping Porcelain Factory that were under its ownership.[1] In the same year Greta-Lisa Jäderholm-Snellman founded the 'Vackrare vardagsvara' department at Arabia to promote the design and production of household and decorative items.[2]

A more permanent arrangement began to take shape in 1931, when Arabia acquired the services of Kurt Ekholm, who had studied ceramics at the 'Konstfack' in Stockholm and trained under Gunnar Nylund at the Rörstrand works. He had absorbed the Functionalist ideals of product design and the Modernist principles of ceramic art.[3]

From visions to a potter's paradise
On his appointment as artistic manager of Arabia in 1932, Kurt Ekholm began to organize the work of the artists attached to the company with the aim of developing an art department and promoting this field of activity in Finland as a whole. The artists involved, in addition to Ekholm himself, included Friedl Holzer, Tyra Lundgren and also Toini Muona, who had joined Arabia in 1931, and Aune Siimes, who came a little later. They had rather modest premises at first, in a wooden building next to the main gate of the Arabia Works, but were able to benefit from the factory's technical equipment, the experience of its staff and its laboratory services. The new feldspar kilns that had been acquired in the 1920s enabled the reduction firing of glazes, which was an essential element in the production of high-temperature materials, porcelain and stoneware.

Arabia had taken part in exhibitions of industrial art at home and abroad in earlier times, but from the 1930s onwards private and joint exhibitions by its

own artists became increasingly common. These served both as sales outlets and as opportunities for public evaluation of their work. Following their success at the Milan Triennial in 1933 and the World Exhibition of 1935 in Brussels, they began to direct their attention more towards the Nordic Countries, as Ekholm's great ambition on the cultural front was closer integration of Finland with Scandinavia.

Art ceramics brought the Arabia Works a good deal of favourable publicity, and so the company was prepared to support and promote it. The department gained new premises in 1937, and was responsible for the designing of household and decorative items for a time. New artists were taken on, notably Birger Kaipiainen and Michael Schilkin. The highlight of that year was the World Exhibition in Paris, and Arabia's collection for the occasion, on the theme of 'Stoneware' met with unanimous approval from the Finnish press. This was also the first occasion on which the art department was mentioned in public as an established concept.

By the early 1940s, Ekholm had gathered around him a group of artists with a wide variety of talents, whose 'national' characteristics could be summed up as a delight in open-minded experimentation unfettered by tradition and a certain 'primitive' quality associated with closeness to nature. Production methods ranged from throwing on a wheel to the modelling of figures and ceramic ornamentation. The department continued its work in spite of wartime conditions, moving into new premises – which it still occupies – on the ninth floor of an extension wing of the factory in 1944. Contacts with the Nordic Countries were strengthened by means of further exhibitions, the most significant of which was an extensive review of industrial arts in Finland at the National Museum in Stockholm in 1942.

A joint exhibition by the Arabia artists in the industrial arts section of the NK department store in Stockholm in 1945 aroused much admiration, but also raised the fundamental issue of the factory's policy in these matters, as the Swedish critics and designers were inclined to question the whole idea of a department concentrating on luxury artistic ceramics within a factory whose main products were everyday crockery and sanitary ware. They stressed the importance of experiences in the artistic field as necessary for the designing of everyday items. Ekholm's defence was based on the notion of differences in artis-

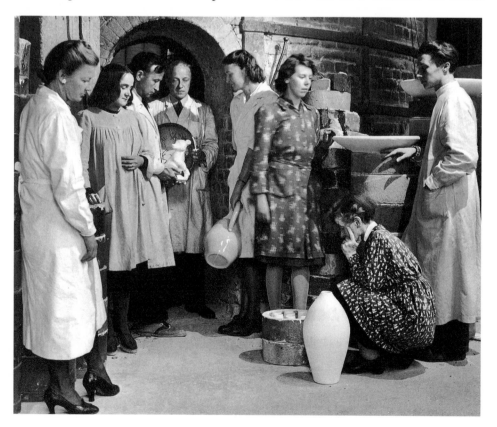

tic temperament, in that some designers felt most at home when they had a free hand to create what they liked and others were better adapted to product development, in which the challenges of the available technology had to be taken into account. Each type of personality would prove most productive when allowed to concentrate entirely on one aspect of the work. It was significant that Kaj Franck had already been taken on by Arabia by that time to raise the quality of the company's tableware.

By the time Kurt Ekholm moved from Arabia to Gothenburg in 1948 to found a ceramics department at the school of the Handicrafts Association there, his dreams of developing Finnish ceramic art had borne fruit to the extent that the best talents in the land were undoubtedly concentrated within Arabia. Before he left, he had also managed to put into effect his plans for creating an Arabia Museum in connection with the Art Department. The factory itself had run into financial difficulties in that same year, and had been taken over by the Wärtsilä Group, which in turn ensured the continuity and development of its art department, now entrusted to the leadership of Friedl Kjellberg.[4]

An ivory tower

The artistic side of Arabia's business was now concentrated in three units: Product Design, Industrial Arts and the art department, which was regarded as 'the potter's paradise'. The artists enjoyed a regular salary, and were also paid commission on the sales of their work, which stimulated their productivity. The ideal working conditions that existed there allowed room for experimentation and thus for constant renewal, and they could receive help from the factory in the preparation of clay bodies and the fabrication of moulds, while the laboratory could be relied on to prepare precisely the glazes that they needed. The department took delivery of a Vistra high temperature reducing kiln in 1951.

New, promising talents came to the art department in the 1940s and 1950s: Rut Bryk, Kyllikki Salmenhaara, Sakari Vapaavuori, Raija Tuumi, Francesca and Richard Lindh and Oiva Toikka. The Milan Triennials of 1951, 1954, 1957 and 1960 were triumphs for Arabia, allowing the art department to increase its reputation and gain recognition as a cornerstone of Finnish design. Almost all the artists won medals, and four of them took the Grand Prix. These successes naturally led to new invitations to exhibit abroad.

Although the department had scarcely any need to worry about its profitability, this question was raised from time to time. Its exhibition successes had aroused interest in artistic ceramics and increased the demand for its products both at home and on the export market. The artists were offered the services of personal assistants in order to increase production, and they were also required to submit a set of at least five suggestions for products or ornaments suitable for mass production twice a year, although production did not benefit greatly from this demand.[5] In practice, the department had developed into an 'ivory tower' isolated from the factory proper and from ceramic artists working elsewhere.

On the other hand, the respect commanded by the artists and the richness of expression that they were able to achieve in their works were still not sufficient to raise ceramics to the level of a true art form. It continued to be thought of as an 'industrial art' in spite of the merits of Birger Kaipiainen's *Sea of Violets* produced for the 1967 World Exhibition in Montreal, or the works of Toini Muona, which were drifting ever further away from utility.

The department lost a number of its founder members during this period, with the deaths of Michael Schilkin in 1962 and Aune Siimes in 1964 and the retirement of Toini Muona and Friedl Kjellberg in 1970, but new blood was obtained from the Industrial arts department, which was working under Olga Osol to produce small series of handmade ornamental and household items. The latter department had developed by this time into a natural first place of work for recent graduates from the School of Industrial Arts, a place where their skills and talents could be put to the test and from where the best of them, such as Liisa Hallamaa, Annikki Hovisaari and Heljä Liukko-Sundström, could move on to the art department. Similarly Aino Anttila and Paul Envalds, who had begun as assistants to

The Milan Triennial exhibitions held during the busiest years of the post-war reconstruction period established Arabia as a national institution. In 1951 the factory's exhibit consisted entirely of artistic ceramics.
Photo: Arabia Museum.

The one-off items produced by the Arabia artists have become popular collectors' pieces both in Finland and abroad. Wentzel Hagelstam is pictured here displaying sculptures by Michael Schilkin.
Photo: Katja Hagelstam.

other artists, went on in time to work independently.[6]

Winds of change, and storms

When the chief designer of the Nuutajärvi glassworks, Kaj Franck, who had been critical of the isolated position of Arabia's art department, was appointed artistic director of Wärtsilä's silicates group in 1968, this also included responsibility for the identity of this department. It was inevitable, however, that he would wish to increase its interaction with others in various directions. He invited guests from abroad, including Zoltan Popovitz and Kent Herschleb from the USA and Kinga Szabo from Hungary, and provided training places for students of ceramic art, a custom that has been continued to this day.[7] The department reached its maximum size around 1970, when it had twelve artists on its permanent staff, and a joint exhibition, the first for some decades, was held at Lappeenranta Art Museum in 1973 to mark the centenary of Arabia.

The factory was experiencing difficulties by this time, however, on account of the oil crisis and the increase in cheap imports, and in 1974 it entered into collaboration with Rörstrand, which was suffering in much the same way. With staff reductions taking place in the Arabia factory as a whole, the question of running down the art department also came onto the agenda. The Swedish partners were in favour of dispensing with this seemingly superfluous branch entirely, but Arabia wished to preserve it because of its value as part of the nation's culture. Kaj Franck had been appointed to a five-year professorship in art in 1973, which meant that he had to relinquish his position with Arabia for that period, but he exercised his authority by demanding that the core and content of the department should be retained and that nothing should be

One of the most significant visiting artists at Arabia has been Rudy Autio, who is of Finnish descent and is one of the pioneers of avant-garde artistic ceramics on the West Coast of the United States. He worked in the art department in 1981 and instructed Finnish ceramists during his visit and in symposia arranged in the subsequent years. Photo courtesy of Jaap Borgers/ Pirkko Räsänen-Borgers.

done to undermine its independence.

In the end, a compromise was negotiated in which Rut Bryk, Birger Kaipiainen and Heljä Liukko-Sundström were allowed to stay on permanently and freelance contracts were signed with Hilkka-Liisa Ahola, Francesca Lindh and Taisto Kaasinen. The others either resigned or went into retirement. The collapse of the Arabia art department was also a shock for many other ceramic artists who had workshops of their own, especially those who had been with Arabia at some time as trainees or assistants.

When the collaboration agreement with Rörstrand came to an end in 1977, Arabia began a fundamental reorganization of its production processes. A new factory hall was opened in October 1979, with two tunnel kilns operating at a temperature of 1260°C. These were intended for mass production purposes, but they would also be suitable for art ceramics in some cases. As a symbol that life and work would go on, Francesca Lindh produced her installation *The Tree of Life* for the new kiln hall.

It took several years for the art department to recover from this setback, although the remaining artists went on working as before, with their sights on future exhibitions. The path charted by Michael Schilkin as a producer of works of art for public places was explored further by Rut Bryk, Francesca Lindh, Heljä Liukko-Sundström and others,[8] and they were gradually joined on the staff by new artists – Pauli Partanen

in 1979, Kati Tuominen in 1980 and Gunvor Olin-Grönqvist, moving from the product design department, in 1982.[9]

Most of the overseas visitors during this period were from the USA: Rudy Autio in 1981,[10] Benjamin Katz and Timothy Persons in 1983,[11] Howard Smith in 1985–86[12] and Jun Kaneko in 1987.[13] The sculptural style that they represented did not in fact have much influence on the department's own artists, but it

did do much to promote favourable attitudes towards ceramics as a visual art form. Visiting Finnish artists included Minni Lukander,[14] Dorrit von Fieandt[15] and Kristina Riska.[16] The Arabia Museum was opened to the public in 1984, and its gallery has established a position for itself as a prominent exhibition space for both modern and historical ceramics and glassware.

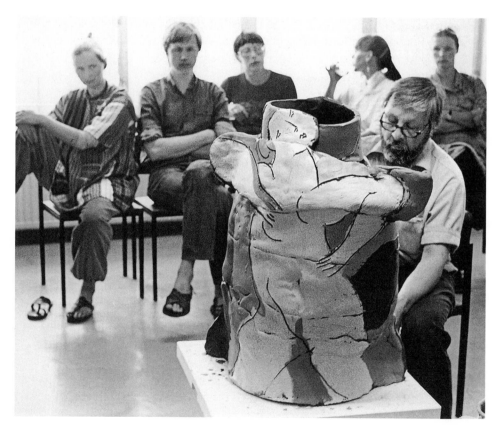

Pro Arte

A further rapprochement between the art department and product design was presaged by the exhibition of Art ceramics 'Earth and Air' held in 1986 by Arabia's principal designer of tableware, Inkeri Leivo. The items of porcelain on display had been made possible by the acquisition of a new porcelain kiln in 1980 in connection with a revival of the production of rice-grain porcelain.[17] The year 1986 was a busy one in other respects, too: a ceramics event entitled 'Clay az Art', involving a workshop and an exhibition, was arranged jointly with the University of Arizona in June,[18] Francesca Lindh held an exhibition 'The Path of Light',[19] and Rut Bryk's extensive retrospective exhibition was mounted at the Amos Anderson Art Museum in Helsinki.[20]

The re-emergence of the question of the economic viability of the art department and the possibility of merging it with product design led to a further reorganization. As Arabia's design manager, Esa Kolehmainen, put it, 'It is a luxury these days to have our own group of artists in-house, but it has become an essential part of Arabia's culture. This cooperation will only work as long as the designers and artists do all forms of work alternately, as is now the case.'[21] All the artists were now given working space on the ninth floor.

The most visible aspect of the reorganization was the commencement of production under the new Pro Arte concept adopted from the Nuutajärvi glassworks to denote the creation of art ceramics in limited series. The first Pro Arte collection, announced by Arabia in 1988, included designs by Dorrit von Fieandt, Inkeri Leivo, Heljä Liukko-Sundström, Gunvor Olin-Grönqvist, Heikki Orvola, Tove Slotte and Kati Tuominen implemented by young potters trained at the Kuopio School of Arts and Crafts.[22]

The Arabia Foundation, intended to sponsor visits by artists, the arranging of exhibitions in connection with these and the upkeep of the Arabia Museum,[23] was inaugurated in 1989, and awarded its first scholarship in 1990, to Fujiwo Ishimoto, who has been among the freelance artists attached to the department ever since.[24]

An eye to the future

Arabia gained a new owner in 1990, following the collapse of Wärtsilä Marine, when the factory was acquired by Oy Hackman Ab.[25] Once more the whole question of the existence of the art department and its role had to be evaluated, leading to the placement of the Arabia, Iittala and Nuutajärvi designers all under the same roof, so that, at least in theory, they all had an opportunity to work with both ceramics and glass.[26] The department itself celebrated its sixtieth anniversary in 1992 in a conspicuous manner, with a seminar and an exhibition in the Arabia Museum Gallery that included Gunvor Olin-Grönqvist's *Ebb and Flow*.[27]

Arabia's art department is still looked on as an elite unit in Finnish ceramics, and its artists continue to be invited to exhibit their work both at home and abroad and regularly gain prizes, the most notable ones in recent years being the Grand Prix awarded to Kati Tuominen-Niittylä in the Mino international competition in 1998, her gold medal in the same competition in 2002, and the prize won by Pekka Paikkari at the Faenza Biennial in 1993. The department has also received recognition from the Finnish government, which has included it in the cultural itinerary for state visits on numerous occasions, purchased impressive state gifts from it and commissioned works of art for public places.

Ceramic art has also flourished in Finland in recent decades outside the confines of Arabia, thanks to scholarships awarded by the state or by private foundations, but this has done nothing to detract from the significance of the department or the esteem in which it is held. The continued wide range of activities pursued by its artists in product design and the creation of unique works of art has helped them to fulfil the purpose for which it was originally founded, that of taking responsibility for the development of ceramics as one aspect of Finnish culture.

HARRI KALHA

In the shadows of the grand narrative

Tyra Lundgren, *The Head of the Medusa*, partially glazed chamotte, Arabia c. 1935. Photo: Arabia Museum.

Face to face with a ceramic sculpture from the mid-1930s, I sense its features pointing away from me, but the hypnotic look in its eyes seems to be addressing my very person. This work, made by Tyra Lundgren in her Arabia studio, depicts Medusa, the monstrous beauty of Greek mythology whose gaze could turn men to stone. Lundgren produced a number of versions of this theme for exhibitions in Paris, Stockholm and London as well as Helsinki between 1934 and 1937.[1] Medusa's formidable eyes also kept watch over the Milan Triennial of 1936, although this time as part of the Swedish contribution, as the architect Alvar Aalto did not want any ceramic art in the Finnish exhibit, which served as an international showcase for the recently established furniture manufacturer Artek. Had Lundgren in fact turned Medusa's gaze towards the Finnish 'Functionalist' stand on purpose?

'There are many who are not happy working with mass production,' Lundgren was to write later, 'and their task is to give us "that little bit extra".'[2] This is basically what the items to be discussed in this article are all about: they give us that little bit extra. This is the case with Lundgren's Medusa, too, although the main reason for choosing it as a pictorial epigram for this article was that it conjures up a certain subversive power. Medusa's transfixing gaze will serve as a metaphor for artistic creativity, not least in ceramics, which is indeed a matter of metamorphosis and transmutation, of 'turning to stone'.

The French feminist Hélène Cixous sees Medusa as a symbol of the independent force possessed by women: 'One need do no more than look straight at Medusa in order to see her, and she is not lethal. She is beautiful and is laughing.'[3] Why bring feminism into an essay on ceramics? Perhaps because gender relations formed one of the many ideological frameworks that governed the narrative of ceramics in the twentieth century. To be sure, women fared well in this 'craftsy' branch of art, but they remained in the shadow of the well-known male virtuosos.[4] In the spirit of the primeval gender mythology, femininity was for a long time destined to represent matter, which was given form by virtue of male creative power. The Functionalist discourse that inspired advances in design served to recapitulate the notion of 'male' knowledge (culture) as a form of control over 'female' matter (nature), a tendency that seems to figure even in design history.[5] As I set out below to recount a (rather than the) narrative of ceramics history in Finland, I would like to bring to the fore a few voices from the shadows of the grand narrative, artist-potters who have remained largely unknown — all of them women — and, on the other hand, to discuss some lesser-known works by better-known ceramicists.

The art of the pot

Gerda Thesleff and her friend Elin Juselius were present when A. W. Finch, having been left with no source of income following the collapse of Iris, began his teaching programme in 'artistic pot-making' [*taiteellinen ruukunteko*] at the Atheneum School of Arts and Crafts.[6] As far as we know, they never actually graduated, but they did study for a number of years and then gradually moved on to work independently.[7] It was Rafael Blomstedt, artistic director of the school, who remarked in 1927 that

Gerda Thesleff decorating a pot by the sgraffito technique in the studio at her home in the 1920s. Photo: Arabia Museum.

ceramics was 'the first among the artistic handicrafts to attract most artists',[8] although one newspaper complained in the very same year that ceramic artists had not yet received recognition from the general public.[9] Ceramics was thus a field that aroused much initial enthusiasm, although its early exponents failed to leave very many historical traces of their endeavours. It should in fact be emphasized how few potters belonged to the trade union for the industrial arts, Ornamo, in the first half of the twentieth century: about three out of a hundred in 1927 (one woman and two men, one of whom was an 'honorary member', A. W. Finch himself). The absence of female potters is surprising given that practically all the students of pottery in the early part of the century were women.

Although Finch was renowned as a Modernist refiner of form,[10] the mode of expression adopted by his pupils right up to the time of his death was a rather more luxuriant variety of ceramic ornamentation. Finch shaped while they decorated: this was the hierarchical division of labour between the master and his students. As Arttu Brummer, one of the most influential educators in the field of design, later recalled, Finch 'was reluctant to explain the mysteries of glazing to clumsy dilettantes, fearing that it would be more difficult to appreciate the merits of really proficient ceramic art if poor, inadequate pieces were to benefit from similar glazes.'[11] Finch thus kept his pupils in the dark to some extent 'out of respect for ceramic art', as it was said at the time.[12]

Gerda Thesleff's personal touch was also to be seen best in the surface treatment of her works. This is partly attributable to technical limitations, as she did at least some of her work at home, transporting the pots by horse-drawn carriage to the Atheneum or the Arabia works for firing. Thesleff's most characteristic feature, the reduced landscape motifs, would seem to have emerged in the early 1910s,[13] and engraved patterns, relief modelling and inlays were other forms of ornamentation that she favoured, although they were apparently not recommended in the teaching provided at the Atheneum.[14] Creating compositions on the round surface and transferring painted sketches of landscapes to the three-dimensional medium presented aesthetic challenges for her. At the same time, surface decoration was a way of attracting public attention to ceramics, of making the art of the pot more 'tangible' as it were. In this sense Thesleff's work has an interesting tale to tell regarding the pot's journey on the way to becoming an art form.

The status of modern art pottery in Finland was influenced by the fact that A. W. Finch, known first and foremost as a Post-Impressionist painter, would present his ceramic works alongside his paintings at exhibitions. The 'art' of the pot was also reflected in its price: the exhibition of the Industrial Arts Association in 1923, for instance, placed a price of Fmk 40 each on hand-painted Arabia bowls, whereas a vase by Gerda Thesleff was valued at Fmk 2,500.[15]

Thesleff's wider popularity, however, as well as her transition to light-coloured faience (from red earthenware) in the early 1920s, was connected with her collaboration with Arabia. Employment on a commission basis was something very unusual at that time, as a substantial gulf existed between the Atheneum potters and the ceramics factories, reflecting a desire to keep idealistic 'art' and commercial 'industry' firmly apart. Finch, a devout spokesman for the arts & crafts ideology, certainly looked down on industry and would warn his pupils against enslaving themselves to it.[16] Thesleff nevertheless came to Arabia at a propitious moment, as the faience material developed there made it possible to adopt a new, lighter, picturesque style and escape from the more sombre tones of red earthenware. In his review of an Ornamo exhibition at around the

Ceramics produced at the Atheneum under Elsa
Elenius. Photo: Pietinen/Ornamo Yearbook, 1936.

same time, the critic Nils Wasastjerna complained that 'wherever I look there are dark, dismal colours: brown, brown and more brown....'[17]

Thesleff's strength lay not in any 'perfect' mastery of form but in the spontaneity of her hand crafting and ornamental approach. The small imperfections one often sees in her work may be attributed to the fact that when producing high-cost unique pieces it did not pay to be too severe in rejecting items. Thus in addition to the successful pieces, the kiln would yield large numbers fit only for the artist's own use or

as presents for friends and relatives. It must also be remembered that Finch himself had stressed the 'imperfect', unpredictable nature of the material as one of the characteristic features of pottery.[18]

The women pioneers of studio ceramics demonstrated with their work that a modern line could very well be found without following the model laid down by Finch. His pedagogical principles only served to confirm the prevailing hierarchy, in that the 'higher' level of expertise in ceramics (that is, glazing and firing) remained the exclusive

province of the master, Finch. Thus despite his rather limited firing technique, Finch tended to be regarded as a master of 'the art of non-ornamental glazing, with complete control over the colouristic difficulties of this technically very tricky branch of artistic handicraft', as Blomstedt put it.[19] As one of Finch's pupils, Tamara Laurén, recalls, 'No, [Finch did not teach us] chemistry at all. We had to work that out for ourselves.... [Elsa Elenius, Toini Muona and I] began to read chemistry on our own and to mix glazes.'[20]

Professor in quotation marks

One reporter who visited the Central School of Industrial Arts in 1930 described the ceramics department at the Atheneum as follows: 'The illustrious chair of the late Professor A.W. Finch has been inherited by his enthusiastic and skilful pupil Miss Elsa Elenius, and led by their new "professor" a number of young ladies were "throwing pots" and painting and "glazing" them. We then saw how they were put into the kiln to bake the next morning, the "pots", that is.'[21] Without dwelling on the disparaging tone that is to be detected in the report,[22] it is clear that following Finch's death the Atheneum pottery workshop had the air of a women's collective enterprise, and that their work bore the marks of a high degree of commitment, as if they wanted to show the world what they were capable of achieving without their professor's 'paternal' supervision. The nucleus of the group gathered around

Items by Kerttu Suvanto-Vaajakallio, produced from a claybody containing red clay, glazed and decorated with reliefs, Kupittaa Pottery Company *c.* 1935, now in a private collection. Photo: Johnny Korkman.

Elenius was formed by Toini Muona, Kerttu Suvanto(-Vaajakallio), Siiri Harjola and Tamara Laurén. It might be worth noting here that seven members of the 'Finch school' were awarded medals at the 1937 World Exhibition in Paris.[23] In addition, the sheer extent of the collection exhibited in Paris testified to the unprecedented interest surrounding ceramics at that time. Notwithstanding Alvar Aalto's disdain, pottery was becoming a part of the ideal 'Functionalist' environment in a rapidly modernizing Finnish culture, a 'respectable' way of enlivening with a touch of material warmth surroundings that were otherwise becoming increasingly ascetic.

Elsa Elenius had begun her studies in ceramics directly after middle school in autumn 1915, but she was unable to make a career out if it at first. She worked as a bank clerk for a while and even spent some time at Arabia, 'painting gold rims on cups'. She also worked as a teacher of art at Iisalmi Lyceum in 1925 and 1926 — at the same time as her work was already representing Finnish ceramics at an international exhibition in Paris.

A leading art critic of the day, Onni Okkonen, was among those who recognized the expressive potential of ceramics in the 1930s. In Elenius's works he perceived something 'soulful, something that spoke of tangible life experiences' and 'a mysterious soul' that could raise pottery to the level of a true art form. Such a level could not be attained 'through regular or exemplary external form, or through superfi-cial fantasies of colour or shape, but it needed something more, a combination of skill and delicate feeling.'[24] Around the same time Elenius's work was commended by Aune Lindström, writing in the women's magazine *Suomen nainen*, who noted that ceramics as an art form 'may well have a future ahead of it once it becomes more widely known'.[25] This put the problem in a nutshell: the modern aesthetics of ceramic art was capable at its best of meeting the most stringent demands of the connoisseur, but there was hardly a public to buy ceramic works outside these professional circles, despite Finch's considerable influence in 'educating' popular taste, for as Tyra Lundgren had put it, he 'inspired a group of collectors within Finnish cultural circles who learned to recognize and value a ceramic work purely for the sake of its genuine beauty'.[26]

Where Finch's ceramics had mainly emulated the nuances of stoneware aesthetics, Elsa Elenius succeeded in obtaining for the Atheneum a high-temperature kiln that made it possible to teach reduction firing. The main aesthetic and technical tools for 'modern' pottery were now to hand — if one can ever say that in the world of ceramics — although there was still little to brag about as far as working conditions were concerned.[27] Elenius had a room of her own in the Atheneum and a potter's wheel (non-electric, of course), and, as a studio potter of the highest rank, she regarded participation in exhi-bitions in Finland and abroad as an important professional challenge — and, perhaps, as a necessary counterbalance to her teaching duties. She gained significant international recognition for her work, although mostly within a rather short period between 1933 and 1939.

'We students practically idolized her,' Birger Kaipiainen recalls with regard to his formative years in the 1930s. 'First of all, she was such a beautiful, stylish woman — and wonderfully tasteful in every way. She taught so much of intellectual value just with her own presence, without resorting to words....'[28] Ritva Karpio, who graduated in pottery in 1945, remarks, 'Perhaps she did not have all the pedagogical gifts one might have expected, but she taught with her whole being. She was an artist from top to toe, and her own work left nothing more to desire....'[29]

'New ideas of beauty, at modest prices' [30]

'Works of art at amazingly low prices!' an advertisement for the Kupittaa Pottery Company announced in spring 1936. 'You don't need to worry in the slightest about their artistic value, as the experts have recognized it many times over, claiming that our factory is working nowadays along the same lines as the independent studio potters. And how inexpensive these pieces are!' The illustration showed a group of objects with no mention of the designer's name, although they can evidently all be attributed to the same person.[31]

Kerttu Suvanto(-Vaajakallio), who has remained virtually unknown in Finnish design history up to now, is the one among Finch's pupils whose works spread most widely into Finnish homes in the 1930s and 1940s. The reason that history has overlooked her is that she died in childbirth in 1939, having worked in the ceramics industry for only seven years. It was during her time at Kupittaa, however, that the company began to come in from the periphery of the design arena and also became more international, with promising incursions into the Nordic, US and German export markets – only to be frustrated before long by the outbreak of war. The Kupittaa works, where Suvanto held the position of artistic director from 1934 to 1939, did not make any great fuss about its designers, so that little documentary evidence has survived on the pioneering work that she did there. It is symptomatic that the factory did not make use of the studio-potter-turned-designer for marketing purposes, so that although its catalogue did mention the name of the sculptor Wäinö Aaltonen in connection with a wall plate that he designed, Suvanto's works remained anonymous – the creations of a 'mere' potter, and a woman at that. There was also a considerable difference in price, although the production costs could not have varied greatly.

Thanks to Suvanto's efforts, the ideals of studio pottery became fused with the Kupittaa company's more pragmatic (that is, commercially orientated) philosophy of industrial production. In fact, the results reflected the democratic ideals of functionalism more strictly than the emphatically artistic contribution of a factory like Arabia, where the studio branch produced expensive unique pieces. It was also thanks to the collaboration with Suvanto that Kupittaa products began to be accepted for design exhibitions, even for the Paris exhibition of 1937, where they were well received in spite of appearing alongside the works of seasoned competitors such as Toini Muona, Friedl Holzer-Kjellberg and Tyra Lundgren. As Valentina Modig-Manuel, another student of the Finch-Elenius school, who worked together with Suvanto at Kupittaa, recalls, 'We certainly had to struggle a fair amount at times, as they would often bring us forms that seemed to have nothing to do with ceramics at all and expect us to paint ornaments on them and sign them as our own.'[32]

'The most natural shape for a pot is round, and the most intrinsic, and at the same time most beautiful, form of ornamentation is the line produced by the wheel as it spins.'[33] This is how Suvanto described her 'ceramic philosophy' to a reporter from the newspaper Uusi Aura in 1938. For her, the finest thing about ceramics was 'the coloured glaze, which is the last word in evolution and calls for techniques in which the Chinese are the masters'. As reduction-fired glazes were not possible at Kupittaa, however, the subtle individualism of the times was represented by a simplified, 'modern' language of forms combined with restrained, classical decoration.

Suvanto's works gain their strength from their sturdy overall appearance and the dialogue between form and subtly ornamental details. Although one should not confuse her work with that of Wäinö Aaltonen (as is often done at art auctions, where her works are sold under his name), there is a certain resemblance between them. The smaller scale and the demands of serial production did not, of course, permit the eloquent plasticity that can be found in Aaltonen's work; indeed, the figures are stylized in a somewhat schematic manner, which conformed to the Functionalist ideal of reduced, compact form. Thus the elongated figure with a hint of flowing drapes and wavy hair that adorns a cylindrical vase by Suvanto may be seen as a highly simplified relative of Wäinö Aaltonen's well-known sculptures Maiden of Finland or Wader (the latter of which, incidentally, did serve as a model for a series of ceramic items produced by Kupittaa). In Suvanto's version, the spiritualized muse of the male sculptors is transfixed into a miniature caryatid proudly carrying the weight of her decorative impression. One sturdy, ponderous urn, to cite another example, is relieved by a series of highly stylized mermaids, while the knob on its stylishly flat lid takes the form of a streamlined bird.

It seems particularly appropriate that these 'ritual objects' in a modern Neo-Classical style should have originated in the city of Turku, which V. A. Koskenniemi described as the Athens of Fin-

A copper-glazed stoneware bowl by Aune Siimes, Arabia *c.* 1946, now in Kyösti Kakkonen's collection. Photo: Kari-Kuva.

land (where Helsinki represented Alexandria). This revival of Classicism may be partly attributed to the need for a ceramics factory regarded by many as 'peripheral' (both artistically and geographically) to create a distinguished profile for itself. But above all it speaks of a desire to create 'modern', that is fashionable but mechanically reproducible 'artistic' works, out of earthenware without any fancy firing or glazing techniques. This may, at least initially, have entailed a certain aesthetic compromise for Suvanto, hence her somewhat 'tongue in cheek' approach, which adds a playful tone to the otherwise sturdy solemnity of her preferred Classicism.

A Little Big Bowl

It sometimes seems that words such as bowl, cup or pot, succinct as they may be, fall far short of doing justice to the objects that they purport to describe. This feeling comes to mind when I look at a bowl made by Aune Siimes in the mid-1940s. Lacking a formal foot, its thick base tapers somewhat towards the edges, and the hand-modelled form evokes a sense of austere negligence or indeterminacy, while affording the little piece a robust strength. The red spatterings of glaze that run down towards the base emphasize the expressive spontaneity of this variation on the Chinese 'peach bloom' glaze familiar to connoisseurs.

One of the cornerstones of modern ceramic aesthetics is to be found in the culture of collecting, in particular the principles on which the ancient

ceramics of East Asia have been valued. The status of these traditional *liebhaber* pieces, the sublime attraction of rarity, is echoed in their modern counterparts. Reduction firing involved a moment of suspense that automatically conferred a certain rarity value, turning successful pieces with fine glaze effects (or 'interesting' flaws) into objects of desire for the collector. Siimes's stoneware bowl is just such a piece: like its historical predecessors, it tempts one to take it in the hand, and invites contemplation.

For the Danish potter Christian Poulsen, acquaintance with the works of Aune Siimes meant 'something very rare, an encounter with a true ceramic artist'.[34] He was presumably referring to the unfettered manner in which she would explore the 'nature' of the material, its expressive potential. The glazing effects, with their transmutations, were – in accordance with the Functionalist ethos – controlled means of 'organic' expression, yet they embraced what was considered the essential power of the ceramic material itself, including its fickleness. Lying behind this ideal of authenticity was the general modernistic principle of autonomy: that every branch of art should prove its independence by developing its own specific modes of expression.

Where people were traditionally accustomed to assessing art forms on a scale extending from material to spiritual, 'down to earth' branches such as pottery were apt to be placed at the lower end of the hierarchy. It was the technically refined, 'abstract' treatment of the material that enabled modern ceramics to rise in status, by demonstrating, paradoxically, that ceramics was more than 'mere matter'. Thus, the unadorned, 'organic' form of a vessel provided a kind of short-cut to abstract art. The ceramic abstraction, in the formal guise of a domestic object, was able to break away from Functionalist convention in the direction of the associative stimuli of art.[35]

Sang de boeuf, or oxblood glazes produced by reduction firing, became the testing ground and the artistic *tour de force* of Finnish potters in the 1930s and 1940s. Aune Siimes excelled in this field

Rut Bryk, the wall plaque *Lilies of the Valley in a Vase*, Arabia, early 1950s, now in Kyösti Kakkonen's collection. Photo: Kari-Kuva.

in the mid-1940s, so much so that the architect Rafael Blomstedt praised the rich imagination of this 'worshipper' of the oxblood glaze.[36] This and other related reduction fire glazes had a 'spiritual' quality about them that corresponded to the grim reality of the 1940s in Finland. The unique pieces made during and immediately after the war, together with the lofty discourse surrounding them, betrayed a longing for spiritual elevation and expressive vitality. In this historical context it was appropriate for aesthetics to find an ally in the ambivalent symbolism of blood, as both the elixir of life and the mark of tragedy.[37]

The Norwegian Svend Erik Møller, in 1947, paid tribute to the 'mighty explosive power' of Finnish design, which, thanks to its 'oriental' overtones, served as a source of inspiration for the other Nordic countries.[38] Siimes's stoneware bowls, noted by the critic, epitomize the 'aesthetic materialism' that gave Finnish design its strong profile within the Nordic sphere in the 1940s, and which earned it wider international recognition in the 1950s. This organicist 'aesthetics of the formless' sought to avoid the precise forms of Classicism, favouring asymmetry and other 'natural' flaws.

The cultural climate in the 1940s and 1950s encouraged a tendency to recognize in the Finnish applied arts a 'primitive' character, a robust strength and an emotional flair. A picturesque image arose of designers 'playing' with their material, so that the Danish ceramist Nathalie Krebs described the Finnish ceramic artists in 1945 as a group of 'talented children of nature doing just as they please, with no knowledge of past achievements'.[39] This (at least partly imagined) lack of tradition was the Finns' weakness, but it was also their source of strength. As Rafael Blomstedt put it in his comment on Krebs's statement, 'What remains is spontaneity, the most essential factor in all genuine art, setting up a rich register of tones ranging from extreme crudity to delicate emotion.'[40] Such contemporary comments also serve to reveal the complex-ridden nature of Scandinavian ceramics, a field where the 'eternal' forms were becoming transfixed in their own perfection.[41]

Where most of the Arabia artists sought expressive power in large size or suggestive imagery, Aune Siimes, who was one of the pioneers of the factory's art department, remained faithful to her 'intimate' approach to the ceramic material and its expressive subtleties. From the mid-1940s onwards she began to work not only with stoneware but also with its diametric opposite, hand-moulded porcelain, and it was in this latter field that she finally made a name for herself internationally. As the aesthetic materialism of the 1940s lost ground to the new immaterial ideal of the 1950s, the 'worshipper of oxblood' was lauded as a poet of porcelain.

Lilies of the valley in a vase

'Finnish Art is permeated by a kind of tough remoteness suggestive of an austere and solemn fairy tale,'[42] the critic M. H. Middleton wrote when reviewing the exhibition 'Modern Art in Finland' that toured Britain in 1953–54, and these words ring in my ears as I look at a wall plaque by Rut Bryk from the early 1950s. The subject matter is very unassuming, a vase containing lilies of the valley, but there is something utterly captivating about it. The refined green tones of the leaves and the coarse, unglazed surface that forms their background appeal to one's sense of touch as well as sight. Depicted with such devotion, these lilies of the valley have something that is at once melancholy and dignified about them.

Bryk had been working on a new technique for making wall plaques from 1948 onwards,[43] at a time when the status of ceramics as an art form – not least due to Arabia's efforts, was reaching new dimensions. Bryk's works were exhibited in art galleries as independent, signed creations, a little like unframed paintings. The focus on the plaque form was a formidable challenge as far as firing techniques were concerned. As Eero Rislakki, writing about the latest plaques by Arabia artists Toini Muona, Birger Kaipiainen and Rut Bryk in the magazine *Kaunis Koti*, pointed out, 'The production and firing of flat tiles is a sufficiently expensive and difficult process that no one outside the walls of Arabia has dared to go further than experimenting with it. But in spite of this, people abroad regard plaques of this kind as especially typical of Finnish ceramic art.'[44]

Embracing her new-found technique, Bryk took to depicting the carefree world of the summers of her youth: cows grazing in the fields, a stove, the realm of the kitchen with occasional fruit or simple household utensils – as if setting out to demonstrate that the value of artistic expression did not depend on lofty subject matter, any more than it did on the material used. While such modest themes can be understood as allusions to modernistic freedom (à la Georges Braque), they also evoke a feminine consciousness: the artist remained modestly 'in the back room', concerning herself with affairs of the kitchen and the intimate realm of the home. This understatement is even reflected in the titles of her works: *Basket of Pears,*

Bowl and Lemon, Fruit and Potatoes, and so on. It is symptomatic that these subjects were in the mode of the still life, a genre with a problematic status in the pictorial arts.[45]

A reporter from the magazine *Saviseppo* described Bryk as 'apparently natural and effortless in her work, as if she were arranging flowers in a vase rather than drawing them on a ceramic tile.'[46] Our plaque with the lilies of the valley, in which she could be said to have literally 'arranged flowers in a vase', does indeed express a certain internalized humility, which can be understood in terms of the historical dynamics of national consciousness in Finland.

'Dark too are the tones of Finnish art: still, cold and hard, yet with an air of fantasy…', M. H. Middleton's romanticizing review (cited above) goes on. Lying behind this 'air of fantasy', of course, was a very concrete need to transform the austerity of everyday life (for Finland was still suffering from widespread material poverty) into a positive factor. Thus Bryk's still-life images in all their everyday simplicity evoke the atmosphere of the home, the rehabilitation of which was part of the post-war reconstruction effort. As in design as a whole, the home and its accoutrements had to be sublimated, projected, as it were, onto a higher plane of spirituality. Although the phenomenology of the home was for a long time to be coloured by the experiences of war and poverty, there was a need to perceive a 'sacred' beauty amidst all the austerity. It was in

fact precisely these words, 'something sacred', that were used to describe the Finnish stand at the Milan Triennial of 1951, where a whole wall was devoted to the plaques of Rut Bryk,[47] in recognition of which she received the Grand Prix, the highest award at the exhibition.

'My intention is to create something of beauty in people's surroundings, for we spend far too much of our time wrestling with the grey, monotonous everyday world,' Bryk maintained in 1953. Her 'everyday world' at that time was a highly subjective one, coloured by her own personal history, but it also reflected the nostalgia for the agrarian way of life that was part of the spirit of the age in Finland. It is perhaps this 'introverted' attitude that explains, at least partly, the successes of Finnish industrial arts during that period: where it appealed to the national identity and nostalgia of the Finns (in the face of accelerating urbanization and a gradual abandonment of rural life), it was perceived abroad in terms of a 'genuine', down-to-earth aesthetic trend that could disarm the strictest proponents of international modernism.[48]

Bryk continued with increasing determination to move towards modern art, however, or perhaps one should say a synthesis of pictorial art and ceramics. As a new, more international and technologically orientated age dawned in Finland, the domestic-nationalistic themes were laid aside. In their place came abstract form, modulization and a 'megalographic' architectural approach. And the rest, as they say, is history.

ESA LAAKSONEN

Ceramic art in modern Finnish architecture

Sun-baked clay bricks with straw added for strength were one of the earliest building materials to be used in our culture, alongside wood and stone, and they are still widely used even today in Africa, Asia and the Middle East. Similarly, fired clay in various forms constitutes an essential construction material almost everywhere. It is natural, therefore, that ceramics should always have been a part of architecture, being used for structural purposes, on walls and as decorative elements. The Islamic architectural tradition in particular makes abundant use of ornamentations based on fired ceramics, whereas modern Western architecture has been unfortunately reluctant to indulge in ornamentation in recent times, which has led in practice to the disappearance of the decorative use of ceramic materials from our architectural grammar over the last hundred years. Artworks executed in relief, which occupied an important place in the Classical architectural tradition, were still in common use in the 1930s, and to some extent in the post-war 'romanticism' of the 1940s and 1950s.

The façades of Helsinki feature large numbers of ceramic reliefs. Perhaps the main artist responsible for these, working chiefly in the pre-war period, was Gunnar Finne (1886–1952), who had himself studied architecture, and who produced numerous works in the Classic style, often depicting human figures. Among these were the brick relief on the wall of the main offices of Alko, the Finnish wine and spirits

monopoly, in Salmisaari (1938), the relief in the entrance to the Finnish Coeducational School (nowadays the National Board of Antiquities) and the particularly fine 'Saver', which grows up, as it were, out of the yellow façade of the Post Office Savings Bank building designed by Antero Pernaja in Fabianinkatu (1942). His post-war successor was Michael Schilkin (1900–62), whose work will be reviewed in more detail later in this article, and others who have been ative in the same field are Taisto Kaasinen (1918–80) and more recently Outi Leinonen (b. 1950), Kerttu Horila (b. 1946) and Johanna Rytkölä (b. 1956). Leinonen completed her work for the gable end of the Kårböle junior school in 2000, and it is to be hoped that this marks a revival of the architectural use of wall reliefs in Finland.

It seems, too, that with the disappearance of ceramic elements, the fired bricks used in building have also become impersonal utility items. Where a Finnish architect fifty years ago had a wide variety of bricks to choose from, fired in different ways, composed of different types of clay, and even glazed for use in façades, the industry nowadays can offer little more than a monotonous range of plain-coloured bricks of standardized, modular dimensions. It also seems that ceramics are frequently used as a form of pictorial art in connection with buildings, i.e. they are part of the furnishings and are commissioned from separate funds set aside for works of art.

There has been much discussion of the combining of art and architecture into a successful symbiosis, perhaps even a single work of art, partly because the choice of works of art for a building in relation to its architecture is often a somewhat controversial matter. Frequently, achieving a discrete final result calls for an exceptional exercise of cultural willpower on the part of the institution commissioning the building, as the inclusion of the work of the artist in the building process proper is apt to be regarded more as a superfluous cost factor. It must be said, in fact, that the major organizations commissioning new buildings, the state and the larger local authorities, have been exemplary in their ability to view the provision of works of art as an integral part of the building process. Art committees and individual architects and artists have sought out opportunities for collaboration, although with variable success. The best results have usually been attained in projects in which the artist and architect have worked together in the traditional way, from the planning stage and first drafts onwards, whereas failures have frequently ensued in cases where the works of art have 'just appeared' on site in the almost completed building as ornamental appendages devoid of any context.

Interesting results have often been achieved where the collaboration has been based on personal friendships between architects and artists. Professor Pentti Kareoja's collaboration with the

35

artist Markku Pääkkönen in the 1990s gave rise to a number of quite original plans for the colours of buildings – in an area of student housing in Vaasa and for the Mustakivi School and the AV Learning Centre in the Arabianranta development in Helsinki, for example. This latter design is built up of standard-sized pieces of enamelled corrugated sheet metal in a number of regular colours. Works in a similar vein, based on 'catalogue materials', have also been produced using ceramics, for the underground concourse at Helsinki central railway station, for example (Terhi Juurinen and Riitta Siira, 1982). Another successful example of such cooperation is the wooden lower ceiling for the council chamber in the second building stage of Helsinki City Hall, the disposition of which was designed by the artist Juhana Blomstedt. There have unfortunately been no examples of architecture-ceramics combinations in recent times to equal that achieved by Antero Pernaja and Gunnar Finne for the Post Office Savings Bank.

Perhaps the best-known ceramic artist who provided works for public places and buildings in Helsinki was Michael Schilkin. It is in his kilns that reliefs were produced for the outside walls of the Arabia factory (1943), where he himself was employed, the Toukola Church Hall (1955) and the Helsinki School of Economics (1950). One of his lesser-known works was his *Market Place* (1947) for the staff canteen in the basement of Helsinki City Hall, a build-

Buildings in which abundant use is made of tiles provide good opportunities for cooperation between architects and ceramic artists. The ceramic animal figures that serve as showers on the walls of the children's pool at the swimming and leisure centre in Siilinjärvi, for which the author was the architect, were designed and produced in 1992 by the ceramic artist Marja Myllymäki (b. 1956). Photo: Jussi Tiainen.

ing originally designed by Carl Ludvig Engel as the Seurahuone Hotel. This relief was in fact dismantled during the fundamental renovations carried out on the building in the 1960s and was stored away in boxes until 2001, when the Aki Davidsson architectural office took on the task of restoring the City Hall once more in the spirit of Aarno Ruusuvuori's renovation in the 1960s. The result is that Schilkin's relief has been reinstated in the staff canteen, now on the first floor, in modern, spacious surroundings which, to judge from old photographs, form a far more suitable venue for this elegant work in chamotte clay than the original, rather low basement. An interesting contrast has been created by placing this pictorial work in a modern environment. Schilkin's problem (as is evident in his relief for the School of Economics) was that his works tended to acquire a certain 'rustic' imbalance. In his *Market Place*, however, he appears to have succeeded, as if by accident, in placing the ship and lorry correctly, with their direction of movement towards the upper right corner, producing an imbalance that generates a sense of movement and gives the whole work its dynamism. One cannot but admire the couple of delicate features by which the artist locates the scene quite definitely in Helsinki and creates an atmophere of a sunny summer's day. The work of conserving the relief has also been successful (two pieces were lost and had to be replaced).

The works of Rut Bryk (1916–99) are an excellent demonstration of the possibilities for symbiosis between an architect and a ceramic artist when cooperation is at its best. Bryk produced a ceramic sculpture for the main staircase of Helsinki City Hall that is perfectly suited in scale and in its handling of colour to the clean lines of the entrance hall and staircase and adds a certain opulence to Professor Aarno Ruusuvuori's minimalist architecture. The theme is the map of Helsinki. The artist also managed to express the possibilities and methods existing in architecture through her work. Her tiled reliefs are usually based on a distinct modular network, but by varying the size of the units, the texture of the patterns, the protrusions and depressions, the details and the colours, she was able to develop them into infinitely rich, ingenious entities that invite one to explore them further – just as one finds elsewhere in the built-up environment. They have a rhythm about them that creates an impression of movement, while their colours concentrate our attention on them and force the eye to move over their surface. The uniformity that they project from afar, at first glance, turns into a wealth of detail when looked at from close to.

Kristina Riska produces large-scale sculpture-like ceramic items by a thin coil technique that calls for an especially demanding hand-glazing process. The result is a fine-grained surface that emphasizes the form and size of the object. Riska's works need plenty of space around them. Detail on a pot from 1997.
Photo: Kimmo Friman

Other works by Rut Bryk are to be found in the Finnish Embassy in New Delhi and in the president's official residence, Mäntyniemi, both outcomes of close cooperation with the architects Raili and Reima Pietilä. The Pietiläs' architecture fits in exceptionally well with Bryk's art, in that her detailed, systematic mode of expression, which gains its structure from the architectural themes, complements their complex, organic and highly idiosyncratic architecture. Her ceramics serve, as it were, as a model for the world-view contained in their buildings. This association between artist and architect was particularly successful in the case of Mäntyniemi.

The large ceramic creations of Kristina Riska (b. 1960) have a power that wells up from the delicacy of the material and the majesty that lies in the sensitivity and diversity of form and content that characterizes the surfaces. The language of forms that she uses makes reference to everyday utility vessels such as vases or plant pots, but the sculptural works themselves are obviously ceramic art and not everyday objects. It is this dialogue between form and scale, emphasized at a micro-level by the glazed surfaces and minimalistic colouring, that lends an archaic but sensitive tone to her work. Her principal commission for a public place is a series of seven large 'vases' for the entrance hall of the Finnish Embassy in Washington. Riska's works depart somewhat from those traditionally intended for use in an architectural context, and they call

for extreme precision in the planning of the space. In this sense the multipurpose demands of the Washington Embassy building are mildly at variance with the nature of the ceramics.

Karin Widnäs (b. 1946) is one of the few artists in Finland actively concentrating on ceramics for installation in buildings. She recounts that she took to designing wall tiles and tiled stoves in spite of the fact that her studies at the University of Art and Design in Helsinki had led her towards the production of unique ceramic items of an artistic nature. She makes her limited series of basic asymmetrical wall tiles out of red

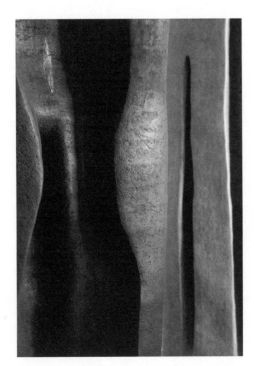

clay by a mould technique and undertakes active cooperation with architects. One example of this is the wall behind the cash desk in the Artek furniture salesroom in Helsinki, which she produced in conjunction with the Valvomo architects' office. In this case the architect and ceramic artist decided together on the sizes, shapes and glazing colours of the tiles. Widnäs also produces perforated bricks of red clay by the traditional moulding method, and has used these together with tiles for the walls of her own studio at Fiskars, a building designed for her by Professor Tuomo Siitonen.

Ceramics are widely used in construction work, and one would imagine that ceramic artists and architects would have a lot in common at this interface between art and building. Unfortunately we have scarcely any ceramic artists in Finland who have specialized in the design of items for inclusion in buildings – with the exception of the interior decoration of a few private homes. Similarly, with the exception of Alvar Aalto, architects have not usually been interested in incorporating specialized ceramics into their designs. As a designer of industrial products as well as an architect, Aalto developed his own series of ceramic tiles which he used to form broad surfaces both inside and out of doors in many of his buildings. Similarly, his rod-like ceramic clinker bricks became a hallmark of his architecture, whereas other architects made little use of these. Industrial manufacture of Aalto's con-

The work of the ceramic artist Tiina Veräjänkorva (1959) is an exploration of time, interfaces, seriality and semiotics in an urban environment. Her *Innumerable Signs* in the yard of Helsinki University's Forestry Building makes use of the eye-catching blue colour used on advertisements and road signs and is situated in a place where art can offer the passer-by new semantic contents. Photo: Museokuva.

structional ceramics was discontinued a few years ago, but clinker tiles are still being used as a surface material (e.g. in many swimming baths). Particular mention should be made of the magnificent clinker-surfaced interior and ceramic sculptures of the Yrjönkatu Baths in Helsinki.

Ceramics constitute a mystical art form in which techniques known throughout history are used to transform a simple raw material that is available almost anywhere into a highly durable object. At the same time a glaze may be added that assumes a colour in the course of firing and becomes an integral part of the object, recording the artistic notions of its creator for posterity. In the same way, of course, architecture – our built environment – is a historical record of our society's traditions and material achievements, a picture of the human mind to be handed down to future generations. Ceramic materials are essentially haptic: they have durable, glazed surfaces that are pleasant to the touch. They also form a natural part of our available building materials, and it would be a wonderful thing if we could learn to make far more extensive use of ceramic art as a mode of architectural expression than we do at present.

The artist Rut Bryk beside her *Ice Stream*. The large ceramic wall took its form from the architecture, adapting to its lines. It was produced at the Arabia studios and was placed in the president's official residence, Mäntyniemi, in 1992. It consists of seven panels, the names of which tell of the primitive forces of nature and the landscape of Lapland. Photo by courtesy of Pertti Nisonen and Maaru Wirkkala.

HANNELE NYMAN

The ceramic artist and industry:
passions, ideals and economic realities

One salient feature in the development of the ceramic arts over the decades has been the accent placed on ideals, combined with the inevitable clashes between these ideals and practical considerations. There have been conflicts that in the best cases have led to renewed creativity, both in the artists' own studios and in their co-operation with industry, although the latter has been beset by constant problems of drawing the line between the authentic discovery of unique designs and the mass production of decorative objects. Is it to be art or industry – or can one combine the two?

The relation between art and industry has been a controversial one ever since the dawn of the industrial age, arousing fiery tempers on occasions. It became a particularly urgent matter in the mid-nineteenth century, with the emergence of the Arts and Crafts movement, and by the end of the century the same polemic had reached the Scandinavian countries, where ceramics was even more emphatically linked with industrial production.

The leading role in the ceramics industry in Finland has been played throughout by the Arabia factory, founded in 1873, which took on its first full-time ceramic artist in 1896, and whose art department has been a legend in its own field ever since its creation in the early 1930s. Kupittaan Savi, founded in Turku in 1918, also employed artists from the outset, and Kera, founded in 1917, did so later, in the 1930s. Other early ceramics companies in Finland, including Suotniemi, Andsten, the Turku Tile Works and

Rakkolanjoki, preferred to base their production on imported patterns or adaptations of these.[1] Another obvious source of inspiration for artistic ceramics in Finland was the studio philosophy initiated by A. W. Finch, who was opposed to any association with large-scale industry.

Artists in industry? The first steps
The dichotomy between industry and ceramic art has been explained in terms of the ideas of Ruskin and Morris, although they did accept the use of machinery to some extent. Morris laid emphasis on the work of the 'artist-craftsman', who worked through the whole process himself, from design to execution and finishing,[2] although from the Nordic perspective he was seen to be concerning himself more with small series of items than with unique pieces, as would be natural in view of the long tradition of studio ceramics in England. On the other hand, as Finch wrote in 1901, referring to the ideas of Ruskin, Morris and their successors, 'The reforms were not intended to apply only to external form but also to content: the aim was to render the whole of life both simpler and more beautiful.'[3] This was intended as an antidote to industry, which was perceived as a source of both complexity and impoverishment.

The notion of the function of the ceramic artist in industry that developed

EXPOSITION UNIVERSELLE DE 1878
FINLANDE

B. K., Éditeur

The first tentative moves towards making use of art in the Finnish pottery industry. Arabia had employed French painters and a graduate in art, Fanny Sundahl-Lundblad, to decorate the main items for its contribution to the Finnish stand at the 1878 World Exhibition in Paris. Photo: Otava Publishing Company photo archives.

The founding of the art department at Arabia in 1932 was the realization of the ceramist Kurt Ekholm's dream of creative artists working freely within industry. The factory manager, Carl Gustaf Herlitz, looked favourably on artistic work as a counterbalance to industrial production and gave it his full support. Ekholm in Michael Schilkin's studio around 1945. On the table is a bust of Herlitz that Schilkin had made. Photo: Arabia Museum.

in France comes closer to that which prevailed in Scandinavia, and went still further in certain respects. Unlike their English counterparts, the French ceramic artists regarded their work as a branch of 'fine art' and exhibited their creations in art galleries alongside the works of painters and sculptors. Thus Auguste Renoir learned the techniques of painting and the use of colours as a child in the porcelain works of Lévy Frères, Auguste Rodin made some extra money between 1879 and 1882 at Sèvres, and Paul Gauguin collaborated with Ernest Chaplet. Gauguin also perceived very clearly that clay had a dynamics of its own, maintaining that although a sculptor might use clay models in his work, it was quite another matter to be aiming from the outset to produce a work in clay.[4] Others who followed the same line of development in their time included Joan Miró, Georges Braque and Pablo Picasso.

Although the development of the ceramic arts side by side with industrial production from the 1880s onwards is a feature common to all the Nordic countries, some differences are to be found. In the opinion of Hård af Segerstadt, the ideas of Ruskin and Morris created the greatest stir in Finland, where alongside literature and painting, design and architecture were also being harnessed in the service of the projection of a specific Finnish identity, whereas these influences were received in a more staid manner in Denmark and Norway, while Sweden gravitated systematically towards Functionalism.[5] It was in Finnish

ceramic art that particular weight came to be attached to the artistic aspect, although the acceptance of ceramic artists in industry, and particularly the degree of freedom afforded to them, has been greatly dependent on the interests and philosophy of the individual factory manager in each case and on his vision or lack of it, a feature that has repeated itself many times over in the course of time.

In the case of the Iris factory (1897–1902), which made a positive effort to combine art with industrial production, the founder, Louis Sparre, and the ceramics production manager, A. W. Finch, shared a desire to apply Morris's ideas in practice. Sparre was in no way averse to the use of machines, and Finch concurred with this: it was the only alternative if one wished to keep prices at a reasonable level and make the products accessible to as many people as possible. As Finch put it in his enthusiasm for the rationale of the Iris factory, 'Times are changing, and industry is moving in new directions, as it is becoming increasingly obvious that art should be understood as one of the essentials of life.'[6] Later, after Iris had closed down, Finch moved to a teaching post at the Central School of Industrial Arts, where his declared aim was to train his students to work as independent ceramic artists outside industry. In the 1920s he was obliged to defend his views in the face of those who would have liked the school to produce industrial workers, and falling back on Ruskin, Morris, van de Velde and his own experiences of vis-

its to schools of art elsewhere in Europe, he declared categorically that it was not the purpose of such schools to train employees for factories that deprecated artists.[7] Finch's emphasis on the gulf between industry and art was a legacy that continued to guide the school's teaching in ceramics for a long time to come,[8] even though many of his pupils eventually became influential figures in industry, including Gustav Adolf Franzén, Valentina Modig-Manuel and Toini Muona.

The management of the Arabia porcelain factory was thinking along much the same lines as the Swedes and Danes in the 1870s and 1880s, when the architect J. Ahrenberg was taken on as artistic adviser, and when Thure Öberg became the factory's first resident artist in 1896. Öberg experimented with Morris's approach most obviously in the form of his crystal and lustre glazes, which were among his most original contributions, but Arabia had to wait until the 1920s and 1930s for its first really innovative artists. Meanwhile, Kupittaa began to produce works in the spirit of the English Arts and Crafts movement in 1918. Their first artist was Gustav Adolf Franzén[9], a pupil of A. W. Finch.

The management of two large factories in Denmark, Den Kongelige Porcelainsfabrik and Bing & Grøndahl, employed art directors from 1885 onwards,[10] among whom Arnold Krog of Den Kongelige developed his own technique of underglaze painting which earned Danish ceramics worldwide fame. There was another, smaller workshop, however, Kähler Keramik, that is of particular interest in this connection, as it used glazed stoneware for one-off items and employed artists in design work from the 1880s onwards, most notably Thorvald Bindesbøll, the pioneer of Danish industrial arts.[11] Finch referred to Kähler as one of the pioneers of cast clay in the 1890s, at a time when 'many industrialists, in spite of their responsibilities, have given in to immature tastes for economic reasons, ignoring with arrogant disdain the advice of artists, experts and other "impartial" observers.'[12] Den Kongelige was also commended by Finch for its proper attitude towards technical advances.

In Sweden, Ellen Key continued to explore the social perspective of Morris and Ruskin in the 1890s with her *Skönhet för alla*,[13] in which she emphasized that industrialists should collaborate with de-

signers in all cases, whether manufacturing matchboxes or larger objects, as beauty and the developing of a sense of beauty were social goals and essentials of life and not luxuries. Both the movement in England and the writings of Ellen Key had a profound influence on the ceramic artists Alf Wallander, who himself offered his services to Rörstrand and was employed as the company's resident artist from 1895 onwards, and Gunnar Wennerberg, who contacted the Gustavsberg company. It was also the case, however, that the managers of both factories had a personal interest in social and artistic matters.[14]

More beautiful objects for everyday use

The items produced by Wallander and Wennerberg were described later as *vackrare högtidsvara* (more beautiful objects for celebration use), as the age of everyday ware dawned somewhat later

in the Scandinavian countries, in the 1910s and 1920s, when demands began to arise for more affordable items. By this time, industrial concerns were beginning to hire artists both to modernize their range of products and (less often) to create unique items. 'Everyday ware' was most prominent in Sweden, where the pamphlets of Ellen Key had prepared the way for such developments, and *Svenska Slöjdföreningen* (the Swedish Handicrafts Association) engaged Gregor Paulsson to write his first propagandist publication, *Vackrare vardagsvara* (More Beautiful Objects for Everyday Use), in 1919.[15] This treatise aimed especially at industrialists announced a programme for producing more beautiful everyday ware and stressed the important role that artists could play in achieving this goal.

Paulsson perceived the essential conflict of interests in this policy: the need for artistic freedom versus the need for adapting to the demands of industry, and at the same time the need for collaboration between industry and artists. There was a demand for industrially manufactured objects of beauty, but these should be designed with mass production in mind and not be imitations of the artist's unique handmade items. Paulsson had an unshakeable faith in both the potential for an artist to influence industrial design and the inspiration of modern industrialists, for whom the factory could be an object of genuine interest and not merely a source of profit.

In Finland, it was Edvard Elenius who deliberated in 1915 on the relation between the products of factories and small workshops in *Kotiemme kauneus* (Beauty in our Homes),[16] a booklet published by the Society for Popular Education. He came to the conclusion that not all mass-produced items were to be condemned, for glass and china objects could scarcely be manufactured entirely by hand or as cottage industries, nor could one manage without them.

The need for developing in an artistic direction intensified in the case of the Arabia factory once it became independent in 1916, and closer collaboration with artists was initiated in the 1920s with the employment of Greta Lisa Jäderholm-Snellman to revise the factory's range of designs and of the Austrian-born artist Friedl Holzer-Kjellberg. Other artists also attached to the factory during this period were Finch's pupils Elin Juselius and Gerda Thesleff and the Swede Tyra Lundgren, who made a number of visits in the 1920s and 1930s. Greta Lisa Jäderholm-Snellman set up the More Beautiful Objects for Everyday Use Department, with the approval of the works manager Carl Gustaf Herlitz.[17] Greta Lisa's idea of a beautiful item was above all that it should be painted by hand, so that she was prepared to combine industrially produced form with hand-painted ornamentation. This department provided many opportunities for students to work in industry, as the painters came from the Central School of Industrial Arts, where Greta Lisa taught porcelain painting. Kurt Ekholm later gave her the credit for being the first modernizer of artistic ceramics in the Arabia factory[18] and the first person to make its items known in the world outside.

A dish (36 x 31 cm) painted by Laila Zink for the
Kupittaa Pottery Company: a picture of the artist
herself at work in the factory, early 1950s.
Owned by Jorma Kivimäki. Photo: Johnny Korkman.

In the late 1920s the architect Rafael Blomstedt was moved to deplore the state of the ceramic arts in Finland and the difficulties encountered in reconciling the views of artists and industrial manufacturers, but noted that 'some hopes exist that certain leading manufacturers may be ready to undertake serious measures to refine their production. This will call for a certain amount of adaptation and understanding on both sides in order to make a good beginning.' Greta Lisa Jäderholm-Snellman, Maija Grotell and Elsa Elenius were all commended for their work so far.[19] Meanwhile, Arttu Brummer wrote of the *Vackrare vardagsvara* movement in Sweden that many factories were engaged in cooperation with artists to these ends and that there were some sales outlets that were committed to this slogan, and Brummer hoped that the same could be achieved in Finland.[20]

Free, creative artists
The emergence of a powerful concentration of ceramic artists in Finland was something that took place precisely in the industrial sphere. Two people were particularly responsible for the creation of Arabia's art department, Kurt Ekholm and Carl Gustaf Herlitz, the former a ceramic artist himself and the latter a factory manager who was favourably disposed towards such aspirations. The purposeful efforts of Kurt Ekholm to build up the department from the early 1930s onwards were grounded in the view that it was essential to develop a national ceram-

ic culture and that responsibility for this lay with the country's largest porcelain works. 'It was my intention to attempt to create a department for independent ceramic artists under the auspices of Arabia, a department that would function on a broader basis than was customary. I believed that it was only in that way that it might be possible to create something new that would mean a step forward in the ceramic arts.'[21]

Prior to coming to Arabia, Ekholm had been an apprentice to Gunnar Nylund, who had just been appointed artistic director of Rörstrand, and it was there that he had become acquainted with stoneware, which was to become one of the basic materials used by the Arabia art department and was later to be adopted for the industrial manufacture of tableware as well. Rörstrand also had a man-

ager who was favourably disposed towards ceramic art, Fredrik Wethje, who had been a trainee at Arabia for a time.[22] Both Herlitz and Wethje possessed some of the qualities that Paulsson was looking for in the 'modern industrialist'.

The fundamental notion behind Arabia's art department was idealistic in the extreme: that the artists should enjoy complete creative freedom and that they should not be encumbered by obligations with regard to large-scale production. Products did benefit greatly over the years from the technical and material innovations introduced by the artists, just as the one-off items created by them benefited from the acumen gained in the factory, especially the services of its meticulously organized laboratory. The department's participation in overseas exhibitions, e.g. the Milan Triennial and various Scandinavian events, forged a worldwide reputation for Arabia. The relationship, as Herlitz put it, was that 'the more we simplify our working methods and standardize our mass production, the more scope we have to give to the power of our artistic expression.'[23]

Herlitz was a prolific writer, and a constant theme of his deliberations was the reconciliation of economic 'realities' with the aspirations of the people who did the work, the optimal combination of the material and human dimensions: 'It is essential to invent a system that transforms production into an elegant art form.'[24] In one brief work on the social impact of industry, Herlitz put forward ideas on the works manager as one part of the working community: 'The true creative longing in a person may take the form of working as an artist, or of concentrating on the shaping of human relations, as a manager, for instance.'[25] He was clearly a disciple of Henry Ford, whose success he referred to on many occasions.[26] The art department gave him great satisfaction on both scores: 'The art department has not remained merely at the level of an inevitable ornamentation for our mass production, but it serves to cherish and develop ceramics as an art form in such a manner that repercussions will be felt before long in our production of everyday utility ware, giving this more refined forms and more artistic ornamentations.'

Tyra Lundgren described Herlitz in the 1940s as a manager 'who lives with china and for china, and even thinks china'[27], a person with a profound mastery over this difficult material. She believed that the strength of the art department lay in its technical management, i.e. in the enthusiasm of Carl Gustaf Herlitz and his belief that anything was possible. Lundgren then went on to consider the relation between the artists and the factory. From a theoretical point of view, the combination is ideal: the artist has more technical opportunities than would ever be possible when working alone, more experience in ceramics of all kinds and at best a feeling of really having some influence on industry. The danger is that the artist may be inclined to overestimate the value of technology, but this can be avoided with a sufficiently powerful artistic identity.

Of the other Finnish factories, Kera employed an artistic manager in the 1930s, and Kupittaan Savi added to its team during the same period. The first trained ceramic artist at Grankulla Potteries (later Kera Oy) was Valentina Modig-Manuel, who was employed there in 1930–36. The management was suspicious at first of the simple forms that she created, and of her refusal to sign items produced with imported moulds, which she had agreed to decorate although she did not approve of their forms. She was nevertheless officially appointed artistic director in 1931. Modig regarded work in a factory as beneficial for a recently qualified potter, as one learned the mixing of clays, the making of moulds and the shaping and firing of pots and had an opportunity to experiment with glazes, all of which made it easier to set up a studio of one's own later. The second ceramic artist to be employed at Grankulla was Kerttu Suvanto-Vaajakallio, in 1932–34, but she soon moved to Kupittaa, luring Modig with her for a time, until the latter founded her own studio, Keramos, in Turku.[28]

Another workshop that operated from the 1930s onwards was that of Gregori Tigerstedt in Helsinki. This combined ceramic art with the small-scale production of domestic ware for sale at the Stockmann department store. Tigerstedt referred to his enterprise as a 'factory' and also offered to fire objects made by other potters and by sculptors.[29] Tigerstedt, as a member of the Terracotta Association, knew the sculptors of the day, so that men such as Ville Vallgren,

Gunnar Finne and Emil Cedercreutz, together with many students at the Atheneum, would bring their works to him for firing.[30] Another opportunity for firing pots of which Vallgren, Cedercreutz and particularly Wäinö Aaltonen availed themselves was at the Arabia factory. Aaltonen evidently experimented with glazes there as well,[31] and some items of his were produced in small series by Arabia.[32]

Industry, art and industrial arts

In his classic, *A Potters Book* (1940), Bernard Leach built up a discussion of the differences between the artist-potter and the ceramic artist on the ideals of Morris and the Asian pottery tradition. He criticized mass production, not on account of the use of machines but because of its false standards of beauty that were based on commercial or conventional tastes.[33] He was fearful of combining the artist/designer with industrial methods unless the designer had a profound feel for the clay. What he was looking for in principle was beauty and honest production, regardless of whether the potter was a Chinese peasant farmer or a celebrated European artist. 'Pots, like all other forms of art, are human expressions: pleasure, pain or indifference before them depends upon their natures, and their natures are inevitably projections of the minds of their creators.'[34]

In Finland, Arttu Brummer was arguing in the early 1930s for a distinction to be made between artistic handicrafts and industrial arts: 'With the invasion of machines into the world of crafts, we are obliged to resolve the relation between the decorative arts and mechanization.'[35] He believed that crafts could come closer to the secrets and emotions of art than could the engineering technology and logic of the industrial arts. We expect industrial products to be utterly rational, but we are prepared to judge handmade items on a more liberal scale. 'The highest level of expression in creative art is that form should be a creed in its own right, a moral conviction, an outburst of the desire for beauty. A language of this kind enables one heart to communicate directly with another. As the world of industrial arts expands and takes on an ever more commercial aspect, we should be ready to tend this delicate offspring of the dark forests and fragrant meadows with gentle care. We will be struggling on behalf of living art for some time to come.'

The post-war situation was exploited to the full by designers in Finland and the Scandinavian countries, and in a manner that encompassed art, the industrial arts and crafts. The outcome was the success story known as Scandinavian Design. The intended appeal of design to the general public had not been fully effective in the age of 'more beautiful objects for everyday use', but in the post-war atmosphere design became a magic word and designers became stars. Ceramic artists rose in public esteem, as the exhibitions that toured the world placed the works of the Arabia artists in particular alongside utility items. One influential figure in this was Herman Olof Gummerus, who was a public relations representative for Ara-

bia and was involved in organizing innumerable such exhibitions.[36] The Arabia artists also continued with their own series of Nordic exhibitions that had begun so triumphantly, and gained much positive feedback, including outbursts of admiration such as that expressed in a letter from Edgar J. Kauffmann Jr of the Museum of Modern Art in New York to the industrial artists of Finland: 'We demand to know who pointed the way for the exceptional programme pursued by Arabia, a large factory employing a group of first-class artists. Who are these people? I do not know of a single American china factory that has been able to gather its earlier work into a museum as Arabia has done. And if someone should try to do so, would our work bear comparison?'[37]

There were also critical voices, however, who wondered at the existence of purely artistic interests in industrial circles, particularly in Sweden where the focus was on 'more beautiful objects for everyday use'. Kurt Ekholm staunchly defended the rights of the Arabia artists to concentrate on their own work, and it was at his initiative that Kaj Franck was taken on in the 1940s to develop a separate Product Design Department. The third link in the chain was the Industrial art department: 'The products of this department are called industrial art because the models and ornamentations are produced in small series'[38] in accordance with the artists' plans. The basic philosophy behind this department had been created by Jäderholm-Snellman, and it continued to take students straight from

the School of Industrial Arts,[39] now partly with the idea of ensuring the continuity of the art department.

Both of the principal influential Finnish figures in this field, Rafael Blomstedt and Arttu Brummer, recognized the high standards achieved by the Arabia artists and the prominence that they enjoyed abroad,[40] but the potter Eero Rislakki[41] was more critical of the indeterminate mass of ornamental objects that had been produced and commented that the best ceramic artists in the land had become to a great extent concentrated in the Arabia factory over the last ten years, so that this company now carried the main responsibility for high-class art ceramics. But had the summit now be reached, he asked, so that more competition was needed? After all, the other Nordic countries had several equally strong enterprises competing with each other in this field.

The Kupittaa works continued to lay emphasis on ceramic art in its post-war output, the main figures being Orvokki Laine, Marjukka Pääkkönen-Paasivirta, Viljo Mäkinen and Heidi Blomstedt. It was above all Viljo Mäkinen (who left to become a freelance artist in the 1960s) who managed to create unique pieces, and the management was encouraged to perceive the value of this activity through the successes achieved in exhibitions.[42] The ornamentation section of the production department, which corresponded to the hand-painting department at Arabia, was a place where many artists would work to earn their keep while studying, and it operated on purely commercial lines, the

What is the future of artistic ceramics within industry? The Arabia artists founded an independent association on 4.11.2003 to continue the work of the art department. From the left: Pekka Paikkari, Heini Riitahuhta, Kati Tuominen-Niittylä, Inkeri Leivo, Kristina Riska, Heikki Orvola, Fujiwo Ishimoto and Heljä Liukko-Sundström. Photo: Timo Kauppila/ Arabia art department association.

sales department dictating what appealed to the public, i.e. what the painters should do.[43] Heidi Blomstedt's vases, on the other hand, were classified as industrial art, while small series were produced in the 'more beautiful objects for everyday use' vein by Marita Lybeck's Emmel workshop in 1947–57. Lybeck was also artistic director of the Kera pottery in 1957–58, again showing a predilection for simple, utilitarian ceramics.

The rejection of purposeless art

Criticism increased in Finland, as elsewhere, in the 1960s and 1970s, perhaps as a reaction to the success enjoyed by this 'purposeless' form of art, or per-haps as a direct hangover after the prizes won at the triennials. Some intolerance of 'crossing the boundary' was also expressed among sculptors and others, but the success of the ceramic artists helped to cast doubts on attempts to draw a sharp dividing line. Thus Sakari Vapaavuori of Arabia and Viljo Mäkinen of Kupittaa were able to pose perfectly naturally as sculptors as well.[44] At the same time, functionality was a universally expressed demand, and industrial design emerged powerfully as a separate concept, spreading to Europe from the USA.[45] Emphasis was placed on the social responsibility of designers and the 'obligation' to express an opinion. To be fashionable, things had to be directed at everyone, and art in industrial circles was something reactionary, to be condemned as no more than decorative. Thus we find the industrial designer Antti Nurmesniemi asking whether Finland can afford to live only for Sundays,[46] and vehemently criticizing the decorative approach, a category in which he clearly included artists such as Birger Kaipiainen, as over-refined, trivial, complacent affectation: 'We do not need to serve up pearls on a silver platter to the wealthy and privileged.' One consequence was that increasing numbers of potters set up studios of their own or went into partnership with others, supported by the advice given by Kyllikki

Salmenhaara in her teaching at the University of Art and Design in Helsinki. Many such potters actively criticized their colleagues who worked in the 'ivory tower' on the ninth floor of the Arabia factory.

Kaj Franck sought to counterbalance the personality cult by criticizing the abundant use of the names of artists for marketing industrial products: 'I would like to proclaim an age of anonymity in our industrial arts.'[47] Teamwork and mass production were the order of the day. On the other hand, he did not deny the value of unique items, and during his period as artistic director at Arabia in 1968–73 he was ready to recognize it as a significant cultural institution in many respects. 'The art department is not directly profitable,' he maintained, 'but indirectly it has always been of the utmost importance for giving Arabia's regular products, Finnish design in general and the whole of Finland a worldwide reputation. The maintenance of this department is an act of philanthropy on the company's part.'[48]

The radical cuts in production at Arabia that took place in the mid-1970s in response to the energy crisis were a trial for the art department, and there were imminent threats of closure. The trend in china and porcelain manufacture all over Europe was for companies to be merged. Thus a collaboration agreement was concluded between Arabia and Rörstrand in the mid-1970s with the aim of forming 'an efficient, medium-sized factory producing household china'. All the 'peripherals' were to be stripped away, including the art department. Franck countered this

by suggesting that it should be converted into a separate institute, and the eventual outcome was a somewhat radical compromise under which only three out of the nine artists retained a permanent position with the company. This aroused a lively discussion in the press, with questions asked in Sweden as to whether Arabia had sold its soul along with its art department and in Finland as to whether the country had lost part of its national heritage, since not only had almost the whole department gone, but also the Kilta (later Teema) and Paradise series of tableware, which the Finnish public regarded as symbolic of Arabia's reputation. The agreement was scrapped after three years, with the comment that 'mediocrity doesn't pay.'[49]

The more we standardize...

The department for creative artists, Arabia's great speciality, has been preserved for the time being. Nowadays it is a synthesis between the creative art department, the Product Design Department and, through the Pro Arte collection, the Industrial art department. Thoughts have nevertheless returned time and again to the theme around which it was founded in the first place, that it is only through creative freedom that something can be achieved that carries art forward. 'Working in this department is not all enjoyment. Often it is mentally very strenuous, as artistic work does not always fit into the picture, so that we find ourselves fighting for our existence.'[50]

But is there a future for ceramic art within industry? Once more factories

are merging, changing ownership and adapting to new situations. It would seem at the time of writing that the Arabia, Rörstrand and Höganäs porcelain factories are about to pass into the hands of an investment company or the equivalent as part of the sale of the Hackman Group, Den Kongelige in Denmark is moving out of its old premises, and Gustavsberg in Sweden has reorganized itself as a cooperative. Most ceramic art is now being produced outside the factories, in separate group workshops, studios or partnerships. Some of the artists are also engaged in teaching, while others live by producing small-scale series of hand-made items.

The conflict between commercial interests and artistic values has not abated, but is still raging as vigorously as ever. The reputation of an art department still represents a significant form of intellectual capital for a factory, extremely valuable in terms of public relations but difficult to classify or to measure financially. The key words today are young, fresh, global (anonymous although possessing a name?), project work by international designers, and a brand name constructed on certain criteria, to which production has to be adapted. The danger is that all the roles will be mixed to form an amorphous globalized mass, resulting in intellectual and artistic impoverishment. But fashions change. What if the next passion is for emphasizing national characteristics in art and design?

ÅSA HELLMAN

The advent of small ceramic workshops in Finland

Gregori Tigerstedt outside the workshop that he set up in the 1930s in a former stable and coach house in the centre of Helsinki. The building has been preserved practically in its original form.
Photo courtesy of Yvonne-Tigerstedt Suonne.

'Finland is not actually a ceramics country although this seems to be the general belief,' wrote Professor Kyllikki Salmenhaara in *Kotiteollisuus* magazine in 1972.[1] She referred to the fact that the Finnish ceramic tradition is limited in comparison with ceramic folk art in other European countries. Local museums contain interesting artefacts in wood and textiles, carried out in a variety of techniques, but examples of ceramic work are rare. Those that exist are generally plain in decoration and form.

Finland lacks natural stoneware clays, and the domestic earthenware clay is difficult to use in workshop production as its melting point is low and its iron content varies even within one region. Early potteries mainly produced bowls, baking dishes, unglazed preserving jars and decorative tiles for stoves. Small workshops passed down from father to son, common in most European countries, were rare in Finland.

A tortuous path

The predecessors of today's ceramic studios were established in the 1930s. Some of the students of Alfred William Finch, the first teacher of ceramic art at the Central School of Arts and Crafts (now the University of Art and Design Helsinki), had their own kilns, but most of these workshops were short-lived and their work is largely undocumented. The most talented and diligent students were for decades allowed to fire their work in the school's kiln. Others took their products to Arabia to be fired. Finch had employed traditional potters as throwers at the Iris factory, and the school's ceramics department also cooperated with potteries in the Tuusula-Kerava area.[2] Some Finnish sculptors, among them Ville Vallgren, had kilns and fired their own terracotta pieces.[3]

One of the first workshops in Finland to specialize in ceramics as art rather than pottery was founded in the 1930s by the sculptor and painter Gregori Tigerstedt, who had studied sculpture in Geneva and Berlin and later became fascinated by ceramics and its firing processes. His studio was located in the centre of Helsinki, in a courtyard in Kruunuhaka. Tigerstedt's concept was to allow ceramists, sculptors and art students to fire their work there for a small fee. Tigerstedt's daughter Yvonne worked for many years in the studio assisting her father. The workshop had a significant status and accepted work for firing even in wartime. The studio ceased operating in the 1970s and was gradually taken over by painter and mosaic artist Bruno Tuukkanen.

An exception was Mirjam Stäuber in Tenhola. Stäuber studied with Finch and used stoneware as well as earthenware, which she for several years fired in a wood-burning kiln. She was highly productive during the 1930s and 40s, and her beautiful, well-thrown ceramics still remain in western Uusimaa. She married and moved to Trinidad in 1954 but continued to work in Tenhola during summer visits.[4]

Ceramist Valentina Modig-Manuel was another studio pioneer, who with

Tor and Ilma Berglöf in their workshop in 1957.
The family made a living from tiny handmade articles
of pottery that would fit into a very small kiln.
Photo courtesy of Tor Berglöf.

In the 1940s Birgit Dyhr lived and worked in a single-
room town flat in which she also had her own kiln.
Photo courtesy of Birgit Dyhr.

her husband Josef Manuel managed a successful workshop, Studio Keramos in Turku, between 1937 and 1981. It produced thrown ware and cast animal sculptures designed by Josef Manuel. Studio Keramos clearly illustrates the fact that family enterprises could often outlive workshops run by single women; a husband's support could mean a lot for a woman ceramist.

Some ceramists set up workshops in their homes, often in basements and sometimes even in blocks of flats. One of these was Birgit Dyhr, who from the 1950s onwards for almost forty years had a studio with a kiln in her apartment.

The chances of enjoying a successful career as a studio ceramist in Finland were minimal up to the 1970s. There were no importers of clays or glazes, and independent ceramists had to buy their materials abroad, incurring transport costs and customs duties. Arabia sold clays to independent ceramists up to the middle of the 1970s, but the factory's clays required significantly higher firing temperatures than the studio kilns of the time could manage.[5] In order to purchase kilns and glazes, Finnish ceramists went to Stockholm's Seeman company, the closest retailer of ceramic materials.

Finnish ceramic art was for a long time closely linked to the Arabia factory and to the artists at the artd epartment on its renowned ninth floor. Arabia's artists were in many ways privileged; thanks to the factory's resources they could wholeheartedly apply themselves to their artistry, escaping the countless technical problems of ceramic processes. Neither were they troubled by mar-

keting issues on a national or indeed international level: Arabia's artists always had a place at international exhibitions. A certain amount of professional envy among independent studio ceramists toward their colleagues at Arabia was inevitable. Naturally there were those who considered any attachment to the ceramics industry to be beneath them.

Independent ceramists had to overcome not only practical problems but also isolation and lack of cooperation within the field. They struggled alone in small studios and were frustrated, having chosen a profession in which it was virtually impossible to make a living.

Another problem was a lack of positive role models. The artists at Arabia seemed to belong to another world. In Finland, in contrast to other countries, ceramic art was chiefly women's work,

with low pay and a relatively low social status. It was difficult for the wider public to associate ceramics with anything other than a hobby. After graduation, male ceramics students generally sought positions in closely related areas: some, like designer Richard Lindh, opted for management positions in the silicate industry; others, notably sculptor Mauno Hartman, eventually chose to work with other materials.

Among other early studio founders were Marita Lybeck, Dorrit von Fieandt, Taina Kurtze and Tor and Ilma Berglöf, all described in detail elsewhere in this book. The way for future studio ceramists was paved by a handful of enterprising and fearless artists. Most often they were women, forced to interrupt their work on the birth of each child and expected to manage their homes and households in addition to carrying out their heavy and demanding ceramic work. Consequently, many female ceramists began working twice as intensively in middle age, once their children had flown the nest. Many, on the other hand, found the financial and social pressures overwhelming and were compelled to leave ceramics as one would an unhappy marriage.

Some strong women

In 1963 Eija Karivirta, a student of Elsa Elenius, founded a ceramics workshop in an old laundry on Töölönkatu in Helsinki, where her fellow student Anna-Maria Osipow joined her a year later. The artists mixed their own clays from powder, and Karivirta had a kick wheel built to size (they happened to be the same height). Their electric kiln, a 'Leinosen-uuni', was built in Vartiokylä, where kiln-maker Reino Leinonen was based. Their production consisted of plates, lamp bases, jugs, mugs and teapots. Health and safety conditions left much to be desired as artists at the time were unaware of the poisonous nature of metallic oxides. Lead glazes were mixed with bare hands.

A breakthrough for Karivirta and Osipow came when Stockmann's buyer, Ben Gyllenberg, placed orders for their work. Stockmann's design department enjoyed a high standing, and having work displayed there alongside that of Arabia employees increased the artists' confidence. In 1966 Eija Karivirta moved to Porvoo and founded a studio; Anna-Maria Osipow also worked independently at studio Prijuutti in Järvenpää, which operated between 1977 and 2002. Both artists gradually abandoned thrown functional ware and successfully concentrated on ceramic sculptures.[6]

Liisa Tahvanainen (later Tarna) trained in Germany to become a traditional potter (*Töpferin*). Her studio, founded in Tikkurila in 1966, was based on German family workshops. She also acquired clays, glazes and a kiln in Germany. As private studios were rare in Finland, hers received a great deal of publicity in the contemporary press. In contrast to other ceramists, she employed an agent to sell the studio's products to craft shops in Finland. Asthma forced Tahvanainen to give up ceramics in 1971.

Generally speaking, studio work demanded an unyielding state of health. The studios had to be heated in winter, making the air dry and dusty. Years of kicking heavy potter's wheels caused hip problems, and toploading kilns taxed the neck and back. The clay and the floors in basement workshops were cold. As a consequence, rheumatoid arthritis was still a common occupational illness in the 1970s.

Piippa Tandefelt was the first ceramist to be awarded a one-year government scholarship for artists. She graduated from the Institute of Industrial Arts (since 1973 the University of Art and Design Helsinki) in 1964 and moved a year later to the island of Suomenlinna, where she founded a studio in a part of the eighteenth-century fortress. From the outside, the historic environment may have seemed idyllic, but conditions were primitive. Water was brought to the studio in a horse-drawn cart, and the scant heat from a small oil stove did not keep the place warm in winter. The clay was ice cold. But as Piippa Tandefelt became established she acquired local contacts, leading to the Pot Viapori group workshop being founded on the island later on.

Financial breakthrough

The 1970s brought revolutionary changes to Finnish ceramic art. The design industry had experienced intensive growth in the 1950s and 1960s, and Finland had become established global-

Private ceramics workshops were rare in Finland until the 1950s, and the lack of kilns meant that some students were allowed to use the school's workshop even after they had graduated. The picture shows ceramics students at the University of Art and Design Helsinki around 1930. Standing, Elsa Elenius, newly appointed head of the department. Photo courtesy of Auli Urrila.

ly as a design country. Industrial designers, notably Tapio Wirkkala and Timo Sarpaneva, had become international stars. By the beginning of the 1970s the situation changed. Increasing competition in the field and a harsher economic climate made factories less willing to invest large amounts in a few big names.

Ceramics factory Kupittaan Savi Oy was declared bankrupt in 1969, having been bought by Arabia – 'clearly in order to drive out the competition', believes ceramist and designer Peter Winquist, who worked at Arabia at the time. The larger ceramics factory also downsized: the first to go were the departments of sanitary porcelain and tiles. The order to reorganize the art department in 1975 came as a shock, especially as an opulent brochure about the department had just been printed.[7]

Arabia's art department was the

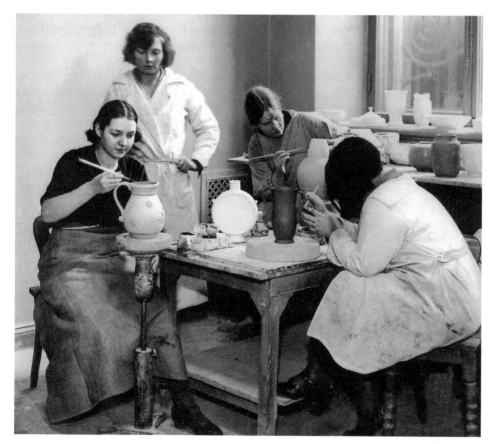

flagship of Finnish ceramics and design. As many prominent artists were now forced to leave, an era in applied art came to an end. Industrial design would increasingly be dominated by purely market-orientated issues. But for independent studio ceramists the events were psychologically liberating. 'Arabia's artists had been so dominant and powerful that it had felt as if small studios could never set themselves free from their shadow,' said Eija Karivirta.

The face of Finnish ceramic art changed. Small, private studios produced work on a smaller scale with lower firing temperatures. The focus shifted from unique exhibition pieces to more intimate, thrown functional items. And every year saw the graduation of a new host of enthusiastic young ceramists....

Capricious Finnish red clay

Paradoxically, it was Kyllikki Salmenhaara, an Arabia artist, who came to play a decisive role in the rise of independent studios in Finland. As head teacher of the ceramics department at the Institute of Industrial Arts she had to tackle the question of career opportunities for her students. She was appointed head teacher in 1963, but it took over a decade for her educational objectives to mature and the teaching at the university to take its ultimate shape, developing into a realistic foundation for independent studio work.[8]

In the 1960s Kyllikki Salmenhaara had a vision of pottery villages where ceramists would work close to local sources of clay.[9] The idea was to make it possible to earn a living by creating small series of functional ware – thrown, cast or press-moulded – and for that, the basement spaces available in larger cities were too dark and cramped. At Arabia, Kyllikki Salmenhaara had worked with high-fired stoneware but encouraged, without any real personal experience, her students to use Finnish red clay. Kaj Franck also spoke highly of the use of the local variety, though partly for ideological reasons. Ironically, these most ardent defenders of earthenware clay forgot that the companies which had earlier used the material – notably AB Iris and Studio Emmel – had been financially unprofitable and forced to close down.

Many ceramists tried to produce earthenware, but the Finnish public was suspicious and demanded quality. Some pots would not hold water and the contemporary press wrote about the dangers of lead glazes. In addition the melting point of the domestic clay varied with catastrophic effects: if the planned firing temperature was exceeded even slightly, the result could be grotesque melted forms. Red clay did not meet the requirements for domestic ware in every aspect, though it turned out to be an excellent medium for terracotta sculptures. Some of Salmenhaara's first successful students included Piippa Tandefelt and Catharina Kajander, who consequently changed paths and began building large works in red clay using the coil technique.

No pottery villages were founded; the capricious Finnish clay could not compete with imported stoneware clays. Kyllikki Salmenhaara's vision was not, however, entirely utopian. Thirty years later, in the 1990s, some craft communities were created in old foundries and factories. A good example is the Fiskars cooperative in western Uusimaa, which has evolved into a lively art and design centre.

In the 1970s it became clear that the ceramics industry could no longer employ all young, recently qualified ceramists, and Salmenhaara increasingly encouraged her students to start their own studios. Courses at the university were revised; material science and chemistry became important subjects to enable future ceramists to mix their own stoneware bodies and glazes. Accomplished male students were appointed teachers in mechanics, technical drawing and plasterwork. It is also probable that Salmenhaara made a conscious attempt to raise the status of the ceramist's profession by taking in more male students; some female students quietly complained that there was favouritism toward the men. Meanwhile the obedient women assistants went about cleaning in their Marimekko aprons.

Nordic models

While these intensive developments were taking place at the ceramics department, at European universities new winds were blowing from the Left. For many young artists, the word 'collective' took on a near-magical meaning. Sweden had pioneered by founding several group workshops for glassblowers, textile artists and ceramists. Their ideological backgrounds varied, but they all helped to teach craftsmen and artists that group work gives strength. The Blås & Knåda group, which ran a gallery in central Stockholm, became an important model and partner for Finnish ceramists. Earlier, ceramics made by Arabia's stars had been sold at the exclusive NK department store in Stockholm; now Finnish studio ceramists could show their work at museums and galleries in Sweden and the public received them willingly.

The Swedish journal *Form* published detailed illustrated articles on small studios and opened the eyes of buyers and collectors.[10] In contrast to Finland, Sweden had a tradition of private ceramics collecting. Pieces by Finnish ceramists were also purchased by the Swedish National Art Council for display in public buildings. *Form* was at the time sharply focused on the Nordic countries, and its editors Gunilla Lundahl and Kerstin Wickman were true friends of Finnish design. Their articles crossed borders and Scandinavian cooperation blossomed. In 1978 Swedish and Finnish artists travelled together to the World Crafts Council's international conference in Kyoto, visiting several Japanese ceramic centres on the way. This would later prove to have had a liberating effect on the creative work of the Finnish participants.

This Nordic cooperation also included group visits to colleagues in the neighbouring countries – in other words, several merry parties where artists sat around discussing professional concerns until the early hours. Comparisons revealed great differences in the countries' ceramic climates. The professional identities of Finnish studio ceramists were still uncertain and ambiguous. Their self-esteem was low and the Finnish public was ill informed about ceramics, believing that handmade items should be less expensive than Arabia's industrially manufactured ones, which had always enjoyed a high status. Qualified ceramists were not happy being described as craftsmen or associated with hobbyists and amateur artists.

Through Swedish influence, the Finnish word *taidekäsityöläinen* (literally 'artist-craftsman') began to be used in the 1970s to distinguish industrial artists and artisans from craftsmen. The debate drew protests from craftsmen, who considered references to art to be pretentious. But the new linguistic definition helped to strengthen professional identities. Potters became known first as ceramists and then gradually as ceramic artists or, when appropriate, sculptors.[11]

Ceramics Cellar in Kallio

The first modern Finnish ceramic group workshop was founded in 1971 at 18 D Aleksis Kiven katu in Helsinki. The workshop consisted of three rooms totalling fifty-five square metres and the space was shared equally between its four founders, Ulla Fogelholm, Åsa Hellman, Olavi Marttila and Pirkko Räsänen. All its members were at that time still students and thus not eligible for grants to equip a studio. An electric kiln was built as college work by Pirkko Räsänen and glass pioneer Heikki Kallio, who later went on to found his own glass-blowing studio. Head teacher Kyllikki Salmenhaara supported the project by letting the group purchase one of the ceramics department's old kick wheels for a nominal sum. Simple shelves and tables were acquired free of charge from a neighbouring shop that was being refurbished. The founders proudly noted that the workshop had been entirely financed by student loans.

At this time the premises at the ceramics department of the Institute of Industrial Arts were unbearably cramped and noisy. The new workshop was an oasis where its participants could practise throwing and learn the practical aspects of the job without interruptions. Finished works were sold at various craft events, mostly without profit, but at least costs of rent and materials were covered. The basic concept presupposed that each member would purchase and thereby own a part of the workshop, acquiring the right to use the premises and equipment. On leaving the workshop, members could sell to an existing or prospective member. A portion of the premises was also rented out to outsiders who were temporarily in need of a studio.

Today's electric kilns have automatic thermostats, but in the 1970s Finnish ceramists used Seger cones, which melt and bend at specific temperatures during firing. The kilns had to be watched carefully, and as it was more sensible to use electricity at night, when rates were lower, this resulted in tiring night watches. During intensive work periods the ceramists wandered about half-asleep. A small camp bed shared a room with the kiln and each firing process let off dangerous gases. There was no ventilation and the street-level windows could not be opened at night as the workshop was located next to Populus, a rowdy workers' pub. The workshop's windows were regularly broken in drunken fights. The ceramists would sometimes spend entire nights throwing just to stay awake.

The workshop produced wheel-thrown, cast, press-moulded and hand-built work. In the 1970s everything rustic was considered modern and there was as yet no real competition from cheaper, imported ceramics. Plain earthenware pottery reminded many urbanites of childhoods spent in country villages and they relished and bought it for nostalgic reasons. Occasionally the workshop held exhibitions with direct sales, which in the long run worked as consumer information events. Could wheel-thrown items be placed in the dishwasher and was it 'dangerous' if a part of a vessel was unglazed?

The workshop, which in time came to be named Keramiikkakellari (the Cera-

There was scarcely any competition in the field of hand-made domestic pottery in the 1970s, and rustic pots produced on the wheel sold well. The photograph is of the Ceramics Cellar, maintained by a circle of potters who produced functional ware to finance their one of a kind art pieces. Photo courtesy of Åsa Hellman.

mics Cellar), enjoyed a long and significant life, although it never became widely known. It was a pleasant and open place to work, not least because the permanent members carefully screened potential participants. The criteria applied were above all reliability and liquidity – the latter by no means common in the profession. A wide range of artists worked at Keramiikkakellari at one time or another until it was shut down in 1993 due to increased rental costs and the premises were taken over by the more prosperous neighbouring company Kumipojat. Artists who passed through Keramiikkakellari include Taija Partanen, Mirja Niemelä, Hilkka Niemi, Marjukka Pietiäinen, Kuutti Lavonen, Liisa Ikävalko, Sinikka Ahla and Anne Virtanen.

Group workshops and collectives

Kaj Franck, artistic director at Arabia's art department, was a Swedish-speaking Finn with close ties to the other Nordic countries, familiar with several Scandinavian group workshops. Although Franck was an industrial designer, crafts, both traditional and modern, remained close to his heart. As a member of various government art committees, he was instrumental in setting up the Pot Viapori ceramics workshop. It was established in 1972 on the island of Suomenlinna, a short ferry ride from Helsinki, and is still active. Its founders were ceramists Ritva Kaukoranta, Minni Lukander, Hilkka Jarva, Tuula Pöyhö and Piippa Tandefelt, and textile artist Eva Manner.

In contrast to Keramiikkakellari, Pot Viapori conveyed a political ideology that some of its founders shared and wished to put into effect. In the 1970s it was considered politically and socially 'correct' in Finnish cultural circles for artists to belong to the political Left. Pot Viapori was seen as a real opportunity to create a utopian community in miniature, a kind of collective where everything was shared. The plans for the project were grand and included a library, image archives and more. In practice it took years of discussions, meetings and arguments to find a functioning concept. Members came and went.

Pot Viapori is located in an old Russian arsenal built in the nineteenth century when Finland was a Grand Duchy subject to the Czar.[12] In this decaying historic building with no running water, which had for a long time served as a storeroom, the artists gradually built a modern ceramics studio. This required strenuous, recurring renovations. In its first decade, almost as much time was spent cleaning and refurbishing as doing creative work. The artists purchased kilns and other necessary equipment with the support of government and municipal grants.

Pot Viapori is a registered non-profit organization with aims to promote ceramics in Finland. The association owns all kilns and other effects, which guarantees continuity, as none of the members can remove any vital equipment when agreements terminate. Annual meetings are held to decide on joint exhibitions and other important projects.

Dilemmas arise in most group workshops from the difficulty of achieving a balance between the naturally egocentric characters of individuals and the compromises required for group work. The prerequisites for the success of a ceramics collective are prosaic but essential, even as simple as ensuring that people tidy up after themselves. The artists in Pot Viapori have found their way forward through trial and error. The workshop has miraculously survived over thirty years of internal setbacks and national economic crises. Its ceramists are pleased that they can work

quite freely as individual artists and private entrepreneurs. The aim is to allow members to develop their personal forms of expression and for their output to be complementary. Mass-production and large series are not possible, as the kilns only cater for around four full-time ceramic artists. Joint sale events in summer and at Christmas open the doors to the public.

In addition to the founder members, many other artists have worked at Pot Viapori for extensive periods. These include Riitta Alho, Åsa Hellman, Outi Leinonen, Riitta Mattila, Soile Paasonen, Marjukka Pietiäinen and Riitta Talonpoika. Visiting artists have included Gudny Magnusdottir (Iceland), Karen Minge (USA), Tina Reuterberg and Eva Bergenheim (Sweden), and Martien van Mens (Netherlands). The workshop's backroom, which now mainly functions as an exhibition space, was for several years rented out as a textile studio.

Many Finnish group workshops have only survived for short periods. Often artists abandon their groups as soon as private studios become financially viable. An exception is Seenat, still active despite the departure of many of its members. The workshop was established in 1976 by Riitta Siira (née Pensanen), Lea Klemola and Terhi Juurinen. Seenat's production consists mainly of cast, serially manufactured functional ware sold in select design boutiques.

The progress of Finnish industrial art

The 1970s constituted a period of great development, and it would be appropriate to call the decade the 'Finnish Arts and Crafts Movement'. During this interesting period Finnish craftsmen began to organize themselves and consider issues related to their profession. The Finnish Association of Designer/Makers TAIKO was founded in 1983 as an independent group within the Finnish Association of Designers Ornamo. Working with ceramics, textiles or jewelry should no longer be seen as an exclusive hobby; it was imperative to earn one's living through a commitment to these fields. For the first time, craftsmen worked together seriously, organizing their own exhibitions, craft demonstrations, lectures and sale events.

The director of Arabia's art department, Kaj Franck, fought isolation by inviting artists to work at the factory for limited periods. Studio ceramists still groped for contacts with each other and with the public, and a paralysing vacuum was avoided as they began to meet regularly. They had common problems and realized that these must be solved collectively. The pricing of handmade ceramics was for the first time discussed on the basis of solidarity. Ornamo members agreed not to undersell their products and ruin the market for those who intended to make a living from ceramics. Despite this it was difficult for independent ceramists to compete with industrial design and inexpensive im-

ported goods. High value-added taxes hampered many artists, especially those who produced functional ware.

Debates with influential art committee members, usually men within the architectural and industrial design professions, were common. For some strange reason even they seemed to uphold a romantic notion that it was a ceramist's duty to produce high-quality functional goods, by hand, *cheaply*. Ceramists – still mostly women – protested, as their incomes were closely related to their professional identities and their increasing self-esteem. Someone quipped that the architects should try to design high-quality houses, to be built cheaply by hand! The public was still irritatingly ill informed. Many people still associated contemporary urban ceramists, who had received many years of expensive education, with self-taught craftsmen. Their products were also compared in terms of price to crafts imported from developing countries.

From the 1980s, an increasing number of studio ceramists turned to ceramic sculpture, receiving commissions for public spaces. This sparked off criticism from sculptors and painters who felt threatened. In time, many Finnish sculptors began to work with clay, acquiring a whole new level of regard for ceramic techniques, which were not quite as effortless as they had thought. Today, ceramic artists are influenced by contemporary movements in painting – and vice versa – and some prominent art galleries now regularly exhibit ceramic work.

The Pot Viapori collective workshop celebrated its twentieth anniversary in 1992. Standing, from the left: Riitta Mattila, Outi Leinonen, Ritva Kaukoranta, Hilkka Jarva, Riitta Alho and Soile Paasonen. Seated: Seppo Nieminen with Marjukka Pietiäinen, Piippa Tandefelt and Åsa Hellman. Photo: Pot Viapori.

With the mushrooming of new workshops, the range of ceramics on offer is growing exponentially. A new generation of urban dwellers is interested in art and design, becoming potential customers of workshops. To avoid gallery commissions, many ceramic artists choose, when possible, to sell directly from their studios, building a network of producers and consumers. Ceramic art approaches people and everyday life; ceramics are no longer just for show or seen as ostentatious gift items. Arabia's monopoly has ended, and what was lost in grandiose exhibition pieces has been gained in a greater variety of materials, techniques and styles for everyday enjoyment and use.

The growing public interest in contemporary ceramic art has inspired an increasing number of adult education centres, vocational and summer schools to include ceramics in their curricula. This benefits ceramists, as it opens up jobs for teachers and extends the public's awareness of ceramics. The greater the number of people working with clay, the more interest in the material and the wider the appreciation of quality and authenticity. Finally there is also a large group of 'friends of ceramics' in Finland.

Once craftsmen became active members of TAIKO, progress was made in leaps and bounds. In 1988 ceramic artists from all continents came together in Porvoo for a historic occasion: the first international Iris ceramics seminar. It was in Porvoo that Alfred William Finch, Belgian-born cosmopolite and the true father of Finnish ceramic art, had started Finnish earthenware production one hundred years earlier, and so the story of ceramics in Finland had finally come full circle.

AIRI HORTLING

The new generation

One of the bone china *Eclipse* lamps (11 x 38 cm) designed by Iiro Ahokas and Johanna Ojanen for the interior of a Paris restaurant in 1999.
Photo: Iiro Ahokas.

Changes and internationalization in education

Changes have taken place in ceramics education in Finland that have had repercussions for the ceramic arts and for industrial design. The University of Art and Design in Helsinki played a pioneering role during the 1990s as the hub of an educational network that comprised an increasing number of colleges and polytechnics. This meant, however, that training was based on a single philosophy throughout, as all the instructors had in principle the same educational background. Modern students of ceramics are inclined to a greater extent than before to consider and evaluate their professional identity in the light of marketing opportunities, and in this sense the status of an admired designer and creator of small, exclusive series of studio items is nowadays more attractive than that of an artisan exhibiting in galleries. The wide range of contrasting experiences, such as hand throwing versus designing on a computer screen, has created tensions that can be perceived in the identity crises suffered by many professionals in this field.

In earlier times the highest level of instruction in ceramics available in Finland was that given at the Atheneum as part of the School of Industrial Arts, which gained university status in 1973, and many people are still inclined to speak of 'Atheneumists' in connection with any experts in the industrial arts. The ceramics department was located in the same building as the museum for

eighty years. The premises it occupied had been declared inadequate for teaching purposes early in the twentieth century, but this did not diminish the students' enthusiasm, and they remained obedient to the master potters and artists who taught them. Marianne Aav, Director of the Design Museum in Helsinki, reminds us that many visiting students from abroad reported afterwards that the facilities were modest and that this evidently detracted from efficient teaching.[1,2] In my own student days we had to explain apologetically to every visitor that the small sizes of the works we produced were due to the restricted dimensions of the kilns available for firing them, so that their quality would be judged in relation to the learning environment. The teaching itself was of a high standard, however, and new aspects were introduced as additional equipment was acquired. One unusual feature of Finnish education was its continuity, so that the ceramic artists responsible for the teaching followed in the footsteps of their own teachers, becoming experts in their own right and enriching the field in accordance with their own interests and resources.

I studied there in the 1960s, when plain Japanese designs were in vogue. These were produced by hand, employing a variety of techniques and the resulting forms were evaluated critically. Thus any talk of successful forms entailed more appraisal of the avoidance of technical flaws than discussion on personal experiences gained. The greatest

praise was reserved for the natural beauty of a fired clay surface, as is still evident among modern studio potters.

The ceramics department was the last to move out of the Atheneum building when it was due for refurbishment in 1983. The professor in charge, Kyllikki Salmenhaara, had died in the summer of 1981, and her successor, Henrik Gröhn, had inherited the task of guiding the department out of the Atheneum to the Arabia premises, with an intermediate stop in Kuortaneenkatu.[3] Gröhn brought about a radical shift towards the West in both the ideals of the ceramic arts and the aesthetic focus of the department's work, and allowed the ceramic artists Timothy Persons and Ben Katz to introduce a US-style spontaneity in the handling of clay into the

The Tonfisk Design range, created by Brian Keany and Tony Alfström, is typical of studio items produced in very recent years in the Kaj Franck spirit.
Photo: Tonfisk Design.

teaching. When Gröhn moved to the Finnish Broadcasting Company, he was succeeded by Tapio Yli-Viikari from Arabia, who had been appointed Associate Professor in 1987. A highly successful international ceramics event had been held at Arabia in the 1980s under his direction, and this provided the stimulus for two conferences at the University of Art and Design in 1992 and 1996, marking a major expansion of international contacts, in line with the prevailing educational policy. The enthusiasm for this branch of art and the wide range of opportunities that it offered gradually became visible in studios and galleries, with a proliferation of works, some inspiring praise and some criticism. Nowadays a higher proportion of graduates than ever before are able to earn recognition as ceramic artists or designers, and these people serve as examples for others and are able to influence the nature and progress of ceramics as an art form.

One pitfall for ceramics students was for a long time the existence of ready-made pigments for surface colouring (red, orange, purple, etc.), as no teaching was provided on the use of these.[4] The philosophy was that students should set out from a knowledge of the chemistry of oxides and raw materials and use colours that they had prepared based on their own research. The breadth of training in the choice of materials had in effect rendered ready-made pigments unnecessary. The teaching of American-style ceramics, on the other hand, required the purchase of such colourants and guidance in their use. In the end, the use of pigments for ornamentation purposes became an official part of the syllabus only in the late 1980s, the necessary materials being acquired in cooperation with the Arabia factory.[5] Even so, Finnish ceramicists have been slow to adopt these ready-made pigments.

The availability of materials was greatly enhanced by the decision of companies such as Bang & Co. to supply kaolin and other chemicals to Finland in the 1970s,[6] and further expansion in the network of importers in the 1980s improved the services provided and simplified the potters' work. The result was proliferation. Small studios sprang up beside the main roads, some founded by professionals and others by keen amateurs. Many of these small workshops collapsed during the recession of the early 1990s, however, in spite of having acquired a discriminating and critical clientèle, and the ones that survived were those that had functioned on sound business principles from the outset or had found a niche for themselves.

Our educational traditions, and on a broader level our general upbringing, may be said to look down on self-promotion, regarding modesty as a virtue and insisting that 'the products must speak for themselves'. Only artisans who have achieved public recognition can speak out about their products, their significance and the ideas behind them. It was only the post-modern reassessment of social values in the early 1990s

The idea of the *Garden* coffee bar (2001), developed by Mirjami Rissanen and Tommi Terästö, was to achieve customer-centred design by discussing the appearance of products and trying them out in practice together with potential purchasers.
Photo: Rissanen & Terästö.

One interesting topic of research around the turn of the millennium was the use of finely ground burnt reindeer bone, a slaughterhouse by-product, to create a translucent variety of bone china.
Photo: Airi Hortling.

that led to a clarification and strengthening of the significance of ceramic art within the field of product design, and to a simultaneous increase in the emphasis placed on the development of an individual mode of artistic expression. It was accepted that ceramic products represented a form of design that should be promoted and publicized through the media. Thus it was at last possible by the end of the decade for the manufacturers of mass-prduced ceramics, artists and designers with an interest in research to communicate on an equal basis as professionals and experts. Finnish ceramicists are now able to speak openly about their products and their materials as is the case elsewhere in Europe. At the same time, student exchanges and other international contacts have increased greatly, and Finland is now receiving a flow of students from China, Japan and Korea who are interested in learning about Scandinavian design. Although general tastes are showing an oriental bent, Finnish ceramics nevertheless continue to be based firmly on the aesthetics of clay as a material and refined simplicity of design.

Enthusiasm for research

Although it had been possible to take a licentiate degree in fine art at the University of Art and Design from 1981 onwards and a doctorate from 1983, the opportunities for postgraduate study were somewhat neglected during the relocation of the department, and new interest arose only in the early 1990s. It was at this stage that research into ceramics as an art form began to gain momentum alongside materials research. The headline claiming that 'Research is rising from the ashes like a Phoenix' reflected well the enthusiasm that abounded at ceramics seminars. An

engineer was employed to help with research projects, and a research community began to form which included people from outside the industrial arts. Apart from postgraduate work, some projects were undertaken with finance from the Finnish Technology Agency (TEKES) and some work was commissioned from outside. Efforts were made to establish broad-based interdisciplinary cooperation between the academic universities and those devoted to the arts. Towards the end of 1999 a total of seven licentiate degrees were awarded in ceramics, after which this degree was abolished under a revision of the statute governing higher education, and postgraduate studies were transferred from the master's degree to the doctorate in fine art, in accordance with the practice in academic subjects. In 2003 there were thirteen postgraduate students of ceramics. However, just as research in this field has diversified, it has also become more a matter of verbal expression than of knowledge arising from practical experience. Seminars and international conferences involving contacts between scientific communities tend to be devoted to the kinds of content and concepts typical of the present day: the aesthetics and ethics of the material, the ecology of recycling, pictorial forms in a virtual world, and elements of design and ergonomics that take account of social limitations.

The range of themes taken up in postgraduate work on ceramics is wide. Helena Leppänen, already a licenti-

ate in Art and Design, took as the subject of her doctoral thesis socially motivated and user-friendly design concepts and their significance for the function of the product, while Raino Ranta, a designer and design coordinator for Pentik Oy, discussed the changes in thought processes and ways of working that are taking place with technological advances as virtual techniques come to replace the material-based design of objects. This theme is central to the Finnish tradition of product design in the industrial arts and reaches the core of the art of ceramics, namely the significance of a knowledge of the material for the work of the designer. By contrast, Maarit Mäkelä produced a set of ceramic pieces for a doctoral thesis in which she examined femininity and 'memories drawn in clay' through the medium of the 'retrospective gaze' that arises in the course of the research process. In another doctoral thesis in fine art, entitled 'Garden in a Garden', Tiina Veräjänkorva assessed her own relation with the environment from the perspective of subjective 'movement in a garden' through a set of ceramic statues that she had produced.

A number of projects were carried out on the eve of the new millennium in the form of commissioned research on material properties. One of these set out to explore the possibility of using reindeer bone from slaughterhouses in Lapland to develop a ceramic material specific to the region.[7] Reindeer bone is regarded as a problematic, slowly decomposing waste product, and thus the ecolo-

gical aim of the project was to utilize it as a clay additive, thereby increasing employment in the manufacture of bone china products.

There have been a number of regional projects aimed at exploiting industrial minerals and stone by-products available in Finland, e.g. the amber mica obtained in the course of quarrying apatite,[8,9] aimed at utilizing these local raw materials and providing employment for the local population once the information gained can be commercialized. The powdered rock remaining from the cutting of soapstone in the quarries and stonemasons' workshops of Northern Karelia, for instance, can be exploited directly for the preparation of clays and glazes for use in pottery,[10,11] and commissioned research into the possibilities in this field have led to the employment of students as research assistants and in design projects. As a result, a regional Soapstone Ceramics Centre comprising five firms has been established under the auspices of a three-year project aimed at training potters as versatile entrepreneurs and at the same time ensuring that these Finnish minerals are exploited to the full in designs that reflect local natural values and culture. The Finnish Stone Centre serves as a regional base for research and information connected with the diversified use of natural stone, and research into the applications of natural minerals in ceramics forms one branch of its activities. A further means of promoting efforts towards an understanding of this traditional Finnish material has been the creation of a laboratory devoted to the study of natural stone and ceramics as materials.[12]

Participation in international engineering conferences has greatly increased my own understanding of how Finnish study programmes in the use of ceramic materials differ from those in other countries, and it is evident that this expertise should be preserved. In other countries materials research tends to be separated from the study of product design and carried out in specific institutions, so that designers are not expected to be aware of the properties of the raw materials they are using. A person responsible for pottery manufacture in the future will nevertheless have to be aware of the importance of ecological and aesthetic product development. Research carried out in Italy in 1999 showed that a total of ten million tonnes of industrial waste and by-products are generated every year. Thus research should be geared towards fashioning these materials into ceramic products through firing processes that convert the compounds contained in this waste into silicates that remain stable at the molecular level and will no longer disintegrate into substances that are detrimental to nature.[13,14] In global terms, the aim is to employ design and research as means of conserving the environment and accepting responsibility for the world in which we live.

The processing of art and the challenges of acquiring skills

Students of ceramics in the early 1990s, their world view shaken by the recession and the demise of ordinary social values, began to consider their own relationships with nature in the course of producing their work. Many degree dissertations were devoted to re-evaluations in the aftermath of this crisis in values, to the relation between the worker and his work and to the implications of this. Riikka Latva-Somppi, in her degree work *Kärsimyskukka*, projects an image of herself as an explorer recording observations on the state of the environment.[15] This may be looked on as a manifestation of the feelings of her generation, hidden on clay surfaces left by the impressions of hands and covered by glazes. As an outcome of society's survival strategy and the re-evaluation of education, a new generation is developing that is becoming more reliant on technical equipment and more aware of the media than ever before. These people are learning to put their work forward in public and are bold enough to respond to new challenges.

In his speech at the opening of the academic year in 1998, the Rector of the University of Art and Design in Helsinki, Yrjö Sotamaa, brought up a number of points of friction in the institution's teaching. Under the title 'Is Finnish design just an empty myth?',[16] he listed the areas of expertise that the designer could be expected to master in order to achieve an interface with the

working community. The list outlines what appears to be the reverse of a good designer and consists of a string of inadequacies: insufficient understanding of commercial requirements, an aversion for customer-centred or market-related thinking, and weak analytical, investigatory and conceptual skills. He also emphasized that a powerful artistic outlook can arouse attention in a potential employer. He ended up presenting a new challenge: 'It is essential that our development work should respect our strong traditions in the field of design, but at the same time it should have the courage to evalute that tradition, critically if necessary, and should be ready to make changes.'

The new generation of designers has indeed adopted more ambitious goals than its predecessors, putting forward new ideas and implementing the notion of concept-centred design, but it was still perplexing to perceive a tension in the air as the new millennium approached, as if everyone was waiting for an aesthetic upheaval of some kind to take place. I remember talking with students at the time about new features to be seen in ceramics. The increased use of white colour and perforations evidently marked a transition towards the unknown, and nowadays such products tend to proliferate, almost to the extent of being commonplace.

In praise of whiteness

When the American Rudolf Staffel held his exhibition at the Design Museum in

Helsinki in 1996, he attempted to purge ceramics of the colour which he had felt as a child to be decorative, examining his own actions through porcelain items by other artists. Staffel's exhibition was one of my most significant experiences in recent years, for at the age of over eighty years he allowed himself to squeeze the clay and leave the imprints of his forceful willpower on it, like symbols that were there to be re-evaluated. Marianne Aav wrote about his works that they were objects that could not contain any other light, since in spite of their immaterial quality they were already full to the brim[17]. The images of fragility, dignity and social status that white porcelain usually carries with it have been stripped away from Staffel's works, which represent the freedom from the shackles of matter that may be regarded as an integral feature of the ceramics of the new millennium.

Porcelain is an adaptable concept: it is white and clean, a symbol of virginity, with a broader significance than the earlier concept of matter. It is no longer an expensive white clay of poor plasticity that is hard to work, but it is now a refined, elitist design culture which is being put into effect at this very moment in the act of creating a ceramic object.[18] There are many kinds of porcelain, as many as there are makers of it, and it is common for these makers to exchange clay formulae. As Iiro Ahokas, who studied the symbolism of white colour in his degree dissertation in fine art,[19] puts it, 'For me, light and whiteness symbolize puri-

ty, goodness, holiness and serenity.' The pair of lamps designed and constructed by Iiro Ahokas and Johanna Ojanen for a restaurant in Paris represent the pre-production development stage, but as Krista Launonen writes in her article 'Uncompromising Young Designers' in the magazine *Gloria*, they speak to one, in the words of the designers, 'of the austerity of nature in the north, of mom-

ents just before dusk, of the moon and of shadows.' In their opinion, designers need a good measure of naïve enthusiasm and audacity.[20]

Eating habits and the usage of kitchenware have changed in recent times, and this is reflected in the production of china works and in the manufacturing environment. Increased production costs have caused many indust-

Page 63

Terhi Vähäsalo's *Ottilia* tableware (1997) explores the identity of a woman designer and her visibility in giving shape to objects. Photo: Terhi Vähäsalo.

Helsinki in 1996, he attempted to purge ceramics of the colour which he had felt as a child to be decorative, examining his own actions through porcelain items by other artists. Staffel's exhibition was one of my most significant experiences in recent years, for at the age of over eighty years he allowed himself to squeeze the clay and leave the imprints of his forceful willpower on it, like symbols that were there to be re-evaluated. Marianne Aav wrote about his works that they were objects that could not contain any other light, since in spite of their immaterial quality they were already full to the brim[17]. The images of fragility, dignity and social status that white porcelain usually carries with it have been stripped away from Staffel's works, which represent the freedom from the shackles of matter that may be regarded as an integral feature of the ceramics of the new millennium.

Porcelain is an adaptable concept: it is white and clean, a symbol of virginity, with a broader significance than the earlier concept of matter. It is no longer an expensive white clay of poor plasticity that is hard to work, but it is now a refined, elitist design culture which is being put into effect at this very moment in the act of creating a ceramic object.[18] There are many kinds of porcelain, as many as there are makers of it, and it is common for these makers to exchange clay formulae. As Iiro Ahokas, who studied the symbolism of white colour in his degree dissertation in fine art,[19] puts it, 'For me, light and whiteness symbolize puri-

ty, goodness, holiness and serenity.' The pair of lamps designed and constructed by Iiro Ahokas and Johanna Ojanen for a restaurant in Paris represent the pre-production development stage, but as Krista Launonen writes in her article 'Uncompromising Young Designers' in the magazine *Gloria*, they speak to one, in the words of the designers, 'of the austerity of nature in the north, of mom-

ents just before dusk, of the moon and of shadows.' In their opinion, designers need a good measure of naïve enthusiasm and audacity.[20]

Eating habits and the usage of kitchenware have changed in recent times, and this is reflected in the production of china works and in the manufacturing environment. Increased production costs have caused many indust-

> Heikki Rahikainen: *Virgin Clay and Self-Portrait*, 2003. Photo: Johnny Korkman.

Circle, a crumbling brick wall constructed by Jatta Lavi, Petra Alankoja and Minna Koistinen, students in the ceramics and glass department of the University of Art and Design, was an entry for the peripatetic exhibition 'Varde' in 1994–96, the theme of which was ecology. The exhibition visited London, Rome, Berlin, Budapest, Barcelona, Linz and Helsinki. Photo: Arto Keksinen.

rial companies to move at least part of their production outside the European Union, and this in turn has given small studio-produced series an elitist character and has increased these studios' market shares by virtue of their exceptional product concepts. Tonfisk Design is one herald of this new trend, with products that tell people in Europe of Finnish timber and of the snow, while Terhi Vähäsalo explores the identity of the female designer through the medium of her *Ottilia* tableware,[21] having dedicated her degree dissertation in 1997 to the women of Ostrobothnia. In 2002 Eeva Jokinen developed an application of the rice-grain porcelain technique to studio production,[22] in a degree dissertation that gave expression to the association between the perforations in the object and its white colour, relating the earlier tradition to a new age of design.

One experimental arena for sounding out the field of the arts is the *Garden* (Tarha) coffee house, the idea of Tommi Terästö (in connection with his degree dissertation) and Mirjami Rissanen[23], intended as a means for determining a designer's identity and for achieving self-assurance. It is a garden in which knowledge and skills can meet, a way in which people can approach each other. It is possible, in conversations over coffee, to ask a consumer whether one is on the right lines as a designer, and in this sense the place represents the collective concept of a designer group, a dialogue between objects and their users. The design objects carry a message, and this is an environment for sounding the message out. Conversation, or simply stopping to listen to one's own thoughts, in this mellow natural environment can serve as a discussion forum on matters of design, or else as a forum for a momentary aesthetic experience. The *Garden* is a place where people are looking for direct information on objects of art at the first encounter. Consumers are asked to regard these objects as products that incorporate valuable ideas, at a point in time when the value placed on everyday articles is tantamount to that afforded to disposable ones.

Many an excellent design object has remained in an obscure cupboard in recent times, like a buried treasure, once its creator has graduated, as pursuance of the topic has been prevented by conscience and a scarcity of marketing mechanisms. No pattern for discussion or action has existed to allow commercialization of these design ideas. The traditional saying that 'the product will speak for itself' no longer works in the information society, where the consumer is unable to distinguish anything more than the most assiduously advertised fashions, which therefore come to control the whole field of consumer behaviour. Graduates of the new generation know that they have to construct presentation portfolios in order to capture the attention of the media and fulfil their dreams as product designers and ceramic artists, aided by the fact that their background training in ceramics is far broader than ever before. Conceptual thinking, mastery of product design and the development of an artistic identity can all provide encouragement in this and enhance the multifarious influence of the ceramics culture.

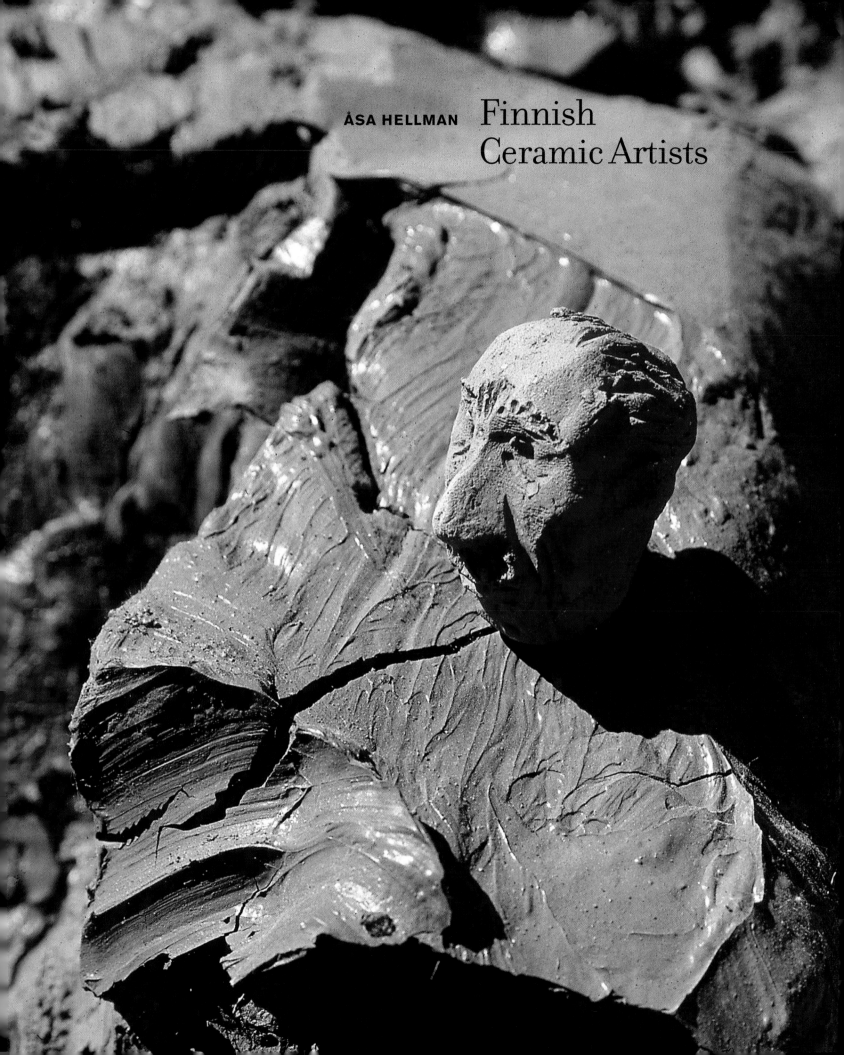

ÅSA HELLMAN

Finnish
Ceramic Artists

The Father of Finnish Ceramic Art

Alfred William Finch

Artist, teacher and cosmopolite

- Born in Brussels 1854, died in Helsinki 1930

- Académie de Bruxelles, art studies, 1878–79

- Début as a painter, Ghent Triennial, 1880

- Faience painting and studies in ceramics, 1890 onwards

- Silver medal for ceramic work, Brussels World Exhibition, 1897

- AB Iris, Porvoo, director of ceramic production, 1897–1902

- University of Art and Design Helsinki*, ceramics dept., head teacher, 1902–30

A.W. Finch, regarded by his contemporaries as a kind, unassuming gentleman.
Photo: Otava Photo Archives.

* The Central School of Arts and Crafts was founded in 1886. In 1949 the name was changed to the School of Industrial Arts and in 1973 the college evolved into the University of Art and Design Helsinki. For consistency, the current name of the institution is used throughout the artist presentations in this book.

When Alfred William Finch arrived in the idyllic, small Finnish town of Porvoo in 1897, aged 43, he was a mature artist, internationally respected as a painter, graphic artist and ceramist. He was invited to Porvoo in his capacity of expert ceramist in order to build up the production of ceramics at the AB Iris design factory founded by Swedish count Louis Sparre. Sparre had first been attracted to Finch's ceramics on his trip around Europe, at the 1897 Brussels World Exhibition. That same autumn, Alfred William Finch accepted Sparre's proposal that he come to Finland on a one-year contract to start up a ceramics workshop at AB Iris.

Painting and ceramics

Alfred William Finch was born in Belgium to English parents in 1854. As a consequence he spoke fluent English and French, and the interesting combination of two cultures undoubtedly contributed to making 'Willy' Finch not only an eminent artist but also a multifaceted cultural personality and cosmopolite.

Art studies at l'Académie de Bruxelles led Finch to join an avant-garde group of prominent artists in Brussels. They were among the first to paint in the Neo-Impressionist style, in accordance with a theoretically formulated colour and form canon. Finch would later make use of these theories in his ceramic work.[1]

At that time Brussels was a centre for the Art Nouveau movement and Finch befriended Henry van de Velde, its foremost representative. As artists, both men were unusually versatile and they kept in touch through the decades, even after Finch had moved to Finland. The British Arts and Crafts Movement – the major contemporary design trend – was also influential for Finch. His work, though most often free and spontaneous, thus had its foundations in a carefully formulated ideological agenda. Alfred William Finch was always both a zealous theorist and an enthusiastic artist.

In 1890, Finch accepted the post of decorative painter at a faience factory in La Louvière. He was probably compelled to do this for financial reasons, in order to receive a regular income. But it was entirely in line with the philosophy of the Arts and Crafts Movement that Alfred William Finch the painter would later push painting aside to become increasingly involved with ceramics over the subsequent years. Clay became his passion; his fascination for the possibilities offered by the medium and its challenging techniques would only grow with time.

As his nature dictated, Alfred William Finch approached the subject conscientiously, acquiring a thorough knowledge of clays, glazes and firing techniques. During the 1890s he studied different aspects of ceramics by practising the craft in workshops. For a while he worked in the countryside at Forges in the Ardennes, an area renowned for its utilitarian pottery. There he learnt the basics of ceramic crafts and worked with traditional potters. This involved both sitting down at the wheel himself and making drawings for professional potters to materialize. Finch would also occasionally purchase bisque ceramics to decorate and glaze himself.[2]

A collection of works by Alfred William Finch in Porvoo Museum. This cupboard made by the AB Iris factory contains typical Iris pottery as well as unique vases by Finch.
Photo: Jan Lindroth/ Porvoo Museum.

Finch's experiments with materials gradually led to changes in form as well as ornamentation. In the spirit of the time he decorated his work with simple curves and dots using engobes, metallic oxides and industrial stains. In firing he used the reduction technique, in which the flames of the kiln, together with a lack of oxygen, cause unexpected and dramatic colour reactions, so-called flambé effects. Finch was successful in exhibiting his wares at various art and design galleries around Europe. Doubtless he benefited greatly from already being an internationally renowned painter, as at that time applied art was considered less worthy. Finch was to play a part in improving the standing of ceramics.

Finch and the forgotten potters

Under Finch's direction, the AB Iris ceramics workshop in Porvoo grew from a simple studio that employed one thrower to an industrial ceramics company with several employees. Finch adopted the traditional Finnish technique of using low-fired, red earthenware for the factory's ceramics production. His earlier experience of working with slips and lead glazes was well suited to common red clay.

The small town of Porvoo is located at the mouth of a river on the Gulf of Finland, and the clay there has a high iron content. Its quality is often unpredictable; later experiments have shown that the melting point of this material varies greatly and that it is almost impossible, even in today's advanced kilns, to achieve an even result.[3] Despite this fact it has always been assumed that Iris ceramics were made of the local Porvoo clay.

Several facts arose during the research carried out for this book, however, which indicate that the products may not have been manufactured in Porvoo clay but in material collected from the Tuusula-Kerava district. That area was an important centre for brick manufacturing and pottery, widely known for its high-quality clay.[4] The railway between Kerava and Porvoo stood complete in 1874 and communication between the two towns was lively, as the journey from Porvoo to the capital had to be made via Kerava. It must have been significantly simpler to transport the excellent Kerava clay to Porvoo by train than to battle with the troublesome local variety.

At least three of the potters who operated in the Tuusula-Kerava area were involved with AB Iris: Gustaf Alexander Franzén, Johan Grönroos III and Johan Artturi Helenius. Of these men the two first will be discussed in more detail later on in this book. A further potter from Kerava, Karl August Ek, also played a part – at least indirectly – in AB Iris.[5]

Martti Saaristo's manuscript for the text 'Savenvalanta Keravalla II' describes how the potter Helenius would regularly supply Finch with various kinds of vases. According to Helenius's own statements, some of these pots lacked drawings and the maker had to work out for himself approximately how to arrive at the final result! This required a true feel for form and shape and a good knowledge of the material – skills that develop over years spent at the wheel. Both Finch and Sparre did business with pottery workshops in the area and we can assume that the Swedish-speaking Sparre often had to act as interpreter during Finch's first years in Finland. Sometimes Finch travelled to Kerava in person to procure bisque ware, thrown in accordance with his instructions.

Traditional potters mastered the entire ceramic production process. On the other hand it is obvious that they would learn a lot about glazes, pigments and decoration techniques by working at AB Iris. The elderly Ek would later mention in an interview that in his glazes he used borax instead of the traditional, toxic lead.[6] Willy Finch, who carefully followed the latest research within silicate chemistry through journals and correspondence, must surely be given the credit for this.

Thus the cooperation between Finch, the international artist, and these local potters was mutually beneficial. Several years later, as a teacher at what is now the University of Art and Design Helsinki, Finch was still in touch with his earlier potters, who seem to have been allowed to study with him free of charge, possibly in exchange for help with throwing.[7]

Finch's first pupils used the same decorative techniques as the AB Iris factory. Sigrid Wiljomaa (Wilskman) on the right, working with an unidentified fellow student at the Atheneum in 1908. Photo from the Wilskman family album.

AB Iris, a short-lived blossom

Between 1897 and 1902 the Iris factory manufactured almost 200 different models of ceramics for everyday use: lidded terrines, tea sets, jugs, vases, plates, etc. These were often made to order in varying sizes and colours, including cobalt blue, copper and chrome green, iron red and manganese black. The colours were normally created by adding metallic oxides to liquid clay mixtures, resulting in so-called engobes or slips. This made it possible to use sgraffito decoration with clearly delimited colour planes. Some of the products were glazed with a traditional transparent lead glaze, which, when applied to the iron-rich clay and fired in a reducing atmosphere, could adopt beautiful olive-green shades. Sometimes red spots or 'roses' would appear on the green surface. The work was often entirely undecorated or adorned in a simple fashion with dots and S-like curves typical of the time. Certain rare pieces displayed plant motifs characteristic to the Art Nouveau style. As Finch was aware of lead glazes' negative effects on health, household goods were covered with imported, lead-free glazes.[8]

In addition to the above-mentioned techniques, the factory produced vessels covered in turquoise and blue-green alkaline glazes. Around the turn of the century, insights into silicate chemistry were not common among ceramists, who tended to keep their recipes secret and progress through trial and error. The Iris factory, however, achieved high levels of technical and artistic quality despite modest equipment and limited access to materials.

The Iris factory gave Finch the opportunity to fulfil his artistic ambitions, based on his aesthetic and social ideologies. We can trace the quotidian, harmonious forms and lively colour contrasts of Iris ceramics back to the Arts and Crafts Movement's theses on 'art in everything and for everyone' and 'joy in everyday life'. Many parallels can also be drawn to Scandinavian design of around 50 years later, with its motto 'more beautiful things for everyday use'. Thanks to Finch's active nature and international contacts, Iris ceramics were displayed at several exhibitions in countries including Germany, Belgium and France. The Parisian gallery La Maison Moderne had a contract for the exclusive resale of Iris products. Finch contributed to the Finnish pavilion of the 1900 Paris World Exhibition with ceramics for the Iris Room.

Master potter Gustaf Alexander Franzén (third from left) was one of Finch's trusted craftsmen. The photograph was most likely taken in Franzén's own workshop in Ekenäs where he employed a handful of people in the early 1900s. Photo from the Franzén family album.

Finch became highly respected as an artist in Finland, but the larger porcelain-loving masses found Iris ceramics all too extraordinary and rustic for them really to succeed. Low-fired items shattered easily and, being porous, could cause water stains to appear on the dark mahogany tables favoured in urban residences. As a consequence it appears that many of the vessels were taken out to decorate summer villas, where they were thought to fit the surroundings better. But Finch's Iris ceramics did occupy the place of honour in the homes of several enlightened and prominent cultural personalities.

Alfred William Finch possessed an exceptional combination of fine characteristics. He did not, however, have any sense for finances and must throughout his life battle with financial problems. The Iris company was ambitious and highly idealistic. It was declared bankrupt in 1902 but Finch decided to stay in Finland, having been offered a post as the first ceramics teacher at the University of Art and Design Helsinki.

Ceramics teacher: a new stage in life

In retrospect it may seem as though Louis Sparre's 1897 invitation to Finch had been determined by fate. The planned one-year visit stretched over several decades, and gradually Finland became a second home for Alfred William Finch and his family. At the same time he made regular visits to central Europe and actively kept in touch with artist friends and galleries abroad.

Finch's work at the university required a large effort on his part, as the ceramics department was newly founded and demanded the installation of new wheels, kilns and other equipment. Finch's broad and deep experience not only in ceramic art but also in other media now came into use to the benefit of the school and its students. He battled tenaciously for the acceptance of ceramics as an art form, also taking concrete measures to force through improvements at the department. He demonstrated his respect for the traditional craft of pottery by proposing to the school's management that potters be allowed to study and use pigments and glazes free of charge.[9]

Besides teaching, Finch continued with his own ceramic work. At the turn of the century his pieces bore a resemblance to Iris products, but as head teacher he began increasingly to experiment with different structures and to apply runny glazes in thick, painterly layers, alternating matte and glossy surfaces. Though fired at low temperatures, his tall vases owe their inspiration to Japanese ceramics and Chinese stoneware.

While working as a teacher, Finch took up painting, graphic work and drawing again, participating in several painting exhibitions in Finland and abroad. The classification of 'foreign' was gradually left out of exhibition catalogues and Finch became fluent in Swedish, which along with Finnish is an official language in Finland.[10] He played an active part on the Helsinki cultural scene, for instance as the curator of an exhibition of paintings by French and Belgian Post-Impressionists.

Finch's career as a pedagogue and well-loved head teacher in ceramic art lasted 28 years. His death in 1930 was in 2003 still fresh in the memory of ceramist Valentina Modig, who at ninety-six was Finch's only surviving student. 'When I arrived at the school one morning, someone shouted: "Finch is dead!" It was awful. He had become like a father for me, always kind and thoughtful. I knew he would have helped me in starting up my own studio. However, it was clear that he was suffering [with rheumatoid arthritis] – he used to stand next to us on one foot, giving instructions while we worked on the wheel.'

Finch's significance for Finnish ceramic art cannot be overrated. The 'cold, maidenly land of the north' needed a man just like Alfred William Finch. Finch's close contacts with prominent members of the central European art and design scene would in great part contribute to bringing Finland, until 1917 a Grand Duchy ruled by the Russian Czar, closer to Europe and its cultural circles.

Willy Finch's first students – forgotten women artists of the early twentieth century

Anna Dahlbeck

The Dahlbeck family was close to the University of Art and Design Helsinki, as the father worked there as a teacher in bookkeeping between 1871 and 1888.[1] Anna Vilhelmina Augusta Dahlbeck is one of many women artists who were once respected in their fields but have since largely been forgotten.

Anna Dahlbeck worked with various materials and actively exhibited her work. She enjoyed a long career, firing her work at the university at least until the 1920s. She was a good thrower but, like her teacher Finch, she also ordered bisque ware from Kerava-based potter Johan Helenius. In the accepted fashion of the time she then decorated, glazed and re-fired the vessels.[2]

Exhibition reviews in the contemporary press mention Anna Dahlbeck in complimentary terms. She participated in the 'Exposition des Beaux-Arts et d'Arts Décoratifs du Premier Cercle Artistique des Dames' held in 1910 on Great Morskaya in St Petersburg. Only women artists exhibited, and Anna Dahlbeck had the honour of selling one of her ceramic pieces to Her Majesty the Empress.[3] In 1919 she showed some ten artefacts at an exhibition of Finnish art in Charlottenburg, Denmark.[4] Later she also took part in fine arts exhibitions.[5]

Her ceramic works were for a long time coveted prizes in the prestigious annual draws organized by the Finnish Society of Crafts and Design and in 1925 she participated in the Society's fifty-year jubilee exhibition. Many of Anna Dahlbeck's heavily glazed bottle-shaped earthenware vases are now in private collections and museums.

■ Born (probably in Helsinki) 1870, died in Helsinki 1937

■ Daughter of Sven Petter Gerhard Dahlbeck and Augusta Rosina Dahlbeck née Wahlström

■ University of Art and Design Helsinki, studies including drawing, decorative painting, advanced ornament drawing, leathercraft and ceramics, 1899–1909

■ Several design exhibitions in Finland and abroad

On the left a low decorated vase by Gusti Franzén. The tall blue vase, the orange bottle-shaped vase and the decorated olive-green vase are by Anna Dahlbeck. The green, matte-glazed vase in the centre was signed by Aina Eklund in 1906. The Antti Laakkonen collection. Photo: Johnny Korkman.

Ellen Borenius

■ Born in 1852, died in 1950

■ University of Art and Design Helsinki, porcelain-painting teacher, 1890–1929

■ Studies at factories and schools abroad, including Paris c. 1892

■ Studies in pottery as additional pupil with Finch, c. 1902 onwards

Preserved in Jean Sibelius's home Ainola is an earthenware vase in typical fin-de-siècle style signed 'E. Borenius 1904'. It was made by Ellen Borenius, a long-time teacher of floral and decorative painting. She was an esteemed artist and also a board member in the Friends of Finnish Handicrafts. She was granted at least two travel scholarships by the directors of the Finnish Society of Crafts and Design (now Design Forum Finland); in 1904 she visited porcelain factories and museums in central Europe. This prominent lady was also an active ceramic artist and created numerous earthenware pots with layered, runny glazes. Her ceramics can be found in museums and private collections.[6]

Collector Antti Laakkonen among some of his treasures, including work by A. W. Finch and his first pupils. Photo: Johnny Korkman.

Elin Juselius

Elin Ingeborg Juselius was the fifth of seven children. She was active as an artist for a long time, but despite the large number of signed works that still exist, she is no longer well known. She made thrown and brush-decorated functional ware in red clay, which she fired at the Atheneum, and other work in white faience at Arabia. Elin Juselius was highly productive and frequently exhibited together with her friend and colleague Gerda Thesleff. Newspaper reviews show that she received both positive and negative responses. An article in *Astra*, a contemporary magazine, dated 15 September 1922, describes an exhibition of 300 works in faience made at Arabia by Thesleff and Juselius: 'The vegetal ornamentation by Elin Juselius was powerful and successfully incorporated, as well as effective in terms of colour.' Another exhibition was reviewed less favourably in *Hufvudstadsbladet* on 12 December 1924: 'Miss Juselius has become set in her ways, which makes her ceramics resemble factory products.'

Elin Juselius's best pieces show a powerful style of ornamentation, full of movement and drama. Plant motifs with wreaths and leaves that follow the thrown forms of the artefacts are typical of her work. At Arabia she decorated with brushes using engobe colours that often partially burnt off during firing, and consequently her faience bowls occasionally appear slightly anaemic. Elin Juselius was one of Willy Finch's most faithful pupils and continued to work at the ceramics department long after graduation. Unmarried and childless, Elin Juselius had no descendants and information about her life is scant. Her abundant work, on the other hand, has been preserved in the homes of relatives, in museums and in several private collections.[7]

- Born in 1872, died in 1964

- Daughter of Justice Emil Victor Juselius and Wilhelmina Juselius née Almqvist

- Trained as a physiotherapist

- University of Art and Design Helsinki, studies including wood sculpture, leathercraft and ceramics, 1901–10

- Arabia, *c.* 1922–24

- Exhibitions in Finland and abroad

Wheel-thrown faience items by Elin Juselius, decorated with strong engobes, produced at Arabia in the 1920s. Private collection.
Photo: Johnny Korkman.

Aili Warén

■ Born in Kuopio 1876, died in Siuntio 1929

■ Daughter of publisher and school principal Uno Wilhelm Telén the younger

■ University of Art and Design Helsinki, studies in ceramics, 1906–10

■ Keen photographer

Towards the beginning of the twentieth century, ceramic art was taught at the University of Art and Design Helsinki five days a week in three-hour sessions. Most students were young women from well-to-do families. Aili Warén (née Telén), on the other hand, was already a married woman with children when she took up her studies in 1906. Her husband, Paavo Warén, was among other things the first Editor-in-Chief of *Helsingin Sanomat* newspaper.

Many of Aili Warén's ceramics are preserved in the family's summer cottage in western Uusimaa. The collection consists of around twenty pieces, carefully signed and dated between 1906 and 1910. They were probably made specifically for use in her home; there are tea and coffee pots, a cheese cover with plate, a creamer, some flower vases and bowls. With few exceptions they are wheel-thrown and decorated with engobes under transparent lead glazes, like Iris ceramics. The painted and sgraffito ornaments represent the Art Nouveau style, although traces of plain folk art are also evident. Some pieces have a traditional, shiny copper glaze, but one lamp base is quite different with a matte, chrome green glaze and relief pattern.

Although these pieces were created at school, the collection is of great interest in art historical terms. Aili Warén had five children and was for practical reasons compelled to give up ceramics. She also had a strong interest in photography and her glass negatives exist in the National Museum's collections.[8]

Aili Warén, in her youth.

Vases by Aili Warén in sgraffito technique. Heights 14 and 13 cm. Tablecloth embroidered by the artist. Private collection. Photo: Johnny Korkman.

Fanny Alina Lindfors

Fanny Lindfors is one of the few women artists of her time whose background was not middle-clas. She was the daughter of Wilhelmina Björkquist, a housemaid, and Karl Fredrik Lindfors, a butcher. It is likely that being of lesser means she was initially allowed to study with Finch free of charge.[9] An indication is that her name is not mentioned in the list of ceramics students until 1907–8, though some of her ceramic works – two vases and a hanging pot – were given as prizes in the lottery organized by the Finnish Society of Crafts and Design already in 1906. Signed earthenware pieces by Fanny Lindfors are highly cherished by private collectors.

■ Born in Helsinki 1879

■ Studies at the University of Art and Design Helsinki, 1898–1908; ceramics with Finch c. 1904–8, degree in 1907

Aina Eklund

Aina Eklund was one of A. W. Finch's most faithful disciples, who used the university's kiln for nearly twenty years. This was entirely in line with Finch's beliefs, as he wrote in a memorandum in 1914: 'Past students who have demonstrated remarkable commitment and talent should be allowed to continue developing their skills at the school. In addition, if they have difficulties on their own (a lack of kilns, etc.). ... The teacher will propose to the Directors which alumni should be permitted to continue here; the Directors will make the final decision. Of course current students will take precedence over old ones!'[10]

Miss Eklund was also granted a scholarship, making it possible for her to train for several months with potter Karl August Ek in Kerava. She introduced several glazes and pigments to this workshop and informed Ek where he could obtain them.[11]

According to Arttu Brummer's notes in the archives of the University of Art and Design Helsinki, Aina Eklund's ceramics were for several years purchased by the university and used as prizes. In 1925 she still took part in the fifty-year jubilee exhibition of the Finnish Society of Crafts and Design at Stenmans Konstpalats in Helsinki.

Aina Eklund also taught leathercraft at the University of Art and Design Helsinki for a long period, replacing Eva Mannerheim-Sparre. This was a unique position, bearing in mind the minimal proportion of women teachers on staff. At Finch's funeral in 1930, Aina Eklund and Elin Juselius had the honour to lay the wreath on behalf of the students.[12] Further details about the life of Aina Eklund, an active ceramist for two decades, are elusive. Many of her signed earthenware pieces, however, remain in museums and private collections. If decorated at all, their ornamentation is executed in dark slips.

■ University of Art and Design Helsinki, studies including wood sculpture, metalwork and leathercraft c. 1902–3, and ceramics c. 1902–9

■ University of Art and Design Helsinki, leathercraft teacher, 1894–1905

Sigrid Wiljomaa

■ Born in Nokia 1881, died in Helsinki 1959

■ Married to Johannes Eliel Wilskman, 1904

■ University of Art and Design Helsinki, studies in ceramics, 1907–10

■ Porcelain painter

Sigrid ('Sissi') Charlotta Wiljomaa, born Sigrid Wennerstrand, came in her lifetime to have three different surnames, as her husband Johannes Wilskman in 1906 changed his name to the more Finnish-sounding Wiljomaa.[13]

Prior to her ceramics studies, Sigrid Wiljomaa worked for a time as an elementary-school teacher. With her husband she later lived in Heinola, where it seems she had a kiln of her own – a rare thing at the time. Her career as a ceramist was short, possibly due to ill health.[14] Sigrid Wiljomaa, like other creative middle-class women, instead found an outlet for her artistic inclinations in her home.

Through uncommonly favourable circumstances, a large collection of Sigrid Wiljomaa's earthenware is miraculously preserved nearly intact at the family's summer residence. The pieces are signed and dated 1907, 1908 or 1910 – the very years when Sigrid Wiljomaa studied with Finch. They bear witness to an ambitious personality who did not shy away from demanding tasks. Unusual jugs with double handles and lidded, handled terrines exhibit an individual style. Their decoration, however, is typical Art Nouveau and the technical execution shows traces of the constant, frustrating battle with the school's miserable kick wheels.[15]

A further miracle is that two photographs survive of Sigrid Wiljomaa working with clay at the University of Art and Design Helsinki. Their author is unknown, but it is possible that it was her fellow student Aili Warén, who was a keen photographer.[16]

Sigrid Wiljomaa at the wheel, c. 1908.
Photo from the Wilskman family album.

Double-handled Art Nouveau vase by
Sigrid Wiljomaa, c. 1908. Porvoo Museum.
Photo: Johnny Korkman.

Sigrid Wickström

Sigrid Wickström (married name Paaer, used pseudonym Siru Wirva) worked with ceramics around the turn of the last century, but later gradually turned her attention to leathercraft and textiles. Early in the twentieth century she embroidered and designed textiles for the Friends of Finnish Handicrafts.[17] She had a kaleidoscopic career in design, and Finch was uncommonly enthusiastic about her. In a letter of introduction to Henry van de Velde he states that 'she is bad at throwing but good at decorating.'[18]

In terms of the history of ceramic art, Sigrid Wickström is especially interesting owing to a well-preserved, large earthenware vase with highly unusual relief ornamentation. Now in a private collection, it can be ascribed to Sigrid Wickström, as it is signed 'S W 1908'. A similar ceramic item figures in a photograph from the exhibition of prizes from the Atheneum's lottery in 1908,[19] and Sigrid Wickström demonstrably participated contributing a vase.[20]

■ Born in 1883, died in 1923

■ University of Art and Design Helsinki, studies including model drawing, leathercraft and ceramics, 1902–4

Vase with relief ornamentation signed 'SW 1908', evidently the work of Sigrid Wickström (Siru Wirva).
Height 31 cm. Private collection.
Photo: Johnny Korkman.

Elsa Kyander-Elenius

■ Born in Jäppilä 1884, died in Turku 1973

■ University of Art and Design Helsinki, studies including ceramics, c. 1905–8

■ Wilhelm von Debschitz's design school, Munich: studies 1908–10, teacher at ceramics dept. 1912–13

■ Draughtsman at München-Hersching am Ammersee ceramics factory, 1910–12

■ Exhibitions include Paris 1909, Munich Trade Fair 1912, Leipzig fairs 1908–13 and the Deutsches Museum, Berlin 1913

■ Works in the Design Museum, Helsinki and several German museums

Artist Elsa Helena Kyander-Elenius is one of the few ceramists whose work during the first three decades of the twentieth century was carefully documented in contemporary newspapers. She married draughtsman and writer Edvard Elenius, and it is likely that her studies abroad and her marriage to an artist active in the area of design contributed to the abundance of publicity she received. On 9 February 1913, *Uusi Aura* newspaper published an article about her under the title 'Finnish Artist Awakens Interest Abroad'. Pictures of Elsa Kyander-Elenius's ceramics were published in 1914 in the German periodical *Die Kunst*, also noticed in Finland.

Having spent five years in Germany and Italy, Kyander-Elenius made her début in Finland with a solo exhibition in the state's craft museum, where she showed ceramics and textiles. With regard to the ceramic work, on 28 February 1916 someone under the signature G. S-ll (most likely the architect Gustaf Strengell) wrote as follows in *Hufvudstadsbladet*:

'When it comes to Mrs Kyander-Elenius's ceramics, which appear at the exhibition without any pretensions, they are artistically on a much lower level than her textiles. Her faience vases are heavy and clumsy, and the glaze decorations, which favour a kind of plaiting or weaving motif, are dry and lifeless. This is a clear sign of the German school of ceramics; as, with certain individual exceptions (Lauger), German ceramics can in no way be compared with the French and the English'.

Eventually Elsa Kyander-Elenius gave up ceramics, probably for purely practical reasons – the lack of a kiln, for instance. She turned to textile work and in 1922 founded the company Oy Taidekutomo, whose director she was until she moved to Turku in 1929.[21]

The vase on the left by Elsa Kyander-Elenius dates back to her years in Munich.
Photo published in *Die Kunst*, 1910.

Anni Brandt

A private collection in Helsinki contains some thirty hand-thrown earthenware pieces created between 1911 and 1915. The artist behind these works is Anni Kristin Brandt, who during those years studied ceramics under the tuition of A. W. Finch. Each piece is carefully signed (following her teacher's example) with the initials A. B. in addition to the month and year in which it was created.

Anni Brandt's ceramic work consists of decorated plates in various sizes and thrown vases and bowls in different shapes. The technical execution of these pieces demonstrates that despite her youth Anni Brandt was truly committed to improving her skills in spite of the school's clumsy kick wheels. The vessels have transparent and coloured glazes applied over coloured slips.

With the exception of a few undecorated items, the collection is remarkable for its rich and free brush ornamentation, stylistically quite different from typical Art Nouveau decoration. We find a young student who already possessed the fluid brushstrokes of an accomplished artist and had an innate feeling for colour. Anni Brandt appears to have made imaginary journeys south: some of her peacock blue and turquoise patterns bring to mind Islamic ceramics from northern Africa.[22]

■ Born in Helsinki 1890, died in Ilola (Porvoo) 1965

■ University of Art and Design Helsinki, studies in ceramics, c. 1911–15

■ Drawing School of the Finnish Art Association, 1908–12

■ University of Helsinki, degree in teaching, 1913

■ Art teacher, Åggelby Secondary School, 1912–53

■ Married 1918 to painter and scenographer Matti Warén

■ Work as painter with participation in painting exhibitions

Decorative bowl by
Anni Brandt executed
in a remarkably modern
manner and signed in 1915.
Diameter 24.5 cm.
Private collection.
Photo: Johnny Korkman.

Ville Vallgren

Founder of the Terracotta Association

- Born in Porvoo 1855, died in Helsinki 1940

- École des Beaux-Arts, Paris, 1878–80

- Honorary mention, Paris Salon, 1886

- Second and first prize, national sculpture competitions, 1887 and 1890; gold medal 1899, Grand Prix 1900, Paris World Exhibitions

- Bronze statues and portraits in Finland and abroad, including the Havis Amanda fountain, Helsinki

Ville Vallgren in his studio in Leppävaara, Espoo. Vallgren often used Finnish earthenware clay to make models for his bronze, marble and plaster sculptures. Photo: Otava Photo Archives.

Carl Wilhelm (Ville) Vallgren belongs to a group of Finnish artists who studied in Paris during the second half of the nineteenth century and made a name for themselves on the European art scene. He was born in the small, southern Finnish town of Porvoo but came to be a central figure in the Nordic artist colony in Paris. He enjoyed great success as a sculptor in Paris but kept in close contact with his homeland, where he regularly put on exhibitions. In 1913 he moved back to Finland, settling down in Leppävaara, around five kilometres west of Helsinki. He then began a new stage in his life as an active and respected sculptor in his native country.

As a sculptor, Ville Vallgren was used to working in clay, as both plaster and bronze statues must first be modelled in clay before making moulds for the final cast. Vallgren was a keen spokesman for Finnish low-fired clay, which he dug up close to his home in Leppävaara and fired in a combined ceramic kiln and baking oven in his studio. In 1924 he founded the Terracotta Association, which among other things campaigned to 'resurrect the popular art of pottery'.[1] Finnish clay was recommended not only for sculpture but also as a suitable material for manufacturing utilitarian ceramics. The members of the association organized several exhibitions of statuettes, vases, urns and plates.

The Terracotta Association's first joint exhibition opened on 23 November 1924 at Salon Strindberg. It displayed the gentlemen's 'sculptural figurative art' as well as glazed pots made by Finch and his students. Ville Vallgren reviewed the exhibition himself:

'I have worked with terracotta in Paris for around forty years and here in our homeland for twelve years. These days I fire pieces in my own kiln. Having tried several types of clay, including ones from Kemiö, Kouvola, Hyvinkää and other areas, I have found that Leppävaara clay is best. Lokomo clay from Tampere, which is the same as Cambrian clay, becomes resoundingly hard and durable. Out of that clay I have fashioned a small vase, which can be found in the Atheneum's collections.'

He goes on to make a fanciful description of Finnish clay:

'The *ordinary clay* or brick clay local to southern Uusimaa has been found to withstand firing at 800–900 °C. *Cambrian clay* 1–3, when fired in an oxidizing, blue flame, will withstand 1,000 °C. Finnish kaolin = china clay. It is red (!) and can be fired at 1,400 degrees Celsius. Yellowy-white kaolin fired at 1,400 °C is extremely beautiful'.[2]

Ville Vallgren's ceramic work consisted mainly of statuettes, urns and tear-shaped bottles in terracotta. Unlike his plaster and bronze casts, these pieces are modelled directly in the final material and display a quality of immediacy and freshness, with sensual marks left by hands and tools. His graceful and sensuous statuettes of female 'dancers' and 'weepers' are shrouded in the draperies typical of the time, and reflect clear stylistic features of the turn-of-the-century Art Nouveau style. Vallgren's treatment of surfaces indicates his special interest in patination techniques.

Several Finnish sculptors worked in terracotta, but Ville Vallgren was genuinely interested in finding out about the specific opportunities offered by the material. He was a defender of popular arts in their various forms, including for instance 'glazed plates, jars, jugs, urns, etc., fired in rich colours'.[3] The significance of the Terracotta Association's activities, which were mentioned in the contemporary press on several different occasions,[4] must not be underestimated. He was also an educator of the people, who, in his own words, each autumn invited fifty elementary-school pupils to his studio to show them how he built and fired his work.[5]

In the 1920s Ville Vallgren donated a large collection of his terracotta, plaster and marble sculptures to the City of Porvoo and the Porvoo Museum. Through his autobiographical writings Vallgren also made himself known as a *bon viveur*, philosopher and chef.

Sigrid af Forselles

Passion for urns

- Born in Evo 1860, died in Florence 1935

- Drawing school of the Finnish Art Association, 1876 to c. 1878

- Académie Julien, Paris, 1880 to c. 1882

- Studies in sculpture with Alfred Boucher and August Rodin, Paris, 1880s

- Bronze medallion for urn, 'The Woman's Exhibition', Earls Court, London, 1900

- Works in Atheneum Art Museum; relief *Progress of the Human Soul* in Kallio Church, Helsinki

- Exhibitions in Helsinki, Paris, London and elsewhere

Sigrid af Forselles in her youth. Photo: Atelier Apollo/ from a family album.

Veiled Women, a vase by Sigrid af Forselles is, like many of her other works, highly symbolic. Height 19.5 cm. Private collection. Photo: Johnny Korkman.

Sigrid af Forselles was one of Finland's first sculptresses. Her contemporaries were fairly unsympathetic to her art, partly because she spent periods living abroad and worked in a style alien to the artistic currents that were common in Finland at the time. There was also more prejudice towards women sculptors than painters of the same sex, who could more easily carry out their work at home. In contrast to her fellow students, painters Helene Schjerfbeck, Maria Wiik and Amélie Lundahl, Sigrid af Forselles has been all but forgotten as an artist.

In addition to her work as a sculptor, Sigrid af Forselles created ceramic works that have also been denied the attention they deserve. At least twenty of her ceramic pieces are still in existence, and many more are documented through photographs. With her art studies in Paris and Italy as a background, around the turn of the century Sigrid af Forselles was creating entirely different work from that of A. W. Finch's students.

Sigrid af Forselles's ceramic work consists of lidded and handled urns as well as glazed wall tiles adorned with religious motifs. These are fashioned in red clay or light faience, often covered with engobes in various colours and transparent glazes. The urns were hand-built on a whirler, which makes them the slightest bit asymmetrical. The wall tiles are linked to the Florentine faience tradition of the Renaissance. Many of af Forselles's pieces are signed and it is known that they were all completed around the turn of the twentieth country, but no records exist of where they were fired.[1] As a student and – according to sources – intimate friend of August Rodin's, it may be that af Forselles became interested in ceramics by his example,[2] as Rodin worked for a time at the Sèvres porcelain factory.[3] She was also friendly with Ellen Thesleff, whose sister Gerda was a pioneer in Finnish ceramic art. Sigrid af Forselles lived in Italy from 1911 onwards.

Viewers today may find Sigrid af Forselles's urns strikingly individual, almost bizarre, despite the fact that they are clearly influenced by the Central European Art Nouveau style. Their shapes are heavily organic and they are adorned with figurative motifs in which parts of plants create handles, and leaves and branches wrap around the pots' forms like draperies. The urns' decorations often consist of figurative mythological images in low relief, depicting for instance groups of bemantled women loaded with symbolism. Although her material was clay, af Forselles's pieces are more reminiscent of Emile Gallé's unique glass vases than of other ceramics. Sigrid af Forselles's work manifests certain shortcomings in technical execution but does reflect the artist's wealth of imagination and deep personal involvement. This is not the work of a ceramic artist, but of a sculptress with a passion for shaping objects out of clay.

> Urn by Sigrid af Forselles. Height 31.5 cm. Hotel Majvik. Photo: Johnny Korkman.

Johan & Anna Grönroos

The potter and his daughter

■ Johan Alexander Grönroos III, born in 1863, died in 1924

■ Anna Augusta Grönroos, born in 1893, died in 1969

Countless books describe artists living in Tuusula around the turn of the twentieth century, but seldom has anything been said about the cooperation between these artists and local craftsmen, the craftsmen's contribution being all too often overlooked. Among the potters in the area, Johan (Janne) Grönroos III and his daughter Anna deserve a special mention in the history of Finnish ceramic art.

Janne Grönroos was a third-generation potter, and, like his father, parish master potter and brick-maker Johan Grönroos the younger (1817–82), he produced not only thrown functional ware but also exceptionally beautiful tiled stoves, extant in many well-known artists' homes, namely Ainola, Halosenniemi, Erkkola and Suviranta. Tiled stoves were important elements in domestic interiors of the Art Nouveau period, and their makers paid close attention to the artists' wishes in the course of production. Painter Pekka Halonen worked with Janne Grönroos and became so enthusiastic about making tiled stoves that he eventually built a kiln where he could carry out experiments with glazes.[1]

Grönroos also worked with Willy Finch and Louis Sparre.[2] He was probably employed for a time at AB Iris, as it is known that he learnt about glazes, pigments and ornamentation there. It is not far-fetched to suggest that this renowned tile-maker created the tile-clad, green stove designed by Akseli Gallén-Kallela for the Iris Room at the Paris World Exhibition. Grönroos also made another stove, taller and red-brown in colour, also shown in Paris at the time; it was returned to Finland after the exhibition and rebuilt at Erkkola in Tuusula.[3]

Wheel-thrown vase by Johan Grönroos with spatter decoration by his daughter Anna. Photo: Toivo Lumme.

Work at AB Iris must have impressed this potter, who for a living was used to throwing simple, undecorated vessels. Janne Grönroos was so taken by forms and colours that he began to make his own functional and decorative items, including jugs and lidded terrines. His youngest daughter Anna (married name Niemi) also turned out to have a talent for art and worked with her father, decorating the freshly produced pots.[4] These are technically comparable to Iris ceramics, but their ornamentation is often individual and bold.

In his book *Taiteen juhlaa ja arkea* Antti Halonen indicates that Anna Grönroos went on to study at the University of Art and Design Helsinki; other sources suggest that she learnt ceramics in Porvoo. Neither of these statements have been corroborated. Anna's son Risto Niemi has said that Antti Halonen repeatedly asked Anna Grönroos to lend her ceramics for the Brussels World Exhibition in 1958. She did not consider herself an artist and refused to do so: 'I just did the decorating and my father fired the work.'

Anna Grönroos favoured bold, modern ornamentation on traditional forms thrown by her father. Private collection. Photo: Johnny Korkman.

Sigrid Granfelt

Bold pioneer

- Born in Turku 1868, died in Helsinki 1942

- Drawing school of the Finnish Art Association, Helsinki, 1886–89

- Académie Colarossi, Paris, 1891–92 and 1895–96

- Calderon's School of Animal Painting, London, 1898–99

- University of Art and Design Helsinki, ceramics studies, 1902–09

- Finnish Artists' Exhibitions, 1894–1905: third prize 1894, second prize 1898

- Works in Atheneum Art Museum, the Åland Museum, the Åland Art Museum, the Turku Provincial Museum and Husö Biological Station

∨ A detail from Sigrid Granfelt's home, Husö Estate, including a pot and a cupboard decorated by her. Photo: Augusto Mendes/Åland Museum.

>> Ceramics by Sigrid Granfelt in an heirloom armoire. Photo: Augusto Mendes/Åland Museum.

When aristocrat Sigrid Maria Granfelt took up studies in pottery with Willy Finch in the autumn of 1902, she had behind her a solid international education as a painter. She specialized in animal painting, the genre for which she is still best known. In 1911 she moved to Bergö island in Åland, where she practised farming in accordance with the popular principle of self-sufficiency. Few people know that during her life Sigrid Granfelt made a significant contribution to design and craftsmanship in wood, textiles and ceramics. Upon her death she bequeathed her home, Husö Estate, to Åbo Akademi University.[1] A large collection of ceramic pieces preserved at the estate bears witness to the fact that Sigrid Granfelt was a versatile and individual artist in the field of ceramics. Some of Sigrid Granfelt's ceramic work can also be seen in museums and private collections.

Sigrid Granfelt's ceramic work dates from between 1902 and 1928, a period of considerable length. The artefacts are mainly made of three types of earthenware: red-burning clay, white faience and beige faience. This final type of material may have been natural clay dug up in Åland by the artist as it displays imperfections in the form of limestone particles, which over the course of the years have expanded, breaking the vessels' surfaces. Decorations are executed in coloured slips, and at least some of the glazes used appear to be borax-based as opposed to traditional lead glazes.[2] Granfelt's earliest pieces were doubtless created at the University of Art and Design Helsinki, and the double signatures on two pieces indicate that someone else threw the pottery according to Sigrid Granfelt's instructions. Later she developed into a skilled thrower, most probably firing her work, after moving to Åland, at local potters' facilities. She may also have worked for a time as a designer for the Turku tile factory (Turun kaakelitehdas Oy).[3]

The collection at Husö consists mainly of functional artefacts with simple, timeless shapes influenced by traditional pottery. Sigrid Granfelt's studies in central Europe also left traces in vessels inspired by southern equivalents. Two styles predominate: freehand brush decoration based on folk art and experimental, more geometric patterns that even today appear modern. The pieces that have survived reveal Sigrid Granfelt as an individual and creative ceramic artist, who in many respects was well ahead of her time.

Gerda Thesleff

Visions of Tuscany

- Born in Helsinki 1871, died in Helsinki 1939

- Stockholm, studies in physiotherapy

- University of Art and Design Helsinki, 1898–1906 and c. 1909–10

- Arabia, 1922–24

- Studio at home in Helsinki; Lallukka artists' residence from 1933

- Design exhibitions in Finland and abroad, including St Petersburg and Copenhagen

7 Faience bowl with handle by Gerda Thesleff from the 1920s. Height 10 cm. Photo: Timo Kauppila/Arabia Museum.

Throughout her life, ceramist Gerda Thesleff remained in the shadow of her more famous sister, painter Ellen Thesleff. Her ceramics have always had a faithful following, however, including designer Kaj Franck: he brought up Gerda Thesleff's work as early as the 1970s in lectures at what is now the University of Art and Design Helsinki. A new interest in this peculiar artist was kindled towards the end of the twentieth century.[1]

Gerda Thesleff created functional pieces: teacups, jugs, vases and bowls. She was not only an artist, like her sister, but also an artisan. This meant she threw, decorated and glazed all her own ceramics in the humble conditions of a home studio without a kiln. She would often transport her fragile work to the Arabia factory to be fired. As one of Finch's early students, she also had the opportunity of firing her work at the university.

Gerda Thesleff participated actively in exhibitions, often together with her colleague Elin Juselius. They worked at Arabia for a time, and the company arranged a joint exhibition for the two artists in 1922. The pieces Thesleff created at the factory feature both the artist's signature and the Arabia stamp. They were built in a light, high-fired faience body, in contrast to the red earthenware clay used at the school.

Like her contemporaries, Gerda Thesleff fought a constant battle against technical problems: capricious colours that would burn away when fired, glazes that would bubble up and crack, and heavy clay bodies that were difficult to work with. Thesleff's treatment of form and her throwing techniques may occasionally show weaknesses but this is outweighed by her powerful artistic expression.[2]

Few of Gerda Thesleff's pieces are decorated in traditional ways, although she did depict flowers and plants. She painted pictures full of movement and drama with powerful brushstrokes, applying engobes under a transparent glaze. She would also dye clays and press them into the base, achieving unusual, relief-like effects. Art historians have found influences of both Fauvism and Orientalism in Gerda Thesleff's ceramics, but her pieces feel modern even today.

Gerda and Ellen Thesleff made several lengthy trips to Italy, which had a significant impact on both sisters' artwork. The Italian landscape – the hills and towns of Tuscany – stands out as a supporting force and inner vision for Gerda Thesleff. She must have spent many inspired moments in these places, as the landscapes appear time and again in her ceramic work.

Earthenware bowl and vase by Gerda Thesleff. Private collection. Photo: Johnny Korkman Heights 10 cm and 17 cm.

Thure Öberg

Finnish Art Nouveau

When Thure Öberg became involved with Arabia at the age of twenty-four, the company was still a subsidiary of the Swedish ceramics factory Rörstrand. His father, sculptor Axel Öberg, worked at Rörstrand and it could be said that Thure Öberg had porcelain in his blood. Öberg profited fully from his technical knowledge in his new role as the first ceramic artist at Arabia.

Thure Öberg's strong roots in the old artisan traditions of porcelain factories were expressed in his decorations with traditional floral and plant patterns carried out in an underglaze technique. Öberg was the one to introduce this manner of decoration to Finland and he also contributed to its development in both technical and artistic terms. His earliest pieces strongly reflect the Art Nouveau style with their organic and sculptural relief elements. Gradually he developed a more refined style, possibly influenced by successful contemporary decorators such as the Dane Arnold Krog of the Royal Copenhagen Porcelain Manufactory.

Several years of experimentation inspired Öberg to use many other methods of decorating, including multicoloured enamels, majolica technique and underglaze colours such as cobalt blue, inspired by Chinese porcelain. Thure Öberg's work is one of a kind and he holds an important position in the history of Finnish ceramics, as a predecessor to artists at the hand-decoration department at Arabia. The Arabia Museum contains an impressive collection of his work.

■ Born in Stockholm 1872, died in Helsinki 1935

■ Technical School (now International Art School), Stockholm, degree in design

■ Arabia, 1896–1935

■ Assistant's prize for painted decorations, Arabia gold medal, Paris World Exhibition 1900

Bold Art Nouveau forms by Thure Öberg from the early 1920s. Height 16 cm. Arabia Museum. Photo: Indav/Arabia Museum.

Karl Hildén

Potter and Naive artist in clay

■ Born in St Petersburg 1873, died in Kokkola 1948

■ Son of master dyer and potter Mathias Hildén

■ Pottery in Kokkola with a varied production from 1910s onwards

Karl (Kalle) Fredrik Hildén, potter-turned-artist and resident of Kokkola, is one of the most fascinating figures in Finnish ceramic art. Nowadays he is less well known outside the Ostrobothnian region even among collectors, although in his lifetime he had customers throughout Finland. Sculptor Ville Vallgren was enchanted by Hildén's products, as was architect Rafael Blomstedt, artistic director of the Central School of Arts and Crafts (now the University of Art and Design Helsinki).[1]

Hildén learnt the craft of pottery from his father, who was a manufacturer of pots and tiled stoves in St Petersburg and Hämeenlinna. Kalle arrived in the town of Kokkola in 1896 to do his military service, married Lydia Helena Nordbäck and founded a small pottery. After the death of the local potter Axel Moring, Hildén took over his workshop at 39 Ouluntie. Encouraged by the surveyor Vaajakallio and artist Leo Korpela, Hildén's innate artistic talents were allowed to blossom.[2]

From mechanical, serial production, Hildén turned to manufacturing unique, hand-thrown functional artefacts such as various vases, plates and bowls, and entire tea and coffee sets to order. He was an intellectually alert character, known for having read all the books in the city's library. Hildén's ceramics show impressions from various cultures, ranging from Chinese ceramics to Islamic art, which he appears to have gathered from the pictures in art books. He was able, however, to transform all these external influences into his own, personal language of form.

Plate with cockerel by Karl Hildén. Diameter 18 cm.
Private collection. Photo: Johnny Korkman.

The foundations of Karl Hildén's work in clay lay in his inherited, superb craftsmanship. He had a kick wheel and generally used transparent lead glazes, firing his work at low temperatures (around 800 °C) in a wood-burning kiln. Following tradition, he used red earthenware clay which he dug up locally from the banks of the river Perho.[3] Free brush decoration and multicoloured slips are characteristic of his work. He also applied engobes in layers, achieving marbled effects. In addition to leaves and flowers, Hildén painted birds, boats and human figures in the spirit of Naive art. He acquired his ceramic stains in Germany and sold his wares directly from his workshop as well as at the market in Kokkola.[4]

Hildén's work displays a natural sense of material and form. He combined these essential qualities for a ceramist with rare artistic freedom of expression and a confident yet spontaneous talent for decoration. As a potter and Naive artist, Karl Hildén is unique. Examples of his work can be found at the K. H. Renlund Museum in Kokkola, at the Ostrobothnian Museum in Vaasa and in several private collections.

Teapot by Karl Hildén, part of a complete tea service.
Height 11 cm. Private collection.
Photo: Johnny Korkman.

Detail with a lizard motif on a marbled engobe dish
by Karl Hildén. Kaarela Local Heritage Association.
Photo: Tapio Väinölä/K. H. Renlund Museum.

Emil Cedercreutz

Equestrian sculptor

■ Born in Köyliö 1879, died in Harjavalta 1949

■ Drawing schools of the Finnish Art Association and the University of Helsinki

■ Sculpture studies with Victor Malmberg at the Academy of Fine Arts, Helsinki*, 1900

■ University of Art and Design Helsinki, pottery, 1902

■ Further sculpture studies, Brussels, Rome and Paris, 1902–13

■ Founding member of the Terracotta Association and the Association of Finnish Sculptors

■ Founder of the Emil Cedercreutz Museum and Cultural Centre, Harjavalta

Few Finnish artists have achieved so much in so many different genres as the sculptor and baron Emil Herman Robert Cedercreutz. In his lifetime he not only travelled, studied and worked in various parts of Europe, but also made great contributions to the Satakunta region, where his studio and home, Harjula, built in 1914, now forms part of a large cultural centre.

Cedercreutz was one of A. W. Finch's first fourteen students, taking up studies in pottery in 1902. He already had a few years' art studies behind him but was probably attracted to the ceramics department by Finch's fame as an established artist. Some early signed pieces in red clay, decorated with engobe colours and clearly thrown by Cedercreutz himself, still survive.[1] Monochrome photographs show larger pieces, thrown by a professional potter and decorated by Cedercreutz.[2] The equestrian motif appears repeatedly in these works. Cedercreutz painted expressive, dynamic images of galloping horses, accentuating details with the sgraffito technique. He also experimented with paper resists in combination with engobes.

Emil Cedercreutz was a skilled silhouettist, sculptor, writer and art collector, who never gave up ceramics, although he only studied the subject briefly. He regularly participated in sculpture exhibitions with his terracotta statuettes, often with equine subjects. Towards the end of the 1920s, Arabia manufactured large vases and sculptures designed by Cedercreutz.[3]

Earthenware pots with slip decoration by Emil Cedercreutz on his favoured equestrian themes. Heights 6.5 cm and 16 cm. Emil Cedercreutz Museum. Photos: Studio Jaakko Ojala/Emil Cedercreutz Museum.

* The Academy of Fine Arts has undergone many name changes over the years. For consistency, the current name of the institution is used throughout this book.

Gunnar Finne

■ Born in Hollola 1886, died in Helsinki 1952

■ University of Art and Design Helsinki, interior design dept., 1907–9

■ Hochschule für angewandte Kunst, Vienna, 1909–10

Sculptor Johan Gunnar Finne expressed his talents in the domain of applied art in glass, silver, textiles and ceramics. He was one of the founders of the Finnish Association of Designers Ornamo and acted for several years as its chairman. As a teacher in modelling he had an influence on later generations of sculptors. He worked with several architects, creating granite sculptures and grave monuments as well as façade reliefs in ceramic clinker for buildings including that of the old Postipankki bank and the Suomalainen Yhteiskoulu school (now housing the National Board of Antiquities) in Helsinki. He also made glazed statuettes that were fired at Arabia.

Faun relief by Gunnar Finne. Kyösti Kakkonen's collection. Photo: Kari-Kuva.

Gunnar Finne working with an assistant on a clay model of a pillar for the Parliament building in Helsinki, *c.* 1929. Photo: Otava Photo Archives.

Gregori Tigerstedt

Versatile artist

Gregori ('Grischka') Tigerstedt started his artistic career as a sculptor and draughtsman. He was introduced to ceramics by his older friend Ville Vallgren, whom he appears to have seen as a father figure. The trio formed by Emil Cedercreutz, Ville Vallgren and Tigerstedt constituted the nucleus of the Terracotta Association, which advocated the use of Finnish red clay in the 1930s.

Tigerstedt had multiple artistic talents. He painted murals, illustrated books and designed heraldic emblems. He had a solid international education in sculpture, but from the 1930s he began to feel most at home with ceramics. Initially he created terracotta sculptures and large hand-built urns using the coil technique. Later he expanded his skills to include serial production of slip-cast tableware which was sold at Stockmann's design department. Tigerstedt's daughter Yvonne helped her father in the studio with the fastidious job of attaching handles to cups, for example. The artist purchased glazes and pigments in Britain but also carried out his own glaze experiments.

Large free-standing urns by Gregori Tigerstedt for Suomi-Filmi company. Private collection. Photo from the artist's collection of press cuttings.

Within ceramics Gregori Tigerstedt was prompted to come up with his own technical solutions, which provided an outlet for his engineering talents. He designed and built three electric kilns, widely known for their reliability – which was by no means a matter of course in wartime Finland. He also built electric wheels, registering their patents.

Tigerstedt's studio at 12 Pohjoisranta in Helsinki played a significant role from the 1930s onwards as an informal art centre where ceramists could take their work for firing. The long list of well-known artists who used the facilities includes Emil Cedercreutz, Marita Lybeck, Valentina Modig, Francesca and Richard Lindh, Dorrit von Fieandt, Robert Hancock and Maija Aaltonen. A young and less well-off Tapio Wirkkala manufactured ceramic jewelry for sale in his student days and fired it at Gregori Tigerstedt's studio.[1] 'Grischka's workshop' functioned for almost forty years as a 'little Arabia'.

Gregori Tigerstedt's gnome finds a spring ladybird.
Private collection. Photo: Johnny Korkman.

Gusti Franzén

Eldest in a clan of potters

■ Born in Tuusula 1892, died in Malmi 1960

■ Lower School of Crafts, Ekenäs, 1907–9

■ University of Art and Design Helsinki, 1911–15

■ Kupittaan Savi, artist and overseer, 1919 to c. 1930

■ Staatsfachschule für Keramik u. verwandte Kunstgewerbe, Tepliz-Schönau, Czechoslovakia, 1923–24

■ Work at Franzén's Pottery, the Terracotta company and Brothers Franzén ceramics factory

The Franzén family is unique in Finnish ceramic art, as so many of its members have played significant roles at important ceramics factories and potteries all around the country. The progenitor of this family, Gustaf Alexander Franzén, was a renowned master potter who won several prizes at art and craft exhibitions – including a silver medal in St Petersburg, where he worked for a time. Towards the end of the 1890s he was employed by A. W. Finch at the Iris factory in Porvoo.[1] In 1900 he moved to Ekenäs and from there to the village of Täkter in Ingå where he founded his own workshop, Franzén's Pottery.

Gustaf Alexander Franzén had ten children, at least six of whom were involved with ceramics. The eldest son, Gustav Adolf (Gusti) Franzén, was the only one to receive art education. The large family lived in poor circumstances, and as the son of an Iris potter Gusti Franzén was probably allowed to study with Finch free of charge.[2] Apart from pottery studies, Franzén's time at what is now the University of Art and Design Helsinki included advanced ornamental drawing, sculpture, art history and bookkeeping. Surviving earthenware pieces dating from Gusti Franzén's time at the school indicate that he decorated with brushes and blue, white, black and chrome green slips. A pot signed 'GF 1912', found at Kullo Manor near Porvoo, demonstrates that this potter's son was already a skilled thrower when he began his studies, altogether in a different category from his fellow students, the 'family girls'. It is covered in a matte glaze that is highly reminiscent of the complete green-glaze coverings adopted much later (in the 1930s and 40s) at Kupittaan Savi.

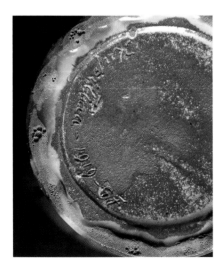

Gusti Franzén's signature 'Kupittaa 1919 GF' on the bottom of the vase on the opposite page. Photo: Johnny Korkman.

Gusti Franzén on the left, modelling a sculpture of a fellow student at the Atheneum, c. 1912. Photo from the Franzén family album.

Gusti Franzén's brothers Frans, Gunnar and Gösta also became potters and all of them, as well as the fifth brother, Georg, were at one time or another employed at the Kupittaa factory. Their sister Edith was hired as a decorative painter, and Frans worked as overseer at Kera Oy.

Gusti Franzén also founded the Terracotta company in Malmi together with his brother Georg. After their father's death in 1922, Frans and Gunnar took over the family business in Täkter. Towards the beginning of the 1950s, all five brothers were working at the Brothers Franzén ceramics factory by Täkter station. Gusti and Frans were particularly skilled at throwing large planters. Hand production gradually gave way to machine manufacture of flowerpots and eventually drainage pipes. The factory officially ceased operating in 1958, though it carried on working on a smaller scale. Gusti continued to make pots until his death in 1960.

Wheel-thrown vase by Gusti Franzén, made during his first year as foreman with Kupittaan Savi, 1919. Height 22.5 cm. The Franzén family collection. Photo: Johnny Korkman.

This contract, signed 1 March 1922, verifies that Kupittaa pottery was produced with Gusti Franzén's slip and glaze recipes.

Wäinö Aaltonen

A sculptor's fascination for clay

■ Born in Marttila 1894, died in Helsinki 1966

■ Drawing School of the Turku Art Association, 1910–15

■ Grand Prix, Paris World Exhibition 1937; sculpture award, New York World's Fair 1939; International Peace Prize, Budapest 1953

■ Statues in many Finnish cities; honorary membership of art academies in Europe

■ Title of professor awarded in 1940

A wall plate portraying a female figure, manufactured by Kupittaan Savi Oy, is the only ceramic work by celebrated sculptor Wäinö Waldemar Aaltonen that the general public knows. This plate was produced from the early 1920s well into the 1940s in different series, each with a different matte, coloured glaze.[1] Few people know that this master of marble, granite and bronze was truly fascinated by ceramic techniques and made clay sculptures from the 1920s onward.

Aaltonen frequently visited the ceramics department at the University of Art and Design Helsinki, maintaining a mutually beneficial relationship with head teacher Elsa Elenius.[2] In contrast to most other sculptors he was not content with terracotta, but glazed and fired ceramic work at the university. Some of his smaller pieces, including a statuette portraying the writer Aleksis Kivi, were produced at Arabia.

In the 1950s, Wäinö Aaltonen purchased a kiln for his studio on the island of Kulosaari, Helsinki. His daughter Maija, who had studied with Elenius, was employed as a part-time assistant. Aaltonen's clay sculptures include *Mahapoika*; a larger version in black stone of this piece belongs to the National Museum in Stockholm. Other works, such as a large mask with the face of a woman, were press-moulded and given varied surface treatments. Aaltonen was fascinated by material experiments, and his genuine penchant for clay lasted throughout his career.

Faience mask of Eeva Arttu by Wäinö Aaltonen, who frequently made several studies of the same subject in different materials. A bronze version of this mask also exists.
Height 33 cm. Private collection.
Photo: Johnny Korkman.

Greta Lisa Jäderholm-Snellman
Exclusive Art Deco

During Greta Lisa Jäderholm-Snellman's career, the management of the Arabia factory began to understand the value of trained artists. Before the 1920s, their products were principally copies of foreign designs; now Arabia began to employ artists, initially for decorative work.

Jäderholm-Snellman was hired by Arabia in 1921 to design and decorate both functional and ornamental ware. Having spent several years in Paris, she had a true insight into Central European culture. As the leader of the department for 'More Beautiful Things for Everyday Use', she designed vases, lidded boxes, bowls and entire dinner and coffee sets.

The designs of Jäderholm-Snellman's work often echo Chinese ceramics with silhouette-like, elegant and stylized human, animal and plant ornaments. Though utilitarian in nature, her work eschews the mundane and reaches for the exclusive and the near luxurious with exquisitely refined, matte glazes. At times these have crackle effects or shades of green reminiscent of jade and traditional celadon glazes. Details are finely rendered and the execution is brought to perfection with advanced manual techniques. Brushstrokes in gold and platinum lustres against a monochrome background intensify the unique and precious character of the objects.

As well as Chinese influences, Jäderholm-Snellman's work reveals a preoccupation with other exotic countries such as Persia and Egypt, typical of the time.

■ Born in Helsinki 1894, died in Alicante 1973

■ Studies in Paris, Scandinavia and Britain

■ Arabia, 1921–37

■ University of Art and Design Helsinki, porcelain-painting teacher, 1929–37

■ Sèvres, France, 1937–39

■ Riihimäen Lasi Oy, 1937–49

■ Monza, Barcelona, Antwerp, Milan, Brussels and Paris World Exhibitions

■ Gold medal, Milan, 1933

A series of perfume artefacts by Greta Lisa Jäderholm-Snellman with decorations in the highly demanding metal etching technique. Heights 7–9 cm. Photo: Timo Kauppila/Arabia Museum.

Emil Rekola

Early artist at Kupittaa

■ Born in Hollola 1895, died in Helsinki 1967

■ University of Art and Design Helsinki, ceramics dept., 1911–15

■ Artist at Kupittaa, 1920s

In 2001 research for this book led to the discovery in a private collection of a large, decorated amphora manufactured at Kupittaan Savi. The vessel is signed 'E. R. -24,' and it is dramatically different from any previously seen. It is clearly made by a highly original, talented artist who worked in a free, painterly style. Its decoration is a far cry from the usual ornamentation. The motif – a female figure and a sea monster with undulating tentacles – has been carried out with expressionistic, confident brushstrokes combined with sgraffito technique, in numerous engobe colours. Who was this unknown artist? After almost two years of tireless investigation including fruitless enquiries through museum journals, the puzzle was solved thanks to an accidental chain of events.[1]

Three further large vases signed by Emil Rekola and manufactured at Kupittaa have since been identified. Admittedly they are cast pieces, but their personal and unconventional decoration in combined sgraffito and paintbrush techniques manifests their position as works of art. We can assume that there are more pieces by Emil Rekola in existence, still undiscovered.

Johan Emil Juhonpoika Rekola was the eleventh and last child of Juho Kustaa Rekola and his wife Wilhelmina Rekola, née Kallentytär, both descendants of ancient farming families. In the course of his studies, Emil Rekola befriended Gusti Franzén, which led to an invitation to work at the newly founded ceramics factory in Kupittaa. He registered as a member of Turku Cathedral congregation in 1926 and in 1933 married Anna Tukia in Valkjärvi. The couple spent some time in Viipuri and moved to Helsinki in 1937.

Edith Franzén and Emil Rekola were colleagues at Kupittaa in the 1920s. Photo from the Franzén family album.

The Woman and the Sea Monster, amphora decorated by Emil Rekola at Kupittaa in 1924. Front view. Height 40 cm. Private collection. Photo: Johnny Korkman.

The Woman and the Sea Monster. Rear view. Photo: Johnny Korkman.

Siiri Hariola

■ Born in Tenhola 1895, died in Järvenpää 1969

■ University of Art and Design Helsinki: porcelain decoration and ceramics studies *c.* 1933–36; porcelain-painting teacher 1938–1950s

■ Bronze medal, Brussels World Exhibition 1935; gold medal, Paris World Exhibition 1937

After graduating, Siiri Sofia Hariola (née Högström) and Tamara Laurén stayed on at the university's ceramics department for almost ten years.[1] Siiri Hariola's work took simple, classical forms and had glaze effects achieved through reduction firing in the school's wood kiln. Hariola enjoyed success at various international exhibitions but appears to have given up ceramics after her appointment as porcelain-painting teacher.

A collection of faience items by Siiri Hariola. Photo from the Ornamo 25th anniversary publication of 1936.

Elsa Elenius

Timeless simplicity

Elsa Elenius and Maija Grotell were two of A. W. Finch's favourite students. Talented and diligent, they were allowed to continue working and using the kilns at the ceramics department after completing their studies. Elenius helped Finch, whose health was already failing, with throwing, and honed her skills at the wheel at the same time.[1]

In the 1920s, in the spirit of the time, Elenius decorated her work with stylized plant and human motifs. These early works clearly project technical virtuosity with the brush as well as a sense of clarity and coherence in composition and form. In 1930 a wood and coke-burning kiln was set up in a wing of the school, allowing faculty members and students to produce large-format works.[2] From this point on, Elenius's artistic development truly flourished.

Elenius succeeded Finch and held the position of head teacher at the ceramics department of what is now the University of Art and Design Helsinki for thirty-two years. She also enjoyed a brilliant career as a ceramic artist and was able to use the kilns and other facilities at the school, achieving periods of intensity and heightened creativity during the summer and at other times when the students were absent. Although Elenius did not achieve wide popular acclaim in Finland, she was the first independent Finnish ceramist to win international recognition. As an artist she was, however, a solitary, reserved figure.

■ Born in Laihia 1897, died in Helsinki 1967

■ University of Art and Design Helsinki, ceramics dept: studies 1915–18, head teacher 1930–62

■ Gold medal, Barcelona 1929; Grand Prix, Milan 1933; Grand Prix, Brussels 1935; gold medal, Paris 1937

■ Pro Arte Utili medal, 1950; Merit Cross of the Order of the Lion of Finland, 1952

Elsa Elenius sledging on the ice in 1943.
Photo courtesy of Auli Urrila-Stenbäck.

Elsa Elenius's work consisted of large plates, bowls, vases and floor urns; only in exceptional cases did she create smaller functional items such as jugs. The large scale constituted a challenge that suited her self-critical, highly demanding artistic temperament. Her pieces are impressive in terms of their size and belong to the crème de la crème of Finnish ceramics. Elenius's major works display a timeless simplicity and harmony.

It can hardly be a coincidence that many of our foremost female ceramists' careers ended by the time they reached middle age. The work was physically taxing, especially for those who worked in their own studios without personal assistants. In 1939 Elsa Elenius sent twenty of her best unique pieces to the New York World Exhibition. Only a handful returned to Finland; the rest were stolen or broken. This setback was too much for Elenius, who lost her motivation for creative work and concentrated on teaching instead. Her students, many of whom became internationally renowned artists, have on several occasions expressed their admiration for Elenius both as a teacher and as an artist.[4]

<< Wheel-thrown works by Elsa Elenius, arranged and photographed in a manner typical of the 1930s. Ornamo Yearbook, 1933.

< A still-life arrangement of ceramics by Elsa Elenius. Private collection. Photo: Auli Urrila.

Tyra Lundgren

Master of form

- Born in Stockholm 1897, died in Stockholm 1979

- School of Industrial Arts, Stockholm, 1914–18

- School of the Royal Academy of Fine Arts, Stockholm, 1918–22

- Periods of work for Arabia, 1925–39

- Rörstrand, artistic director, 1929–30

- Studio AB Gustafsberg, 1940–50

- Diplôme d'Honneur, Milan 1933; gold medal, Milan 1951; Litteris et Artibus gold medal 1950

Swedish painter Tyra Lundgren visited Arabia's factory in 1924 and accepted an invitation to decorate some ceramic tea tables for the company. This was the beginning of a long-term, fruitful relationship between the parties. Lundgren developed into one of the most admired ceramic artists in the Nordic countries, and in time her work also came to encompass textiles and glass. An art critic, she reviewed art and crafts in design magazines, but ceramics was her medium of choice.

Lundgren's talents in the ceramics field were broad. Studies in Central Europe had brought her into close contact with period styles. Her early decorative painting shows traces of Italian faience traditions; her small statuettes from the 1930s are closer in style to Rococo porcelain figurines. Some of her decorative birds for Arabia dating from 1930 to 1934, on the other hand, augur the figurative yet starkly stylized motifs favoured in the 1950s. Lundgren's larger sculptures, some of which are portraits, evoke antique, including Etruscan sculpture. Her work is masterful, with perceptive treatment of form and a restrained yet effective use of glazes. From the 1940s she worked primarily in Sweden on commissions for public art, especially monumental reliefs.

Bird with copper red glaze by Tyra Lundgren from the 1930s. Kyösti Kakkonen's collection. Photo: Kari-Kuva.

Maija Grotell

Finnish ceramist in the New World

Majlis ('Maija') Grotell presumably inherited her talents from her mother, Selma Wiens (b. 1863), who had studied at the Atheneum. Her relatives still recall a set of furniture she had made, complete with intricate wood carvings.¹ As a talented student with A. W. Finch, Maija Grotell enjoyed the privilege of being allowed to continue firing her work at the ceramics department of the school after completing her studies. Grotell's ceramic pieces were often listed as prizes in the prestigious draws organized by the Finnish Society of Crafts and Design. The examples of Grotell's work that have survived in Finland are generally made in red earthenware clay, which was the material used at the school's pottery department. These pieces are decorated with spirited brushstrokes using motifs found in folk art. Her soft, low-melting lead glazes sometimes caused the underlying slips to dissolve, causing blurred, dynamic impressions that contribute to the strong ceramic character of her work.

Maija Grotell emigrated to the United States in 1927, making an exceptional career as a ceramic artist and teacher. It is not far-fetched to draw parallels between Grotell and her fellow student Elsa Elenius, who remained in Finland making a similar contribution to ceramic art, although in considerably smaller circles. These strong women were pioneers, achieving great successes and dedicating their lives to clay. This also required personal sacrifices with regard to family life and health.

Through no less than twenty-five important prizes and distinctions, Grotell secured her position as one of the most significant names in modern American ceramic art. The United States offered the opportunity of working with stoneware clays fired at high temperatures.² Nevertheless, she continued to use coloured engobes for decoration, applying them now to stoneware. Jeff Schlanger describes his teacher: 'Maija Grotell's works have great posture. They stand with glory and without arrogance. They are powerful, secure and stable, yet they stand softly.'³

In addition to her own creative work in clay, Grotell made a significant contribution as the educator of future generations of American ceramists. As head teacher in ceramics at the prestigious Cranbrook Academy of Art, she also worked with several internationally renowned designers, including her fellow countryman, architect Eliel Saarinen.

■ Born in Helsinki 1899, died in Pontiac, Michigan, 1973

■ University of Art and Design Helsinki: painting, sculpture and ceramics studies

■ Inwood Pottery Studios, New York City, 1927–28

■ Union Settlement, New York, 1928–29

■ Henry Street Craft School, New York City, 1929–38

■ School of Ceramic Engineering, Rutgers University, New Brunswick, 1936–38

■ Cranbrook Academy of Art, Michigan: ceramics dept., head teacher, 1938–66

■ Diploma, Barcelona 1929; silver medal, Paris 1937; several prizes, mentions and medals, USA

Earthenware by Maija Grotell, 1923, fired in the kilns of the Atheneum. Vase height 16.5 cm. Bowl diameter 22.4 cm. Private collection. Photo: Johnny Korkman.

Maija Grotell in 1918, aged 19. Photo from the artist's family album.

Michael Schilkin

Slavic temperament

- Born in Trubino, Russia, 1900, died in Helsinki 1962

- University of Art and Design Helsinki, general art course, 1924–28

- Arabia art dept., 1936–62

- Royal Copenhagen Porcelain Manufactory, 1947

- Gold medal, Paris 1937; Diplôme d'honneur, Milan 1951; silver medal, Milan 1954

- Several monumental wall reliefs in Finland and Sweden

∨ Fox with copper red glaze by Michael Schilkin, 1945. Height 29 cm. Arabia Museum. Photo: Katja Hagelstam.

> Figures of African women in grogged clay by Michael Schilkin, mid-1940s. Kyösti Kakkonen's collection. Photo: Kari-Kuva.

>> Michael Schilkin's studio at the Arabia factory, photographed after his death in 1962. Photo: Arabia Museum.

Michael (Mihail) Nikolayevich Schilkin is usually described as a natural talent. The son of a stonecutter, he was born in Russia and moved to Finland in 1921, where he gradually became one of the brightest stars at Arabia's art department.

Having finished his art studies, Michael Schilkin worked for a time as a wood-carver at the Boman furniture company in Helsinki. This work helped him to develop his feeling for form, making him confident and swift with his hands. His sculpture *Samson and Delilah* won the top prize in a Fenno-Russian artists' exhibition held in 1936. This piece was created in Arabia clay and fired in the factory's kiln. At that time Schilkin only made sculptures in the evenings, working as a truck driver during the day to provide for his family. It was only when he received a permanent contract from Arabia in 1937 that he gave up his day job.

Schilkin became known to the general public mainly through his expressive animal sculptures in a coarse, grogged stoneware body. He used traditional Chinese glazes such as celadon and copper red. Works from his exhibitions were often bought as business gifts. Schilkin's mythological figures are dynamic and dramatic, in contrast to his religious subjects, which appear to have been inspired by medieval church sculptures. His large public wall reliefs, on the other hand, show impressions from objects as remote as Babylonian brick gates.

As an artist, Michael Schilkin absorbed a worldwide cultural heritage, depicting moods that ranged from the calmly meditative to the burlesque and humorous. His multifaceted and rich production is united by a strong Slavic form of expression and vitality. His approach to clay was at the same time that of a sculptor and a ceramist.

Kurt Ekholm, director of Arabia's art department, saw the need for employing an imposing artistic personality to create unique works and function as an ambassador – someone with public relations value. Michael Schilkin met these criteria perfectly: he was productive and had a predilection for large formats. In Sweden, where the interest in ceramic art was strong and well established, Schilkin was seen as an exotic talent who overthrew conventional notions. In Finland as well, although he was highly admired, Michael Schilkin was considered out of the ordinary.

Friedl Kjellberg

With a Chinese touch

■ Born in Loeben, Austria, 1905, died
in Porvoo 1993

■ Industrial Design School, Graz

■ Arabia: artist 1924–70, director of art dept.
1948–50

■ Silver medal, Barcelona 1929; gold medal,
Brussels 1935; silver medal, Paris 1937; gold
medal, Milan 1954; silver medal, Cannes 1955

During the 1930s, contacts were lively between ceramics professionals in the Nordic countries. Swedish ceramists, including Tyra Lundgren, were offered the opportunity of working at Arabia in Finland, and the two countries cooperated closely in organizing exhibitions. Nordic ceramists shared an interest in classical Chinese ceramics of the Song dynasty. One such artist was Friedl Kjellberg, born and trained in Austria but active in Finland.

Friedl Kjellberg (née Holzer) carried out comprehensive experiments with glazes and materials and developed her own techniques at Arabia. She is bestknown for having created, through an endless process of trial and error, objects in the Chinese rice porcelain technique. Initially Kjellberg used this complex and time-consuming method for individual pieces, but later she designed a complete elegant and costly dinner set in rice porcelain. Eventually an entire department was founded at Arabia for this type of production.[1]

During her time in Arabia's art department, Kjellberg threw plates, bowls and tall vases in simple shapes, inspired by Chinese ceramics. Her material was generally a pure white porcelain body, which sets off the striking colour effects of glazes such as oxblood red or shimmering peacock blue. Kjellberg also used other traditional East Asian glazes, including celadon and crackle varieties. Arabia's large kilns made firing possible in a reducing atmosphere at temperatures of up to 1,400 °C and were an essential requirement for achieving Kjellberg's results, which were spectacular in technical as well as artistic terms. Through her participation in major international design exhibitions in the 1950s, Kjellberg contributed to the concept of Finnish Design.

∨ Rice porcelain and a sculpture by Friedl Kjellberg at various stages of completion. Photo: Felix Forsman/Arabia Museum.

⌐ Large porcelain plate with copper-red glaze by Friedl Kjellberg, 1946. Arabia Museum. Photo: Indav/Arabia Museum.

Rakel Bäck-Usvaala

Rakel Bäck-Usvaala is one of Finland's earliest studio ceramists. With her husband, decorative painter Lauri Usvaala (né Kettunen), she founded a workshop close to their hometown of Kronoby. In a large wood-burning kiln with clay from a nearby field, Bäck-Usvaala primarily made thrown earthenware, functional as well as decorative pieces. In addition she employed casting methods for serially produced work. Stockmann's department store in Helsinki was one of her principal outlets, but she also sold directly to customers and reached others through agents. Rakel's brother Göran, who later became a renowned designer for Arabia, learnt the art of throwing at his sister's workshop.[1]

■ Born in Kronoby 1908, died in Kronoby 1988

■ University of Art and Design Helsinki, ceramics dept., c. 1934–36

■ Arabia and Gustavsberg, 1930s

■ Studio in Kronoby, 1939 to c. 1960

Vases by Rakel Bäck-Usvaala from the 1940s.
Photo courtesy of Lena Serenius.

Toini Muona

Drama and harmony

■ Born in Helsinki 1904, died in Helsinki 1987

■ University of Art and Design Helsinki: studies 1923–26, postgraduate 1926–32

■ Atelier Vigil, textile designer, 1929–31

■ Arabia art dept., 1931–70

■ Gold medal, Brussels 1935; gold and silver medal, Paris 1937; silver medal, Cannes 1955; Pro Arte Utili medal, Faenza 1955; National Design Award 1970

Toini Muona's talent shone through when she was a student, and she was one of the chosen few allowed to continue working at the ceramics department several years after graduation. Muona was hired by Arabia's art department in the early 1930s and stayed there until her retirement in 1970. There she had the opportunity to concentrate on her artistic creations without any constraints and was spared the frustrating technical problems that hamper ceramists in independent workshops.

Muona did not fear challenges. Her work is permeated by a longing for the extreme, for stretching the boundaries in both technical and artistic terms. She pushed her materials – clay and glazes – to their absolute limits in what was technically possible. A skilled thrower, from the 1960s onwards she was assisted by professional throwers at Arabia. She built the tallest and narrowest vases and bent them until they almost lost their balance, and designed the flattest and thinnest plates. Muona strove to achieve the most spectacular colour combinations: brilliant turquoise with intensive oxblood red. Once she had reached her goals, she began to gamble with her work

> Toini Muona sketching at the Arabia art department. Photo: K.-G.Roos/Arabia Museum.

7 Flambé-glazed plate by Toini Muona. Diameter 55 cm. Photo: Indav/Arabia Museum.

>> Ovoid plate by Toini Muona, 1969. Kyösti Kakkonen's collection. Photo: Kari-Kuva.

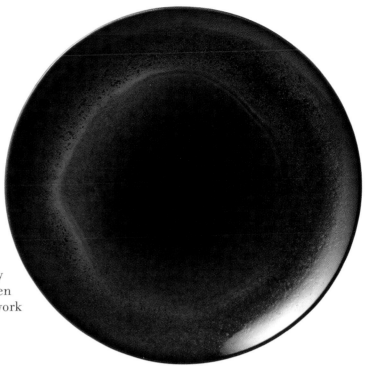

increasingly — experimenting, taking risks, invoking the god of the kiln. She never lost sight of the capabilities of her materials, however. Her sense of what is truly ceramic never failed, though some of the credit for her striking glazes must doubtless be given to the skilful chemists at the factory's laboratory.[1] In addition to her thrown pieces, Muona developed cast forms, more geometric in character, often with white or black glazes.

Active at a time when Finnish design became known worldwide, Muona was recognized at international exhibitions. She received several international awards and is seen by many as the Grand Dame of Finnish ceramic art. The contrasts between calm, harmonious shapes and dramatic glazes in Muona's work still fascinate today.

Marita Lybeck

Simplicity and function

- Born in Helsinki 1906, died in Kauniainen 1990

- University of Art and Design Helsinki: art teaching and textiles 1930s, ceramics dept. 1931

- Design for various companies, including Artek

- Studio Emmel, Kauniainen, 1947–57

- Silver medal, Milan Triennial, 1954

- Kera Oy, artistic director, 1957–59

- Stockmann design dept., manager, 1962 onwards

- Medal of the Arts Council of Uusimaa, 1988

Marita Lybeck's education included training to become an art teacher, a textile artist and a ceramist, but it was in the area of utilitarian ceramics that she became known as a pioneer. A resident of Kauniainen, she gained an insight into the manufacture of ceramics at the nearby ceramics company, Kera Oy, whose production was based on local earthenware clay. This sensitive but demanding material constitutes a challenge in itself: to produce items rooted in tradition yet up to date and suitable for modern, urban homes with their cramped spaces.

Aino Aalto and the interior design company Artek were the catalysts for Lybeck's career as a reformer of designs for utilitarian ware. In the mid-1930s she was asked to design ceramics and upholstery fabrics for the newly opened Artek shop. Her work was later shown at the 1937 Paris World Exhibition in conjunction with Aino and Alvar Aalto's interiors. The ceramic pieces were fired at Kera Oy. Even then, it was functional rather than unique pieces that were closest to her heart. In 1947 Lybeck took a step in a new direction by establishing her own workshop, Studio Emmel in Kauniainen. This company became one of the pioneers in Finnish design, comparable to AB Iris at the turn of the century.

Marita Lybeck made a consistent effort to use only Finnish clay. Studio Emmel produced handmade domestic ware in limited series. The professional thrower Sigurd Kjellberg produced the pots from Lybeck's three-dimensional models, and

Ceramics by Marita Lybeck.
The white tin-glazed pitcher
measures 14 cm.
Private collection.
Photo: Johnny Korkman.

glazes were imported from Denmark.[1] Vessels with restricted ornamentation were covered in unusual, bold glaze colours such as lilac, pastel blue and sunflower yellow, which gave the red clay a fresh and modern appearance. Marita Lybeck also made use of black-and-white glazes, both separately and in contrast with each other. Her simple, often geometric designs represented the kind of toned-down, functional ideology that Kaj Franck would make use of soon after in the industrial environment of Arabia.[2] Following the slogan 'More Beautiful Things for Everyday Use', Lybeck worked with the materials on their own terms. Despite critical acclaim and consumer demand, Emmel could not compete with mass-production price-wise and was forced to close down after ten years.

Lybeck then worked as artistic director at Kera Oy for two years until this company too gave in to competition. She found a new career as the manager of Stockmann department store's design department, where the lively and energetic artist was able to develop her creative and administrative talents on many levels. Lybeck's greatest impact on Finnish ceramics lies in creating new concepts for functional ware using domestic red clay.

Marita Lybeck's Emmel workshop in Kauniainen. From left to right: (throwing) Sigurd Kjellberg, Marita Lybeck and Kjellberg's daughter Sonja. Photo: Maja Eklöf.

Tamara Laurén

Tamara Laurén (née Sandman) graduated as an art teacher in 1939, but became so committed to ceramics that she remained at the Atheneum's ceramics department for some ten years.[1] Her high-fired stoneware is harmoniously shaped, and the refined glazes show resemblance to classic Chinese ceramics.

Together with Toini Muona and Siiri Hariola, Laurén won first prize for floor urns in the national competition for the Finnish pavilion of the Paris World Exhibition.

■ Born in Lepsinsk, Russia 1906, died in Helsinki 1986

■ University of Art and Design Helsinki, teaching and ceramics dept., c. 1926–39

■ Arabia, 1932

■ Bronze medal, Milan Triennial 1933; silver medal, Brussels 1935; gold medal, Paris 1937

Kerttu Suvanto-Vaajakallio

■ Born in 1906, died in Turku 1939

■ University of Art and Design Helsinki, decoration and ceramics dept., *c.* 1924–33

■ Grankullan Saviteollisuus 1932–34

■ Kupittaan Savi Oy 1934–39

Ceramist Aune Kerttu Valentine Suvanto-Vaajakallio studied with Finch and was a skilled thrower. Together with her colleague Valentina Modig-Manuel, she was employed first at Grankullan Saviteollisuus and later at Kupittaa. She favoured engobe and underglaze decoration and her keen eye for form is evident in sculptures and vase reliefs, which radiate grace, rhythm and dynamism. As her artistic career was cut short by her untimely death, she never became widely known, but was nevertheless one of the reformers of Finnish ceramic art in the 1930s.[1]

Heidi Blomstedt

Geometric forms

■ Born in Tuusula 1911, died in Helsinki 1982

■ Arabia, traineeship, 1928–29

■ University of Art and Design Helsinki, ceramics dept., graduated in 1932

■ Studio in Munkkiniemi 1950s onwards, Tapiola from *c.* 1960

■ Uppsala-Ekeby factory, Sweden, 1950

■ Bronze medal, Paris World Exhibition, 1937

The daughter of composer Jean Sibelius and his wife Aino, Heidi Blomstedt grew up in a cultured home, surrounded by contemporary painters and sculptors. Her childhood home Ainola, in Tuusula, contained ceramics by Willy Finch's first students and may at least indirectly have sparked Heidi Sibelius's interest in ceramics.[1] The Tuusula-Kerava district provided abundant red clay and had appealed to earlier potters, including Johan Grönroos who made the tiles for the impressive stoves in Ainola.[2]

One of Elsa Elenius's many renowned students, Heidi Blomstedt began working in earthenware, using brush decoration in simple lines and a variety of colours. Her early works indicate an attraction to stylized geometric forms and in the 1960s her tall, square and rectangular vases for Kupittaan Savi in blue, black, yellow and white became collectibles. Heidi Blomstedt was also known as a glass designer and founded the Interdesign interiors company in Helsinki in 1965. Her work is frequently seen at applied art exhibitions in Finland and further afield.

Heidi Blomstedt at the wheel in her Tapiola studio *c.* 1970. Photo from a private collection.

Kurt Ekholm

Kurt Ekholm, known as Kurre, was a Swedish-speaking Finn educated in Sweden. Having trained at Rörstrand porcelain factory, in 1932 he was hired as artistic director by Arabia. The factory's art department was founded that year on Ekholm's initiative, and in this way he had a decisive impact on the development of ceramics in Finland. He defended the right of Arabia's artists to put their ideas into practice as freely as possible. At the same time he advocated quality and beauty in domestic design.

As an artist and designer at Arabia in the 1930s, Ekholm created plates and urns in austere, manly forms, glazed in various colours. His simple shapes in thrown stoneware are in many ways precursors of the rustic ceramic art which would later (in the 1950s and 60s) be produced at Arabia's art department. Ekholm's white and brown vases from the 1930s have simple lines and are similar to his serially produced dinner sets, including the popular everyday set *Blue Ribbon* ('Sinivalko').

Ekholm's name appears in many contexts within Scandinavian design history. As the creator and later leader of Arabia's art department, he made a significant contribution as a kind of ambassador for Finnish design in the other Nordic countries. He was a well-known exhibition organizer in Sweden, Norway and Denmark. In addition he wrote several newspaper articles on crafts and design, often under the signatures 'Kem.' or 'K. E-m.'. Ekholm was a remarkable man who built up an exceptional career, first in Finland and then in Sweden.

- Born in Helsinki 1907, died in Gothenburg 1975

- School of Industrial Arts (now International Art School), Stockholm: degree, 1931

- Arabia art dept., artistic director, 1932–48

- University of Art and Design Helsinki, teacher, history of ceramics, 1938 onwards

- Founder of Arabia's art dept. and museum

- Rörstrand porcelain factory, 1949–50

- Bronze medal, Milan 1933; Diplôme d'honneur, Brussels 1935; silver medal, Paris 1937

- School of Crafts and Design, Gothenburg: head teacher in ceramics 1948–62, principal 1950–66

Kurt Ekholm's production was centred on glazed stoneware in brown, green, white, oxblood and cobalt blue glazes. Height of the tallest vase 16 cm. Photo: Timo Kauppila/ Arabia Museum.

Valentina Modig-Manuel

From factory trainee to studio pioneer

- Born in Minsk, Russia, 1907

- University of Art and Design Helsinki, 1927–30

- Grankullan Saviteollisuus 1930–36, Kupittaan Savi 1936–39

- Bronze medal, Paris World Exhibition, 1937

- Adult Education Centre, Turku: ceramics teacher, 1956–77

- Studio Keramos in Turku with Josef Manuel, 1937–81

- Exhibitions in Paris, New York, Copenhagen, Cologne and Stockholm

Encouraged by her teacher A. W. Finch, Ruth Valentina Modig established her own workshop. 'Just find yourself any old shed,' Finch would say when his students were doubtful about becoming studio potters without a fixed monthly income. It was not until one became famous that it was possible to make a living off ceramics, Valentina Modig explained in summer 2002.

Modig worked for several years at ceramics factories, learning the technical aspects thoroughly. At Grankullan Saviteollisuus Oy she was the only unpaid trainee with a degree in ceramics. Eventually she became the artistic director and received a salary. Initially she decorated imported copies; later she was allowed to design items to form the foundation of the factory's production. In 1936 she, together with her colleague and friend Kerttu Suvanto, her co-worker at Grankulla, moved to Kupittaan Savi Oy. There she could design as well as decorate. A special technique devised by Modig involved painting with the help of ear syringes (acquired at pharmacies), which she filled with coloured slips. In this way she could draw thin lines freehand.

Valentina Modig-Manuel and her husband Josef Manuel, who worked together for some forty years, in front of their home in 2002. Photo: Åsa Hellman.

Plate, 1946, and pitcher, 1939, by Valentina Modig-Manuel. The colour effects were obtained by reduction firing in a gas kiln. Height of pitcher 49 cm. Private collection. Photo: Johnny Korkman.

At her first studio in Turku, Modig had a gas kiln. There she developed copper red glazes, which were very rare outside the Arabia factory. Her pieces from this period have simple, often undecorated shapes and interesting glaze effects. In addition to unique pieces, the workshop produced small moulded animal sculptures, from which she was able to make a living. These were designed by Modig's husband Josef Manuel and sold to stores all around Finland. They became tremendously popular, but the couple decided to stop manufacturing them when the work began to resemble mass production – a 'dangerous business', as Modig herself put it.

Valentina Modig was often the only studio ceramist to take part in exhibitions where all other work was by Arabia artists. In 1952 she founded a new workshop at Itäinen Pitkäkatu in Turku and began firing her work in an electric kiln. In the 1960s her style changed with the times to become more rustic. She made vases in a rough grogged clay, with surfaces worked into relief-like structures. Her ceramics were for several years sold in the design section of the Stockmann department store, and she continued to work as a professional ceramist until 1981.

Modig's career is remarkable for encompassing so many different aspects of the profession. There is no doubt that Modig and her husband led a hard-working but full life. 'We thought it was so much fun making ceramics that we put off having children and all that until the last minute', laughed Modig, aged ninety-five.

Valentina Modig-Manuel's vase was inspired by man's first moon landing in 1969. Its surface structure was achieved by applying several layers of clay. Private collection. Photo: Johnny Korkman.

Birgit Dyhr
Melancholy and wisdom

■ Born in Haapavesi 1908

■ Kotiahkeruus shop 1930, Norna kotityö shop 1940–46

■ University of Art and Design Helsinki, evening school, 1946–48

■ Arabia art dept., 1946–47

■ Studio in Helsinki, 1950–98

■ Swedish Adult Education Centre in Helsinki, ceramics teacher, 1975–85

■ Exhibitions in Copenhagen, Faenza, Stockholm, Munich, Oslo and Reykjavík

Birgit Dyhr only realized that clay was the right material for her in a roundabout way, in her later life. When she was very young, she studied music in Rome with the intention of becoming a singer. Then she worked for several years at craft shops in Helsinki, designing textiles and straw items. A ceramic Christmas manger she had created for a display window attracted attention and this led to studies in sculpture and employment at Arabia.

Dyhr built a studio in 1950, in a room in her apartment. She worked for over forty years as an independent artist, battling with countless practical problems at a time when all materials – including the kiln – had to be imported. Her joy in working with clay kept her going. She created her own world in clay, full of cunning animals and images from her early years in Italy.

Dyhr's animal sculptures radiate human melancholy and wisdom. Their designs are based on nature studies, but their simple, sculptural shapes are stylized. In contrast to most ceramic sculptures, these are solid, which lends them a pleasant yet monumental weight. The surface of the rough clay is treated with metallic oxides, showing traces of glazes which have been almost entirely scraped off. The same dynamic surface treatment can be found on the artist's wall plates, often playfully Naive in style. They depict joyful Italian building façades with washing flapping on lines and grapevines with ripe, dark-purple grapes. In addition to these southern scenes, Dyhr made relief portraits of Finnish buildings, notably the town hall in Helsinki.

In order to secure an income, Dyhr supplied small series of animal sculptures to Stockmann department store's design section for several years.[1] Their shapes were press-moulded and she carried out the surface work and details by hand so that each animal acquired its own character. She was active in ceramics until she was ninety. In 1993 the Design Museum organized a retrospective exhibition of her work.

Arthur, a rhinoceros in grogged stoneware by Birgit Dyhr. Length 35 cm. Private collection. Photo: Johnny Korkman.

Robert Hancock

Painter who discovered clay

Robert Hancock became known as a painter, but he also worked as a ceramist, designer and art critic. His 'favourite uncle' was Grischka Tigerstedt, in whose ceramics studio he worked during his school days in Helsinki. This gave him the impulse to rediscover clay as a mature artist.

In 1963 Robert Hancock moved to a small cottage in Eckerö, the Åland islands, where he and his wife Kaja lived close to nature, fishing to provide for themselves. Between 1963 and 1973 he worked mainly with ceramics, having found a type of yellow-burning local clay, which he diluted and cleaned. He built a small electric kiln inside his old baking oven. Åland was already a tourist destination and Hancock was the only professional ceramist on the island. The family made a significant part of its living by selling small, press-moulded fish and bird figures. Hancock's lumpfish (a local 'ugly fish') was tremendously popular, becoming a kind of symbol for Åland.

Robert Hancock's small, modest ceramic souvenirs belong to the cream of the genre. He created matte glazes that fused with the clay in a skin-like way, causing his simple, stylized shapes to look like stones from a beach, polished by the tides of millennia. His unique fish sculptures, on the other hand, display an expressive and more realistic style. In 1998 the Åland Art Museum organized a memorial exhibition of Robert Hancock's work.

■ Born in Helsinki 1912, died in Eckerö 1993

■ University of Art and Design Helsinki, 1931–35

■ Académie Libre, Stockholm, 1946–47

■ Further studies with André Lhote and Ferdinand Léger, Paris, 1948–50

■ Exhibitions in Sweden and Finland

Greedy Pike by Robert Hancock. Length 33.5 cm. Private collection. Photo: Johnny Korkman.

Aune Siimes

Profile in porcelain

■ Born in Wärtsilä 1909, died in Helsinki 1964

■ University of Art and Design Helsinki: studies 1929–32, postgraduate 1933–36

■ Arabia hand-decoration dept. 1932–37, art dept. 1937–64

■ Silver medal, Paris 1937; gold medals, Milan 1951 and 1954

■ Works in the National Museum, Stockholm, the Röhss Museum, Gothenburg, the Design Museum, Helsinki, the International Museum of Ceramics in Faenza and the Arabia Museum

Aune Siimes was trained as a draughtsman but also studied porcelain painting with Greta Lisa Jäderholm-Snellman and ceramics with Elsa Elenius. At Arabia she initially spent five years at the hand-decoration department. A move to the art department in 1937 signified the beginning of her career as an artist, and her first works included animal and human statuettes modelled in a rough chamotted clay in typical 1930s style.[1]

When Aune Siimes discovered that porcelain was her preferred material, she began to develop an individual profile from the 1940s onwards. Her first significant pieces include jewelry and floral ornaments made of thin white porcelain. Despite their sophisticated material, her unique porcelain necklaces are reminiscent of primitive jewelry made of seashells and animal teeth – the kind found at ethnographical museums. Aune Siimes's hands also transformed porcelain clay into delicate, small vessels. Tiny holes and perforated patterns create barely visible structures, as on old, lace-embroidered sheets. Occasionally she would mix pigments into the clay, achieving squares or stripes on almost eggshell-thin vessels. Anja Jaatinen-Winquist worked as her assistant.[2]

Aune Siimes made use of the transparency of her material by casting the liquid porcelain in layers so that fine, semitransparent patterns would appear. Her ribbed vases and elegant lidded cups striped in low relief represented a whole new style in porcelain, bearing scant resemblance to traditional European china. Her delicate, effeminately fragile vessels come across as modern even today. Aune Siimes's career was unfortunately cut short, but nevertheless she stands out as a significant artist who used porcelain in fresh and unexpected ways.

> Aune Siimes used reed thread for the porcelain flowers of her necklace. Photo: Pietinen/Arabia Museum.

>> Vases in delicate porcelain by Aune Siimes, mid-1950s. Heights 12.5 and 20 cm. Arabia Museum. Photo: Timo Kauppila/Arabia Museum.

Mirjam Stäuber

Early workshop pioneer

- Born in Tenhola 1912, died in Zurich 1969

- University of Art and Design Helsinki, ceramics dept., 1922–28

- Study trips to Denmark, Estonia and Sweden

- Work with potters in Kyyrölä

- Bronze medal, 'Brussels International Fair', 1936

- Exhibitions in western Uusimaa

Mirjam ('Miu') Stäuber(-Wessman) was the daughter of a wealthy Swiss dairy man who moved to Tenhola in Finland, where he founded a private dairy. She was one of the first female ceramists to face the challenge of practising their profession in their own workshops, independent of Arabia. First she built a studio at her childhood home, Alphyddan, in Tenhola; later on she built a whole house, called Sandbacka, which included a ceramics workshop.

Countless homes in western Uusimaa still contain ceramic pieces by Mirjam Stäuber. Unmarried until her later years and with a stable financial situation, Stäuber enjoyed unusually good conditions for working independently with ceramics. She rarely produced anything serially: her work was diverse, consisting of unique sculpted and wheel-thrown artefacts. Some of these were carried out in imported light-coloured clay; others were built of a local variety with a high iron content, dug up by the artist herself. She used both wood-burning and electric kilns for firing.

Mirjam Stäuber's ceramic pieces include teapots and mugs, lidded terrines and storage containers, candleholders, bowls and plates. She also created decorative items such as thrown or press-moulded birds, piggy banks, hedgehogs and fish. The artist's sculptures and reliefs, such as a christening font for Bromarv church, are more elaborate and often have religious links.

Owing to her training in Kyyrölä, Mirjam Stäuber became an exceptionally good thrower: her lids fit perfectly and her pieces are light and thin. Varied decoration techniques and interesting details contribute to their individuality. All of Stäuber's work bears witness to the artist's enjoyment of creating things by hand and mastering different techniques. Locally she was highly admired, but she would certainly deserve more attention from art historians. By the 1970s Kaj Franck, director of Arabia's art department, was very keen to see Mirjam Stäuber's work documented.[1]

Having married sea captain Jarl Wessman, the artist spent the last seven years of her life in Trinidad. In 1973 the Ekenäs Museum organized a memorial exhibition of Mirjam Stäuber's ceramics and paintings.

Tin-glazed terrine with irregular copper patterns by Mirjam Stäuber, 1943. Height 16 cm. Private collection. Photo: Johnny Korkman.

Teapot by Mirjam Stäuber, 1936. Height including cane handle 16 cm. Private collection. Photo: Johnny Korkman.

Annikki Hovisaari

Rustic beauty

Following graduation, Annikki Hovisaari was a summer trainee at a private workshop in Töölö, Helsinki, before entering Arabia's design department. In the 1950s, she was one of some fifty people who designed, made and decorated there.[1] In 1962 Hovisaari won the first prize in Gualdo Tadino, in a competition entitled 'Man as a Conqueror of Space', which gained her entry to Arabia's art department.[2] Her work consisted of thrown pieces, including large platters, floor vases and candleholders in rough, chamotted clay. For glazing she generally favoured natural shades but also used cobalt blue and turquoise stains containing copper sulphate. Simple patterns distinguish some pieces, but as a rule she let the shapes and materials speak for themselves.

Annikki Hovisaari was at Arabia at a time when Finnish design enjoyed considerable international renown. Her rustic, high-fired ceramics embody the essence of that time. When Arabia's art department was restructured, Hovisaari was asked to stay on but she chose to retire in 1975.[3]

■ Born in Tampere 1913

■ Foto AB photography studio, Tampere, 1930s

■ University of Art and Design Helsinki, ceramics dept., 1945–48

■ Arabia: design dept. 1949–63, art dept. 1963–75

■ Grand Prix de la Ville de Vallauris 1972 (with R. Bryk and P. Envalds); 'Ceramics International '73' medal, Alberta, Canada

Pots by Annikki Hovisaari for an exhibition at the Arabia showroom in 1967. Height *c.* 50 cm. Artist's own collection. Photo: Pietinen.

Birger Kaipiainen
Master of colour and ornament

■ Born in Pori 1915, died in Helsinki 1988

■ University of Art and Design Helsinki, 1933–37

■ Arabia art dept., 1937–54 and 1958–88

■ Rörstrand, 1954–58

■ Public works include *Sea of Violets*, made for the Montreal World's Fair 1967, now in Tampere

■ Diplôme d'honneur, Milan 1951; Grand Prix, Milan 1960; gold plaquette, Gualdo Tadino 1961; City of Helsinki art award 1970; Illum award 1972; Pro Finlandia award 1963; Prins Eugen medal 1982

Birger Kaipiainen joined Arabia's art department when he was twenty-two, following exceptional success as a student at the University of Art and Design Helsinki. His fellow students described him as 'quiet and dreaming with a unique and personal colour sensibility'.[1]

Arabia gave Birger Kaipiainen total freedom to develop his artistry. During the 1940s he produced large, rectangular wall plaques and plates with undulating edges that incorporated romantic motifs. These works display medieval influences as well as inspiration from the Rococo and Renaissance periods. In the 1950s Birger Kaipiainen created elongated, heavily stylized human figures and birds with certain Byzantine connotations. This is the only period when Kaipiainen's work seems to have been influenced by contemporary ceramic trends. Gradually his shapes and forms became ever more resplendent and his colour schemes evolved dramatically. He created an extensive series of unique plates and platters with narrative themes as well as flowers, fruit and ornaments, often stylized. From a delicate Rococo sensibility Kaipiainen's work evolved into a jubilant, princely Baroque, frequently featuring blue pansies to add a touch of melancholy.

Centrepiece by
Birger Kaipiainen with typical
Baroque details and colours,
1968. Height 40 cm.
Arabia Museum.
Photo: Gero Mylius/
Arabia Museum.

Pearly Bird by Birger Kaipiainen,
featuring hundreds of pearls,
fragments of mirror glass and
enigmatic clock faces.
Kyösti Kakkonen's collection.
Photo: Rauno Träskelin.

Plate with typical lustre effects by Birger Kaipiainen, 1970s. Photo: Osmo Thiel/ Otava Photo Archives.

Baroque trees and metal structures for *Pearly Birds* in Birger Kaipiainen's studio in the 1960s. Photo: Pietinen/ Arabia Museum.

At Arabia's art department, on the famous ninth floor, Kaipiainen was in many ways highly privileged. For a period of thirty years he had an assistant and friend in Terho Reijonen who was able to take detailed instructions and realize Kaipiainen's ideas. In spite of this favourable arrangement, it is evident that Kaipiainen's works exhibit an unparalleled virtuosity, not only artistically but also in his profound knowledge of ceramic techniques.

Many of Birger Kaipiainen's contemporaries developed resplendent glazes for their thrown, rustic forms, whereas Kaipiainen excelled in narrative and ornamentation. He was a master of line and figurative work and used both underglaze and overglaze colours to harness the most volatile ceramic pigments, refusing to allow their innate glow to be dimmed by the flames of the kiln. Gold, copper and Iris lustres add accent and drama to his compositions.[2] The hardship of polio, which prevented him from engaging in thrown work, challenged him to seek his own language of form.

Sleeping Beauty Guarded by a Peacock, a wall plaque by Birger Kapiainen from the 1940s. Kyösti Kakkonen's collection. Photo: Kari-Kuva.

Kyllikki Salmenhaara

Queen of clay

- Born in Tyrnävä 1915, died in Helsinki 1981

- University of Art and Design Helsinki, ceramics dept., 1938–43, head teacher, 1963–81

- Saxbo ceramics studio, Denmark, 1946

- Arabia art dept., 1947–61

- Ceramic Training Institute, China; Productivity and Trade Center, Taiwan, 1961–63

- Lecturer, USA, Canada and Japan, 1956–76

- Silver medal, Milan 1951; honorary diploma, Milan 1954; Grand Prix, Milan 1957; gold medal, Milan 1960

Within Arabia, a major ceramics factory, artists carried out the most complex projects and technically advanced material experiments. One of the artists who did the most for the international reputation of Finnish ceramics was Kyllikki Salmenhaara. In many ways she gave her all to clay, dedicating her life entirely to this material. She built two noteworthy careers in the genre: first as an internationally renowned ceramic artist and then as head teacher of the ceramics department at the University of Art and Design Helsinki.

Salmenhaara strove to understand her material thoroughly by conducting methodical research on the chemical reactions that take place during the firing process. Over several years she carried out comprehensive experiments with materials and made use of the knowledge acquired in her own artwork. She not only developed glazes but also prepared clay bodies according to her own recipes. Her plates and vases often have a patina of oxides and layer upon layer of half-removed glazes. Some of her pots have the appearance of ancient artefacts that have survived for centuries at the mercy of the harsh elements. 'The more brilliant the colours and the more exciting the glazes, the less of them I tend to leave on the pots,' Salmenhaara explained to her students.[1]

As an artist at Arabia, Kyllikki Salmenhaara went in for creating one-of-a-kind exhibition pieces. Her speciality as a thrower was in building large, impressive vases out of several smaller sections thrown in advance. This is a demanding technique, especially when firing at high temperatures where the works will vitrify, easily losing their symmetry and balance. In many ways Salmenhaara's form of expression expands on classical Greek traditions, where perfume bottles and wine vessels were constructed from separate thrown forms, joined and placed on slender feet.

Wheel-thrown pot by Kyllikki Salmenhaara that has assumed a certain asymmetry and beauty of imperfection in the course of firing. Kyösti Kakkonen's collection. Photo: Johnny Korkman.

In the genre of ceramics, Salmenhaara was a multi-talented artist and could in many ways be likened to Renaissance man. She was an independent artist, a researcher, teacher and administrator as well as a widely travelled cosmopolite with countless international contacts. As a teacher she was at times categorical and conceited but at the same time skilful, energetic and inspiring. Her work is, in technical and artistic terms, at the cutting edge of Finnish ceramics. Her charisma lives on in the ceramic artworks she created.

> Plates in chamotte stoneware by Kyllikki Salmenhaara, 1957.
Arabia Musueum. Photo: Arabia Museum

∨ Gracious thrown vases and bowls by Kyllikki Salmenhaara.
Photo: Pietinen/Arabia Museum.

Rut Bryk

Pictorial to monumental

■ Born in Stockholm 1916, died in Helsinki 1999

■ University of Art and Design Helsinki, graphic art dept., 1936–39

■ Arabia art dept., 1942–92

■ Awards include Grand Prix, Milan 1951; International Design A.I.D. Award, USA 1960 and 1962; Premio Ravenna, Faenza 1967; Grand Prix, Vallauris 1972 (with A. Hovisaari and P. Envalds); National Design Award 1974

■ Monumental reliefs at the Finnish president's official residence (Mäntyniemi), Helsinki town hall, the Rosenthal factory, Germany, the Finnish Embassy in New Delhi, etc.

'Birger Kaipiainen is teaching me ceramics,' Rut Bryk proudly announced in the early 1940s when she met an old fellow student from the Atheneum.[1] Bryk, a graphic artist, had recently been hired by Arabia and shared a room with Kaipiainen, who was already a respected ceramist. Technical and stylistic parallels between these two outstanding artists' work at this period are discernible, but Rut Bryk went her own way soon enough. While making use of the technical expertise offered by the factory, she applied a graphic artist's talent for illustration.

Among Rut Bryk's early achievements are wall plates with figurative motifs executed in a mildly Naive style. She was moved by fairy tales and domestic comforts, making still lifes and telling simple stories in clay. She also painted birds, fish and tender mother-and-child scenes. Her material was faience and her soft, liquid glazes looked like glass, occasionally featuring crackle effects on the porous underlayer. She applied powerful, contrasting colours – turquoise, grass green, lemon yellow, purple and pink – in clearly delineated planes to emphasize the pictorial quality of the objects. Unglazed parts are treated with browny-black metallic oxides, which together with graphic carvings form an effective contrast to the bright colours, almost comparable to medieval stained glass. In Rut Bryk's wall plaques of Gothic or Romanesque façades, we can also discern religious motifs such as church doorways.

In contrast to most of her female counterparts, Rut Bryk created several large reliefs for public spaces. Her long-time assistant, Kirsi Bruun-Micklin, participated in the time-consuming work of these commissioned pieces.

By the 1950s Rut Bryk had turned her attention to bricks and developed ornamental bricks that could be used as architectural modules. Initially these were decorated with butterflies, for example, but she was already approaching the abstract. In the 1960s she went for large, geometric compositions made up of square elements with inset circles and triangles. These monumental reliefs are highly decorative and detailed in form and colour, and represent a consistent and logical form of abstraction akin to modern architecture. Rut Bryk's work evolved over the course of her career, going from intimate, plain narrative to include monumental, architectonic concepts.

Venetian Palace, wall plaque by Rut Bryk, 1955. Kyösti Kakkonen's collection. Photo: Kari-Kuva.

Butterflies by Rut Bryk, c. 1960. 38 x 50 cm. Photo: Arabia Museum.

Taisto Kaasinen

Large wall reliefs

■ Born in Savonlinna 1918, died in Vantaa 1980

■ Private studies in art 1938–47, ceramic studies with Olga Osol 1947–51

■ Uppsala-Ekeby, Sweden, 1953–62

■ Arabia 1947–53, art dept. 1962–74

■ Works in the Arabia Museum, the Hasselblad Collection, Gothenburg, and the Design Museum, Helsinki

■ Several public reliefs in Finland and Sweden

Taisto Kaasinen specialized in ceramic work for public spaces, especially reliefs and mosaics. As Arabia was part of the Wärtsilä shipbuilding corporation for many years, many of Kaasinen's works are found on Finnish passenger ferries, including MS Ilmatar and MS Botnia, and the icebreakers Kiev, Hanse and Njord. In addition to these large-scale pieces, he made sculptures in smaller formats, often stylized, funny animals and human figures. Kaasinen's sculptures are generally glazed in brown tones, but his wall plaques tend to be brighter.

Taisto Kaasinen exhibited independently and collectively in Finland and abroad. At Uppsala-Ekeby he gained remarkable success in competitions, which enabled him to secure over thirty weighty Swedish commissions.

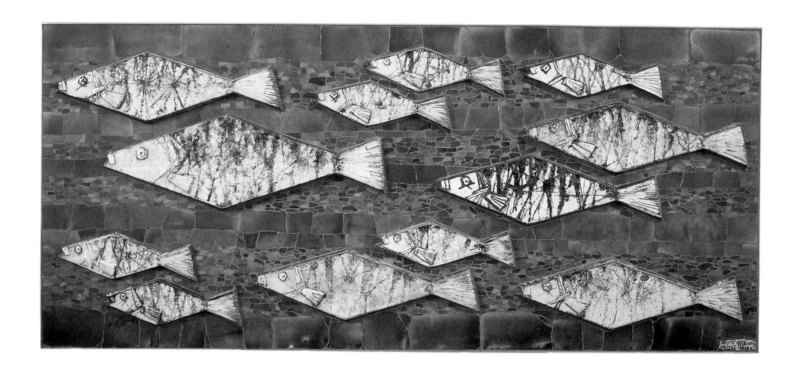

Wall composition by Taisto Kaasinen, 1973.
200 x 90 cm. Photo: Arabia Museum.

Hilkka-Liisa Ahola

Hilkka-Liisa Ahola belonged to Arabia's design department for several years and executed romantic human motifs in brush technique. After her success at the Faenza Ceramics Biennial, she was, in 1968, offered a position at the factory's art department. She created plates and tile compositions in which she combined methods such as sgraffito and brush decoration with glazes and lustre technique. Her most impressive works include two large reliefs for the luxury cruise ships Song of Norway and Nordic Prince.

Ahola is known for superb colour and ornamentation. She is also associated with an intensive blue colour palette, encompassing all shades from cobalt to turquoise and purple.

■ Born in Helsinki 1920

■ University of Art and Design Helsinki, studies incl. model drawing, ceramics and porcelain painting, 1936–41

■ Arabia: traineeship 1943–44, design dept. 1947–74, art dept. 1968–74

■ Nuutajärvi glassworks, 1950s

■ Grand Prix, Faenza 1968

Wall plaque assembled from small tiles by Hilkka-Liisa Ahola in the early 1970s. Photo: Indav/Arabia Museum.

Kupittaa 1918–69

Early manufacture

Ceramic workshops and brick factories are generally established close to clay deposits. A brick factory was already in operation by the river Aura at Kupittaa, near Turku, in the early eighteenth century. The area offered a rich supply of red clay, and in the mid-eighteenth century two brick factories – Kupittaan Ylinen and Kupittaan Alinen – operated there.[1] Kupittaan Saviteollisuus Oy was founded in the same location in 1918 and became renowned for its domestic ware and ceramic art, although its main production consisted of bricks and drainpipes. In the past it was assumed that the company did not employ artists until the 1930s, but recent research has shed new light on the subject.

A hand-thrown, green-glazed vase with the signature 'Kupittaa – 1919 – G F' can be attributed to Gusti Franzén, who would then have been twenty-eight years of age. In the

same year, he had been hired as artist and overseer by Kupittaan Saviteollisuus Oy (changed in 1921 to Kupittaan Savi Oy). The vase is still owned by the Franzén family.

Gusti Franzén graduated from the Central School of Arts and Crafts (now the University of Art and Design Helsinki) in 1915 and had, in addition to the practical experience gained at his father's workshop, received a broad education in art and crafts.[2] Surviving correspondence shows that the energetic young artist and the company's managing director and major shareholder Kalervo Koponen formed a perfect team from the very beginning. Together they purposefully developed the factory's operations.[3] Franzén was above all responsible for production (design, clay work, glazes, firing, etc.) and also seems to have made good use of the bookkeeping skills he acquired at school.

The period after 1918, with the end of the civil war that had raged in Finland, was difficult. With the death of his father in 1922, Gusti Franzén as the

Edith Maria Franzén, nicknamed 'Maja', decorating for Kupittaa in the 1920s. Photo from the Franzén family album.

eldest son shouldered the main responsibility for a family of ten children. As the volume of production at Kupittaa grew, five of Gusti's siblings were employed and given various tasks. His sister Edith Maria (married name Lindholm, 1923) became a skilled decorator using brush and sgraffito techniques. Artist Emil Rekola, a fellow Atheneum student and good friend, was also employed at the company. The factory's price list of 1 June 1921 highlights how artefacts were decorated by accomplished artists: 'Our goods are liberally adorned by artists specifically trained for the task. Thus all decorations are different, products of each artist's free imagination.'

Gusti Franzén designed statuettes and artefacts that could be produced serially using plaster moulds, but also threw items when he had time.[4] He had already begun to use matte glazes on his own earthenware. They resembled stoneware glazes and were thought to be superior to the traditional, glossy lead-based glazes used by most potters. In a letter dated 1 March 1922, signed by Kaarlo T. H. Koponen, Franzén sold all his recipes for clay bodies, slips and glaze mixes to Kupittaan Saviosakeyhtiö for FIM 10,000.

The earliest Kupittaa production consisted of red earthenware with slip decoration. The pots were first bisque-fired and then gloss-fired with a transparent glaze. In addition the factory used coloured glazes; in other words, the technique was in principle the same as that of Iris ceramics. A wall plate with patterns in relief, designed by Wäinö Aaltonen and produced some time before 1924, is an exception. It has previously been assumed that Wäinö Aaltonen became involved with ceramics at the beginning of the 1930s because of his friendship with ceramist Elsa Elenius (newly appointed head teacher of the Atheneum's ceramics department). However

An unusual hybrid of Rococo-inspired form and sgraffito decoration presenting a Chinese motif, made at Kupittaa, evidently by Kalle Akkola. Signed 'A'. Height 32 cm. Private collection. Photo: Johnny Korkman.

Kupittaa pot signed 'K 8.2.1945'. Matte; glaze over underglaze decoration. Height 40 cm. Private collection. Photo: Johnny Korkman.

he spent a great deal of the 1920s in Turku, and in 1923 he built his own studio in Hirvensalo, close to his childhood home.[5] His early contact with the Kupittaa factory may have come about through Gusti Franzén, who was interested in sculpture, and in his key position at Kupittaa was probably responsible for producing Aaltonen's early (and since then highly acclaimed) wall plate.

There were as yet no copyright laws applicable to design. Models were freely copied and borrowed, and elements from different periods of art history merrily combined. Rambling hybrids without any consistency in style were common. But there are also Kupittaa ceramics from the early 1920s showing individual artists' free and unconventional ideas. Today these seem refreshingly original and contemporary. The contrast between naive imitations and individual artists' pride in personal expression can be appreciated as more than a mere curiosity. Alas, as was the case with the Iris factory two decades previously, the expressive sgraffito method turned out to be too labour-intensive and after a few years the company adopted faster, more productive decoration methods. The earthenware clay also brought up specific technical issues, which were hard to resolve.

Gusti Franzén was aware of the limitations of low-fired goods. He wanted to learn more about ceramic theory, glazes and the combination of clay bodies, as well as *Steinzeug* (high-fired stoneware), and he pursued further education in Central Europe. His letters demonstrate that he applied to no less than five art schools and was accepted at the Staatsfachschule für Keramik und Verwandte Kunstgewerbe in Teplitz-Schönau, Bohemia. He studied there in 1923 and 1924, supported by a FIM 5,000 grant from Kupittaan Saviosakeyhtiö. In exchange, he agreed to continue working at Kupittaa for at least three more years.

In the 1920s the Finnish market was flooded with imported porcelain, especially from Germany. In 1929, when the global economy crashed culminating in the Depression,[6] Kupittaan Savi was not spared, and a new period of economic growth did not take place until the mid-1930s. The factory's ceramics department grew and new artists began to work there. Finds of high-quality kaolin in Soanjärvi also led to improved conditions for the expansion of the company's brick-manufacturing side.[7]

There is strong evidence that it was Gusti Franzén's ambition to introduce high-fired stoneware to Kupittaa. After his return to Finland, the company began to purchase white clays from England, which when mixed with local clay resulted in a light-beige faience. In retrospect, there are many indications that despite experimentation with different clay mixes the factory had problems achieving even results in the kilns available at the time. An electric kiln, then a piece of high technology, was taken into use in 1936. *Åbo Underrättelser* newspaper stated on 18 March 1937 that the electric kiln, the pride of the ceramics department, could successfully manage temperatures of up to 1,200 °C. The cost of electricity must have been prohibitive and the main production at Kupittaa was soon carried out in faience, which was financially more viable. This was a popular and acceptable alternative to Arabia's porcelain and stoneware. In addition to faience, Kupittaa occasionally manufactured smaller and more unique collections in vitrified stoneware and eventually in red clay.

The enterprising Franzén left Kupittaa during the Depression to start his own company. During his later career he became involved in diverse projects in the ceramics field. Current members of the Franzén family remember him not only as a master potter and ceramic artist, but also as the first person in Finland to own a truck with a motorized tipper!

Franzén was interested in photography and documented Kupittaa's largely unknown early period. He left behind written records of his work at the factory, which bears witness to his pride in his work. He was highly conscious of what he was doing and has earned a place of honour in the history of Finnish ceramic art.

Jorma Kivimäki, a collector of Kupittaa pottery, with some of his prized possessions in 2004.
Photo: Johnny Korkman.

Viljo Mäkinen

Bold artistic temperament

■ Born in Kisko 1920, died in Turku 1985

■ Drawing school of the Turku Art Association, 1937–39

■ Kupittaan Savi Oy, 1939–64

■ Works in Atheneum Art Museum, the Wäinö Aaltonen Museum, the Amos Anderson Art Museum, the Ariana Museum, Geneva, and the Pittsburgh Center for the Arts, USA

■ Silver medal, Faenza 1956; first prize, Gualdo Tadino 1960; gold and silver medals, Prague sculpture exhibition 1962

Viljo ('Ville') Mäkinen was a designer and artist at Kupittaan Savi Oy for over twenty years, progressing from the decoration of standard products to focus on terracotta and stoneware sculpture. His wife Helena (1921–98) was employed at the factory as a supervisor for some ten years, from the late 1930s onwards.

Mäkinen's work was shown with great success at Finnish and international exhibitions. It has a sketch-like quality and skilfully makes use of the plasticity of clay in depicting animals and humans, often together. He was regarded in the 1940s and 50s as an exceptional talent in Finnish sculpture, and critics were reluctant to point out that his work oscillated between sculpture and applied art. He was influenced by Modernists such as Picasso and Henry Moore but created a personal form of expression which combined a witty Naive style with Primitivism. Viljo Mäkinen had one of the boldest artistic temperaments at Kupittaan Savi Oy, and became a full-time artist after his departure from the factory in 1964.[1]

Taking a break at Kupittaa in the 1940s. In the centre, Helena and Viljo Mäkinen. Photo courtesy of Sini-Meri Niinikoski.

Sakari Vapaavuori

Non-figurative sculpture

The University of Art and Design Helsinki has bred many outstanding Finnish sculptors, including Sakari Vapaavuori. From 1950 to 1980 his abstract ceramic sculptures, made of Arabia's vitrified, coarse façade-brick clay attracted attention at international exhibitions. These outdoor sculptures were made to withstand freezing temperatures. Vapaavuori has also worked in various capacities within the silicate industry and as a teacher at the university.

In the 1950s, artists working with ceramic sculpture were not yet seen as 'real' sculptors.[1] When Vapaavuori showed large stoneware pieces at the Helsinki City Gardens during the 1952 Summer Olympics, he was in many ways transgressing accepted boundaries with new materials and forms. Neither did his work, created at Arabia's art department, then seem appropriate for design exhibitions.[2] The non-figurative, non-decorative ceramic sculptures were strange, hard to define at a time when art was still labelled according to category. Today Sakari Vapaavuori is remembered as a Modernist ceramist and one of Finland's first non-figurative sculptors.

■ Born in Tyrvää 1920, died in Espoo 1989

■ University of Art and Design Helsinki, ceramics dept., c. 1942–45

■ Studio in Helsinki, 1945–47

■ Arabia 1947–74: art dept. 1947–63, director of design dept. 1963, exhibition architect 1965–69

■ Second prize, Gualdo Tadino 1961; Diplôme d'honneur, Milan 1954 (for jewelry)

Outdoor sculptures by Sakari Vapaavuori, mid-1950s. Photos: Pietinen/Arabia Museum.

Karl-Heinz Schultz-Köln

- Born in Cologne 1921

- Cologne International School of Design and the Academy of the Arts Nuremberg

- Arabia 1950–62, art department 1954–62

- Silver medal, Cannes 1955

Karl-Heinz Schultz-Köln was Birger Kaipiainen's assistant before acquiring his own studio at Arabia in 1954. He debuted in 1955 with an exhibition of non-figurative ceramic wall plaques which reflect his original ambition of becoming a painter. Their abstract language of form attracted the attention of critics who considered them less appropriate for domestic interiors than for public spaces such as lobbies, corridors or stairwells in offices or municipal buildings.[1]

Despite his clear indebtedness to Modernist painting, Schultz-Köln skilfully adopted the use of ceramic techniques. He created structured planes by fusing sand or grog onto surfaces with the help of glazes. He also designed functional ware such as invertible cylindrical vases. Schultz-Köln left Finland in the 1960s and now lives in Sweden.

Multicoloured Composition 1 by Karl-Heinz Schultz-Köln, 1953. Photo: Pietinen/Arabia Museum.

Milja Aarnio

Charming warmth

Milja Aarnio's sources of inspiration can be traced back to ancient Egypt and Mesopotamia. Like her colleague Viljo Mäkinen, she discovered red clay as a sculptural medium early on, fully taking into account its opportunities. Aarnio's earthenware sculptures have an individual charm, distinct from what is generally thought of as the Finnish Naive style. The features of her robust, slip-decorated human figures convey archaic ceremonial solemnity, while they simultaneously radiate irresistible contemporary warmth.

■ Born in Polvijärvi 1923

■ University of Art and Design Helsinki, 1947–49

■ Drawing School of the Turku Art Association, 1961–63

■ Works in the Wäinö Aaltonen Museum of Art, the Sundsvall Museum, Sweden, the Hyvinkää Art Museum, the City of Turku's collection and the Yrjö A. Jäntti Art Collection

Small Sailing Boat by Milja Aarnio.
The museum collection of Yrjö A. Jäntti in Porvoo.
Photo: Jan Lindroth/Yrjö A. Jäntti's collection.

Marjukka Pääkkönen

Artist and designer

Ceramist Marjukka Pääkkönen(-Paasivirta) was one of several innovative artists employed by Kupittaan Savi in the 1950s. She helped to phase out outdated models and create new functional ware better suited to contemporary needs.

Pääkkönen designed lidded casseroles, teapots and baking dishes. She threw the originals, which were then mass-produced in plaster moulds. In addition to the factory's usual light faience, she made use of a body similar to red clay for jugs and spice jars. She applied an opaque white tin glaze and Majolica decoration, occasionally combined with sgraffito. By varying the colours and hand-painted ornaments she could give serially produced items a more individual appearance. First and foremost Marjukka Pääkkönen was a designer, who only infrequently concerned herself with decoration.

In addition to designing lines for mass-production, Pääkkönen occasionally made unique salt-glazed stoneware pieces fired in the factory's brick kilns.[1]

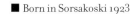

■ Born in Sorsakoski 1923

■ Traineeship, Rakel Bäck-Usvaala's studio, Kronoby, 1945

■ University of Art and Design Helsinki, ceramics dept., 1945–48

■ Kupittaan Savi Oy: artist 1949–50, artistic director 1950–60

■ Silver medal, Milan Triennial 1954; honorary mention, Faenza 1956; silver medal, Milan Triennial 1957

Jug with sgraffito decoration by Marjukka Pääkkönen, 1950. Height 16 cm. Turku Provincial Museum.
Photo: Katja Hagelstam.

Raija Tuumi
Archaic austerity

- Born in Kiukainen 1923

- University of Art and Design Helsinki, ceramics dept., 1946–49

- Arabia art department, 1950–74

- Studio Jousapot, 1974–77

- Works in Stedelijk Museum, Amsterdam, the National Museum, Stockholm, the Arabia Museum, the Design Museum, Helsinki, and the Alberta Potters' Association, Canada

- Medal, 'Ceramics International '73', Alberta, Canada

Raija Tuumi worked for twenty-four years at Arabia's art department, throwing large platters and bowls as well as smaller artefacts such as candleholders, mugs and plates. Her work is characterized by simple, unpretentious forms and plain, coarse stoneware clays occasionally patinated with dark metallic oxides. Her range of glazes is sparse and consists of fairly ascetic colours. High-fired and vitrified, sometimes metallic browny-black surfaces bestow an austere, almost archaic quality to Raija Tuumi's ceramics.

As a contrast to this spartan style, the artist sometimes used intensive cobalt blue glazes with tinges of purple and green. Playful small handles that curl upwards, one of Raija Tuumi's signature elements, give her pots a distinct character. The scale of her work varies from miniatures measuring just two centimetres across to large plates with diameters closer to eighty centimetres.

Plate by Raija Tuumi with typical perforations. Diameter 80 cm. Photo: Indav/Arabia Museum.

Raija Tuumi is drawn to rustic wheel-thrown forms in which circular imprints of her hands bear witness to the strong centrifugal force inherent in the work. Her basic, stout shapes are reminiscent of archaeological finds, pots and storage jars in everyday use in prehistoric times. This impression is strengthened by Tuumi's particular decorative technique harking back to ancient ceramics in the National Museum's collection. Her pots have rows of tiny perforations which let in light and reduce their mass, and her works are always thrown, not coiled: 'Throwing has seemed to me the only right way to make ceramics,' Raija Tuumi explains.[1]

When Arabia's art department was reorganized in 1974, Raija Tuumi went on to establish studio Jousapot where she carried on throwing, although switching to earthenware clay and reducing the scale of her work.

Pot with curled handles by Raija Tuumi, 1969. Arabia Museum. Photo: Arabia Museum.

Maija Aaltonen

From clay to paint

- Born in Helsinki 1924

- University of Art and Design Helsinki, ceramics dept., 1943–46

- Bjarne Engbertsen's painting school, Oslo, 1947–49

- Studio Kjerringvik Keramik, Norway, 1950–52

- Exhibitions in Finland and abroad

Expectations would have been exceptionally high when Maija Liisa Aaltonen, daughter of Finland's great sculptor Wäinö Aaltonen, took up studies in ceramics with Elsa Elenius. In line with these expectations, her studies progressed well and she was awarded a scholarship from the university. After graduation, Maija Aaltonen moved to Norway to work as a ceramist. In 1950 she established a studio in Kjerringvik, Sandefjord, firing her work in a reducing atmosphere achieved by the addition of naphthalene balls and small wooden blocks to her electric kiln. She threw unique pieces, which she showed independently and in exhibitions arranged by Landsforbundet Norsk Brukskunst. In 1953, in Oslo, one of her flower vases was named the 'most beautiful serially produced item of the year'.

Later Maija Aaltonen returned to Finland and worked with her father in his workshop between 1964 and 1966. Her work included pressing clay by hand into plaster moulds and responsibility for firing. Later she worked in Porvoo, turning her talents to painting in 1971. She also learnt the art of icon decoration.

Ceramics students at the University of Art and Design Helsinki, in 1944. On the floor: Maija Aaltonen. Front row: Ritva Karpio, Maila Lapila and Vilkka Aunio. Back row: Sirkka-Liisa Rautava and Maija Järvinen. Photo courtesy of Ritva Karpio.

Liisa Hallamaa-Walden

Generous forms

Large hand-thrown pots constitute a measure of a ceramist's strength and, paradoxically, in Finland women artists have usually created the largest thrown work. Between 1950 and 1970, Arabia's art department employed a handful of women artists who seemed to compete in creating oversized bowls and vases on the potter's wheel. Among them was Liisa Hallamaa-Walden, one of the most prominent artists at Arabia during the golden age of Finnish design.

Numerous impressive ceramic pieces bear witness to Hallamaa-Walden's creative prowess. They were made in coarse stoneware clay with added chamotte, which gave stability while they were thrown, and which withstood high-temperature firing with ease. Open, generous forms which, like flowers, appear to grow upward and outward characterize this artist's thrown work.

Liisa Hallamaa-Walden is one of the few to have made a significant career as an independent studio ceramist after working at Arabia. She moved to the countryside, established a workshop in an old school in Alamaa, and markedly changed her style, producing functional ware, decorative objects and sculptural forms with colourful plant motifs. Two large outdoor reliefs for Saarijärvi school in Kuopio were completed in 1979.

■ Born in Helsinki 1925

■ University of Art and Design Helsinki, ceramics dept., 1947–49

■ Arabia: design dept. 1950–57, art dept. 1957–71

■ Studio in Alamaa 1974–79, Perniö 1979–96

■ Silver medal, International Academy of Ceramics, Cannes 1955; Diploma di Collaborazione, Milan 1961; Prix de l'Usine l'Hospied Vallauris 1970; gold medal, Faenza 1971; gold medal, Nagoya, Japan 1973 and 1974; Doctor of Art, HC Albert Einstein Intl. Academy Foundation 1990

Gigantic bowls by Liisa Hallamaa-Walden at her exhibition at the Arabia showroom, 1970.
Photo: artist's own collection.

Okki Laine

Clay Modernist

■ Born in Turku 1925

■ Drawing School of the Turku Art Association, 1940s

■ University of Art and Design Helsinki, ceramics dept., *c.* 1947–50

■ Kupittaan Savi: artist 1950–60, artistic director 1960–64

■ Silver medal, Milan Triennial 1954; silver medal, Faenza 1956; honorary mention, Milan Triennial 1957; gold medal, Sacramento 1960

Orvokki ('Okki') Laine(-Taitto) began working at Kupittaan Savi Oy soon after graduation. In the 1950s and 60s she was responsible for renewing the factory's image by introducing Modernist shapes and geometric patterns indicative of the time. Her ceramics can generally be described as joyful and unpretentious; among notable designs are the teapots in the *Karjala* series, with stripe and dot patterns.

Laine, one of the most successful artists at the factory, frequently exhibited unique works in Finland and abroad. She specialized in ceramics of a browny-black clay with a high manganese content. Her striking, stylized ceramic dolls became so popular that they were also manufactured in lathed wood. Under Okki Laine's direction Kupittaa began to include both the designer's and the decorator's signatures on their ware.[1] In addition to industrial design, Laine made thrown earthenware bowls and vases with vigorous painted slip decoration.[2]

Yellow vase with stamped decoration by Okki Laine. Vanhalinna Museum. Photo: Katja Hagelstam.

Ritva Kaukoranta

While at Arabia, Ritva Kaukoranta participated in several domestic and international exhibitions. She used the factory's high-firing clays for thrown bowls and platters with beautiful glaze effects, typical of stoneware. She was a founding member of the Pot Viapori group workshop in Suomenlinna in the early 1970s and was active there for a few years. Her preferred material during that time was red clay and her products included smoke-fired hanging 'baskets'. Ritva Kaukoranta's work can be seen in several collections, including those of the Design Museum and the Arabia Museum.

■ Born in Helsinki 1926
University of Art and Design Helsinki, ceramics dept., 1944–47

■ Arabia art dept. 1948–52

■ Studio in Helsinki 1966–72

■ Group workshop Pot Viapori, 1972–77

■ Gold medal, Milan Triennial, 1951

Detail of a bowl by Ritva Kaukoranta made at Arabia
c. 1950. Photo: Johnny Korkman.

Dorrit von Fieandt

Garden in the sun

■ Born in Helsinki 1927

■ University of Art and Design Helsinki:
textile dept. 1944–45, ceramics dept. 1945–48

■ Free Art School, 1956–57 and 1959–60

■ Studio work, 1949–54 and 1965–86

■ Arabia art dept. 1986 onwards, since 1987 as
freelance artist

■ Several exhibitions in Finland and abroad

■ Works in the Design Museum, Helsinki,
the Arabia Museum, the Trollhättan Museum,
Heinola City Museum and Helsingin Osuuspankki

■ Second prize, Stockmann's 125-year jubilee
contest 1986; Pro Finlandia medal 1993

Dorrit von Fieandt's career has been long and diverse. After completing her studies, she founded her own studio, and is one of the earliest studio ceramists in Finland. She worked in a figurative style with brush decoration and a generous use of ceramic colours, initially applied onto a white tin glaze. Later she created hand-thrown, ornate dinner sets and wall plaques. She often used a dark background in powerful cobalt, creating an effective contrast and accentuating the intensity of the pigments.

In terms of technical opportunities, employment at Arabia's art department opened new doors for Dorrit von Fieandt. There she worked with high-fired stoneware, painting her motifs directly onto unfired surfaces and then applying transparent glazes. In addition to unique items, such as large platters and jugs, she designed and decorated industrially produced dinnerware. Dorrit von Fieandt's colourful, painterly ceramics differ greatly from the rest of the factory's production and from other, typically Finnish styles.

The world portrayed by von Fieandt evokes southern warmth and sunshine. She creates verdant tropical gardens, exotic birds, fountains and fluttering butterflies. She also depicts dreamlike circus and ballet scenes, galloping horses and puppets. A connecting thread that runs through von Fieandt's art and appears as a leitmotif in her work is a garden in the sun: resplendent flowers in clear, strong colours against a warm yellow background.

A feast of colour at Dorrit von Fieandt's exhibition at Gallery Forsblom in Turku, 1990. Photo: Timo Kauppila.

Gunvor Olin-Grönqvist

Harvest festival

■ Born in Espoo 1928

■ University of Art and Design Helsinki, ceramics dept., 1948–51

■ Arabia: design 1951–68, product planning 1968–75, art dept. 1976–93

■ Works in the Victoria & Albert Museum, the Design Museum, Helsinki, the National Museum of Sweden, Stockholm, the Arabia Museum and the National Museum of Finland

Gunvor ('Nunne') Olin-Grönqvist is an artist who sees 'the big in the small' and lets objects and situations from everyday life inspire her. Her career at Arabia, spanning over forty years, allowed her to design dinner ware and decorative patterns. As an artist, she had the freedom to create sculptures and unique objects. Her leisure time in the archipelago inspired a range of motifs – the sea, gardens and vegetable markets found their way into her work.

Having designed functional ware for some thirty years, Olin-Grönqvist took to sculpture and had her first solo exhibition in Helsinki in 1982. She chose the harvest festival as her theme, perceptively depicting apples, onions, potatoes, flounders and herrings – all produce from the nearby market. Onions became a kind of emblem for Olin-Grönqvist, and her leeks and garlic bulbs were coveted by the wider public and collectors alike. Her unique pieces utilized ceramic decoration techniques, which she had embraced in the course of her long career as an industrial designer. Olin-Grönqvist's approachable and friendly sculptures exude realism and strong graphic awareness.

Pikes and Baltic Herrings by Gunvor Olin-Grönqvist. Photo: Timo Kauppila/Arabia Museum.

Gunvor Olin-Grönqvist surrounded by animal and plant studies in her studio at the Arabia art department in 1992. Photo: Timo Kauppila/Arabia Museum.

Howard Smith

■ Born in Moorestown, New Jersey, 1928

■ Pennsylvania Academy of Fine Arts, Philadelphia, 1960–62

■ Works in the Arabia Museum, the Design Museum, Helsinki, and the Hämeenlinna Art Museum

■ Ceramic wall on display at Jukolan Lintukoto in Hämeenlinna

Howard Smith moved to Finland in 1962. He navigates between materials like a fish in water, exhibiting with painters, designers and artisans with equal ease. Between 1985 and 1987 he worked as a visiting artist at Arabia and then (1988–95) at Studio Arteos in Tervakoski. At Arteos he created unique sculptures with technical assistance from Erna Aaltonen. Since 1996 he has worked at Fiskars, receiving the Finnish Government's design award in 2001. Smith's artwork has a joyful, whimsical undertone.

Gateway by Howard Smith, 1989.
Hämeenlinna Art Museum. Photo: Timo Kauppila.

Minni Lukander

Minni Lukander was known in the 1970s for her handled stoneware casseroles with ribbon-like reliefs. She also slip-cast reclining bottles on which she inscribed verses from famous poets using the sgraffito technique. A large selection of her works was exhibited with other Nordic ceramists' work at the Stockholm House of Culture in 1976. Lukander also worked for a time making ceramic sepulchral urns.

At Arabia, Minni Lukander began in the mid-1980s to focus on big architectural compositions, making square and rectangular modules slip-decorated with stylized geometric patterns. Her work, exhibited extensively in and outside Finland, is characterized by a fine execution and a sculptural language of form.

■ Born in Joensuu 1930

■ University of Art and Design Helsinki, ceramics dept., c. 1958–61

■ Studio in Helsinki, 1961 onwards, Pot Viapori group workshop 1973–80

■ Arabia art department, visiting artist, 1983–85

■ Public works include wall relief at Suursuo Home for the Elderly (first prize in Helsinki relief competition)

■ Works in the Arabia Museum, the Design Museum, Helsinki, the National Museum, Stockholm, and the City of Helsinki collection

Urn with an ornament relief band by Minni Lukander. Made at Pot Viapori in the 1970s.
Photo: Åsa Hellman.

Raili Aaltio

The Somero region is known for its fine clay and has long been home to brick factories and potteries; this is why Raili Aaltio insisted on fetching red clay all the way from her home region when she worked in Helsinki between 1960 and 1975. She made her living from small thrown earthenware flasks sold at Artek, but her artistic inclination actually veered towards unique sculptures and reliefs.

■ Born in Somero 1931

■ University of Art and Design Helsinki: ceramics dept. 1950–53, postgraduate studies 1953–54

■ Works owned by Nordea Bank, Litorex and the Somero Congregation

■ First prize in Somero souvenir competition, 1975

Evaluating a throwing competition in the early 1950s. Around the table are Elsa Jämsä (in the front with glasses), Sirkku Kumela, Pirkko Hovila (in patterned dress), Anja Jaatinen, Riitta Kerppola, Maj-Britt Heilimo, Raili Lindén-Aaltio, the teacher Elsa Elenius (top), Anja Virkkunen, Francesca Mascitti Lindh, Inkeri Iissalo-Toikka, Tamara Aladin (extreme right), Mirja Mikkonen and Mauno Hartman (centre). Photo courtesy of Raili Aaltio.

Francesca Mascitti Lindh

Southern warmth in the cold north

- Born in Anversa degli Abruzzi, Italy, 1931

- Liceo Artistico delle belle Arti, Rome, 1946–48

- University of Art and Design Helsinki, 1949–52

- Studio in Helsinki with Richard Lindh, 1953–55

- Arabia art dept., 1955–89

- Works in the International Ceramics Museum in Faenza, the Arabia Museum, the Design Museum, Helsinki, the National Museum, Stockholm and the Museum of Modern Art, New York

- First prize, Gualdo Tadino 1961; gold medal, Faenza 1973 and 1977; National Design Award 1981; gold medal, Gualdo Tadino 1987; Maestro del lavoro 1981; Commendatore II classe 2003

Francesca Mascitti Lindh at her wheel in the Arabia art department in the 1950s. Photo: Pietinen/ Arabia Museum.

Pots by Francesca Mascitti Lindh from the 1970s, with organic forms and pressed plant motifs. Arabia Museum. Heights 39–50 cm. Photo: Indav/Arabia Museum.

On her mother's side Francesca Mascitti Lindh descends from a Finnish family of artists, but her father was Italian. She studied art in Rome and Helsinki, and this double cultural influence would later be expressed in her work.

In the 1950s and 1960s Francesca Mascitti Lindh threw simple, round-bottomed shapes, occasionally featuring two spouts, which were reminiscent of traditional Mediterranean water pitchers. She also experimented by cutting up closed, thrown forms to give the vessels basket-like handles. Later her expression became increasingly sculptural, though focused on ceramic materials. She rolled out clay for wall plaques with delicate, poetic natural motifs. The surfaces come alive with accents in pastel-coloured glazes and shimmering lustres. Gradually she expressed herself more freely, creating vegetal, wound shapes in playful rhythm reminiscent of architectural façade reliefs from the Rococo era. She also pressed plants into soft clay and mixed coloured bodies to create a marbled effect in white, grey, sand and browny black. This abundance of powerful, meandering forms and richly structured surfaces in Lindh's later work takes us back to Baroque Rome and the artist's first home in Italy.

Lindh worked as a ceramic artist at Arabia's art department for over thirty years, participating with great success in a long series of exhibitions in Europe and further afield. Though the artist works and lives in Finland, her ceramics reflect a more southern, generous climate.

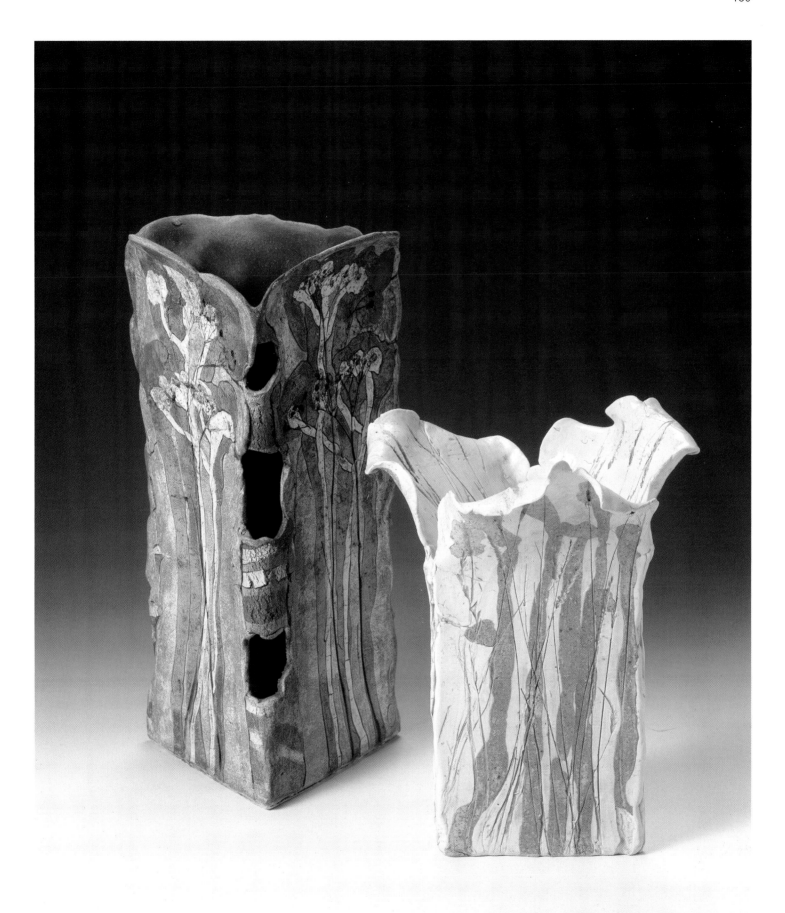

Oiva Toikka

Penchant for clay

- Born in Viipuri 1931

- University of Art and Design Helsinki: ceramics dept. 1953–56, art teaching dept. 1959–60

- Arabia 1956–59, Nuutajärvi glassworks 1963–93

- International Art School, Stockholm, 1990–93

- Lunning award 1970; National Design Award 1975; 'World Glass Now '85' honorary award, Japan; Kaj Franck design award 1992; Prins Eugen medal 2001

During the 1950s, Oiva Toikka worked at Arabia's art department where he created stylized animal and human figures in grogged stoneware. Despite making his name in blown glass Toikka has returned to clay time and again. He cooperated with Swedish ceramist Kennet Williamsson, who created clay artefacts for Toikka to decorate. Toikka is a modern pioneer in the use of the demanding Majolica technique. His patterns are free-flowing and playful, yet disciplined. He has created many pieces for public spaces and his ceramics and glass can be found in Finnish and foreign museums.

Oval dish with fish motif by Oiva Toikka from the 1950s. Private collection. Photo: Johnny Korkman.

Hilkka Jarva

- Born in Viipuri 1932

- University of Helsinki, literature degree, 1964

- University of Art and Design Helsinki, ceramics dept.: studies c. 1968–70, assistant c. 1970–71

- Studio in Helsinki, c. 1970–73

- Pot Viapori group workshop, 1972–98

Hilkka Jarva has experimented with a number of techniques and materials but she is best known for doll-like sculptures of human figures with billowing dresses made of thin clay sheets. They sometimes relate to art-historical periods such as the Etruscan era or the Renaissance. Her fanciful, narrative style has a romantic undertone. She also makes stoneware vases and jugs with thrown bases and slab-built walls.

Jarva has exhibited her work internationally on many occasions. In 1972 she was one of the founders of the Pot Viapori group workshop on the island of Suomenlinna.

Trees by Hilkka Jarva, late 1970s. Slab-built branches on wheel-thrown trunks, Photo from the Pot Viapori archives.

Eija Karivirta

Like many of her colleagues, Eija Karivirta mostly made wheel-thrown functional items before focusing on sculpture. She has worked in several European countries, including Hungary, where she was an assistant to well-known artist Imre Schrammel. Membership of the Kecskemét group has also brought cooperation with other European artists. Karivirta builds her pieces from clay slabs into free, billowing forms. In 1956 she received an honorary mention in a relief competition for Kilteri school in Vantaa. Since 1994 she has had a studio at Taidetehdas in Porvoo.

- Born in Lahti 1933

- University of Art and Design Helsinki, ceramics dept., 1954–57

- Studio in Helsinki 1963–64, Porvoo 1966–72 and Kreivilä elementary school 1972–94

- Works in Hetjens Museum, Düsseldorf, Museum le Manoir de Ville Martigny, Switzerland, the Siklós Ceramics Art House, Hungary and the cities of Porvoo and Mikkeli

Slab-built vase by Eija Karivirta, 1982. Height 40 cm.
Photo courtesy of Eija Karivirta.

Liisa Kurki

Liisa Kurki (née Seitsonen) worked in Sauvo from 1965 to 1969 before moving back to her family's farm in Tervakoski, Janakkala. She built a studio in a barn, where she created wheel-thrown objects as well as sculptures and reliefs. She exhibited in Finland and abroad and sold her works in Helsinki showrooms such as Vokki Virkki and the Finnish Design Center. One of Kurki's ceramic sculptures is owned by Janakkala Congregation.

- Born in Antrea 1936, died in Janakkala 2002

- University of Art and Design Helsinki, ceramics dept., c. 1958–61

- Traineeship at Theodor Uschanoff's studio, 1961

- Diploma, Faenza 1973

Ulla Sangervo-Lappalainen

Ulla Sangervo-Lappalainen makes large raku-fired sculptures and wall plaques, which she hand-builds using grogged clay strips or slabs and decorates with ceramic pigments. Black dominates as a colour, while female figures are the main subjects. Her earlier figures were dreamily romantic but lately they have become increasingly dramatic, almost aggressive.

Ulla Sangervo-Lappalainen's work has been seen abroad at several exhibitions and can be found in the Finnish Government collection, the Baltic Sea Centre in Tuusula, the Arla Institute and Kellokoski hospital.

- Born in Turku 1936

- Kupittaan Savi Oy, 1955–57, Rörstrand, Sweden: porcelain painter, 1959–60

- International Art School, Stockholm, 1960–62

- University of Art and Design Helsinki, ceramics dept., 1963–65

- Kenneth Clark's Pottery, London, 1962–63

- Studio in Helsinki, 1978 onwards

Anna-Maria Osipow

Surrealism, feminism and Pop Art

■ Born in Sortavala 1935

■ University of Art and Design Helsinki, ceramics dept., 1956–59

■ Studio M. Barrier, Paris 1959–60;
studios in Hyrylä and Järvenpää 1962 onwards

■ Commissioned works in Church of St Matthew, Helsinki, Mikkeli town hall and Uusimaa county council

■ Works in the Helsinki City Art Museum, the Röhss Museum, Gothenburg, the Archie Bray Foundation of Ceramic Arts and the Pennsylvania Museum of Art, USA

■ Finnish Government's fifteen-year artists' scholarship, 1986

Anna-Maria Osipow has worked with painters from an early stage in her career. She was trained as a ceramist and started by throwing functional ware. Her breakthrough, however, came in the 1970s with sculptures she exhibited alongside the work of artists in other media, in a crossing of boundaries that was unusual for the time.[1]

Osipow uses clay in a free and unorthodox style, challenging conventional norms. Her work is characterized by large formats and a brisk, spontaneous touch. She often builds her sculptures from clay coils, modelling them boldly, adding pieces or carving them off where necessary. She uses grogged stoneware clay and treats its surface with metallic oxides, slips, glazes and pigments. Her subjects include human figures, mythological animals and various symbolic tableaux involving hands, feet, chairs and horns. Some pieces express feminist themes. Osipow also creates installations consisting of ceramic elements combined with objects in other materials, such as wood. Humour blends with irony, aggression with warmth, producing an individual cocktail of Surrealism, Pop Art and Realism.

In stylistic and thematic terms Osipow's ceramic work mirrors various expressions of twentieth-century fine art and is in many ways unique in its genre. In 2002 the Design Museum in Helsinki arranged a retrospective exhibition of her work.

Striped Woman by Anna-Maria Osipow, 2001.
Photo: Juha Ilvas.

Wall relief in stoneware by Anna-Maria Osipow for the baptistry of the Church of St Matthew, East City Centre, Helsinki, 1985. Photo courtesy of Anna-Maria Osipow.

Eira Savolainen

- Born in Viipuri 1936

- Savitorppa, 1955–58 and 1976–86

- Studio Sävysavi ky, Nahkela, 1977–2001

Eira Savolainen is one of the few Finnish ceramists who have had a long-term commitment to underglaze decoration with brush technique. She makes thrown platters, bowls and lidded boxes using pure white clay, often decorating them with painted flowers and leaves but also still lifes and dragonflies. With careful brushstrokes Savolainen creates intricate compositions that envelop an artefact's entire surface.

The End of the Game by Eira Savolainen, 1988.
Diameter 55 cm. Photo: Advertising Agency Iquistus.

Jack Johnsson

- Born in Helsinki 1937, died in Turku 1991

- Åbo Akademi University School of Business Studies, 1960–65

- Traineeship in studios in Gotland, Sweden, 1970s

- Studio Ruukkupaja, Turku, 1974–91

Jack Johnsson and his wife Marre ran a workshop in Turku for almost twenty years. The production consisted of both thrown utilitarian series and unique pieces. They brought clay from Gotland and patinated its surface with copper oxide before glaze firing at around 1,120 °C. Glossy blue, yellow and green glazes were favoured. Ruukkupaja completed commissions for a number of companies and for the City of Turku, and also won second prize in a gift item competition organized in 1977.

Heljä Liukko-Sundström

Playful fantasy

Heljä Liukko-Sundström's art encompasses a wide range of genres: she is not only a ceramist but also a graphic artist, illustrator and children's author. She has been at Arabia her whole working life, creating sculptures, serially produced objects and slip-cast functional ware, including the *Tuuli* dinner set.

Liukko-Sundström is very productive, and man is one of her favourite themes. She has created several large wall plaques with dream-like, Naive subjects depicted with playful fantasy. The images in these pieces are often executed in finely carved line drawings; areas of colour are applied with a spray technique. Heljä Liukko-Sundström has developed her own graphic methods, which has enabled her to mass-produce her pictorial work. Since the late 1970s she has also published children's books with her own illustrations, printed from pictures originally created on paper-thin clay.

■ Born in Vehmaa 1938

■ University of Art and Design Helsinki, ceramics dept., 1959–62

■ Arabia: design dept. 1962–67, art dept. 1967 onwards

■ Several commissioned works in public buildings

■ Works in the Victoria & Albert Museum, the Design Museum, Helsinki, the Turku Art Museum, Museum Boymans van Beuningen, Rotterdam and the Helsinki City Museum

■ Illum design award 1977; gold medal, Gualdo Tadino 1979; Finnish Government award for Merits in Children's Culture 1982; Pro Finlandia award 2001

Safe, sculpture by Heljä Liukko-Sundström, 1971. Photo: Gero Mylius/Arabia Museum.

Sirkka-Liisa Sarasjoki

Sirkka-Liisa Sarasjoki worked for a long time in Ostrobothnia, western Finland, making wood-fired earthenware. Since 1997 she has concentrated on one-of-a-kind stoneware artefacts in an austere style, reminiscent of industrial design. Her work is often decorated with geometric reliefs and precisely executed carvings. Sarasjoki's works adorn Kronoby municipal building and Halkokari school in Kokkola and can also be found at Kokkola Art Museum and the Jarva Jaani municipal building in Estonia.

■ Born in Kokkola 1941

■ University of Art and Design Helsinki, ceramics dept., 1962–66

■ Studio in Kälviä 1968–97, Fiskars 1997 onwards

■ Ceramics teacher in Kapenguria, Kenya, 1983–90

Piippa Tandefelt

Winged bowls

- Born in Sortavala 1939

- University of Art and Design Helsinki, ceramics dept., 1962–65

- Studio in Suomenlinna, 1966–72

- Arabia art dept., visiting artist, 1973

- Group workshop Pot Viapori, 1972–76

Piippa Tandefelt was the first Finnish ceramist to be singled out for the prestigious one-year government scholarship for artists. Despite her brief career as a ceramist, she is undoubtedly one of the most significant figures in modern Finnish studio ceramics. She also co-founded the Pot Viapori group workshop in Suomenlinna.

At the end of the 1960s, Finnish studio ceramists only really had local earthenware clay at their disposal.[1] Tandefelt used red clay for thrown, cast and hand-built pieces and exhibited her work widely. She is best known for large, unique bird-themed bowls with folk art connotations, which she smoke-fired to achieve different colour nuances.

Tandefelt joined Arabia's art department on Kaj Franck's invitation, but she was only there for four months before returning to Pot Viapori. This move was in many ways taxing: having enjoyed such privileges as ready-made materials and help from professional throwers and laboratory personnel, it was disconcerting to face the practical problems and physically demanding conditions of studio ceramics.[2] Tandefelt eventually gave up clay entirely and went on to found a doll museum on Suomenlinna, her home island.

Smoke-fired bird vessels by Piippa Tandefelt for the 'Pottery takes Flight' exhibition in the early 1970s. Photo courtesy of Piippa Tandefelt.

Taina Kurtze

Studio Kurtze was originally a family workshop where Taina was responsible for design and other family members participated in the practical execution. Their production included thrown functional ware and wall decorations sold at Stockmann. Kurtze now has a large wood-firing kiln and focuses on artworks such as wall reliefs and sculptures, which have been shown at exhibitions both at home and abroad. She often prepares her own clay bodies. Public commissions for reliefs have come from Mäntsälä health centre, Perniö sport centre and Kerava fire station.

- Born in Loviisa 1937

- Academy of Fine Arts, Helsinki, 1955–56, University of Art and Design Helsinki, evening school, 1956–58

- Arabia, traineeship, 1956–57

- Studio in Helsinki 1964–70, Mäntsälä 1970–83, Perniö 1983 onwards

Ulla Parkkinen

Ulla Parkkinen (née Hakala) is known for her thrown functional items in high-fired stoneware. Between 1968 and 1990 she worked in her own studio in Puotila, and during the summer months between 1982 and 1994 she also shared a workshop (Gamla Mejeriet, Fagervik, western Uusimaa) with her colleague Pirkko Räsänen. Ulla Parkkinen's work has been exhibited nationally as well as internationally.

- Born in Kokkola 1940

- University of Art and Design Helsinki, ceramics dept., 1959–62

- Finnish Adult Education Centre of the City of Helsinki, ceramics teacher, 1977–98

Geometrical stoneware plate by Ulla Parkkinen. Photo: Johnny Korkman.

Katy Hertell

Sculptor Katy Hertell worked with concrete, wood and stone before discovering clay as a medium in 1992. She favours the use of stoneware for her animal sculptures, which are decorated with coloured glazes and fired in an electric kiln. Her work has been exhibited in several countries and can be found in the collection of Linköping county council in Sweden.

- Born in Helsinki 1941

- Studio in Laajasalo, 1995 onwards

Marri Penna

- Born in Helsinki 1940

- University of Art and Design Helsinki, graphic design dept., 1959–62

- Studio in Siuntio, 1984 onwards

Marri Penna uses a prehistoric firing technique of the Pueblo Native Americans for her thrown pottery and sculptures in earthenware and stoneware. The firing takes place in a primitive open kiln with horse dung and wood as fuel. This method, based on archaeological finds, turns the pottery black during firing. Unmalleable substances such as sand are added to the clay to prevent cracking in the rapidly rising heat. Burnishing with jasper stone together with carbonization in the course of the firing makes the pots impervious to liquids – as if they had been glazed.

Penna's works have been exhibited nationally and can be found in the University of Helsinki, the Design Museum, Helsinki, Loval Oy in Loviisa and the M. K. Ciurlionis National Art Museum in Lithuania.

Marri Penna smoke-fires her work following in a technique used by ancient Pueblo potters. Photo: Marri Penna.

Fujiwo Ishimoto

A fusion of cultures

Fujiwo Ishimoto comes from a small village in the Ehime region, Japan, which is the home of ancient ceramic traditions. Qualified as a graphic artist, he moved to Finland in 1970, intrigued by Finnish design, particularly Marimekko. He was a successful, established textile designer when he entered Arabia's art department in 1989, where he adapted to clay naturally.

Ishimoto works intuitively, with the material as a starting point. He makes full use of the clay's plasticity, leaving traces of the process through tool and hand marks. Thick, glossy glazes contrast with dry, matte clay in a sensitive and at the same time generous manner. His large, slab-built dishes form three-dimensional ceramic scenes or landscapes of sorts and reflect a variety of moods, ranging from dramatic, stormy nights to sunny summer meadows.

In Fujiwo Ishimoto's ceramics we can trace Finnish as well as Japanese influences. He makes flat plates with folded, smooth planes resembling origami and colourful lidded boxes reminiscent of traditional Japanese lacquer work. However, he is equally sensitive to Finnish nature and its changing seasons. His work evinces a demonstrable fusion of Japanese and Finnish dispositions and temperaments — a harmonious crossing of cultures which, despite being so far apart, have a lot in common.

■ Born in Ehime, Japan, 1941

■ Tokyo National University of Fine Arts and Music, design and graphics, 1960–64

■ Marimekko, designer, 1974 onwards

■ Arabia art dept., 1989 onwards

■ Roscoe Award, USA; National Design Award 1991; Kaj Franck design award 1994; City of Helsinki cultural award 1997

■ Works in the Design Museum, Helsinki, the Cooper-Hewitt Museum, New York, the Röhss Museum, Gothenburg, the Montreal Museum of Decorative Arts and the Art Gallery of Western Australia, Perth

↖ Stoneware dish by Fujiwo Ishimoto, 1994. Photo: Timo Kauppila/Arabia Museum.

Grooved stoneware plate by Fujiwo Ishimoto, 1995. Photo: Timo Kauppila/Arabia Museum.

Zoltan Popovits
Multimedia sculptor

- Born in Eger, Hungary, 1940

- School of Architecture, University of Colorado, USA, 1959–63

- Kansas City Art Institute, USA 1963–65

- Academy of Fine Arts Helsinki 1965–66

- Arabia art dept. 1969–71; Lapponia Jewelry 1975 onwards

- Sculptures at the Baghdad Conference Palace and the Forum block, Sanomatalo and the Uusimaa Provincial Government building, Helsinki

- Regione Emilio-Romagna award, Faenza 1978; first prize, glass design, Nuutajärvi 1978; first prize, Hyrylä market square sculpture competition; gold medal, 'Gdansk International Triennial for Portrait Sculpture' 1989

When Zoltan Popovits settled in Finland in 1965 he had received a comprehensive art education, and his international experience allowed him to test the clay in ways that were new and refreshing for Finland. Arabia's art department provided him with technical resources for independent sculptural work, which he carried out in porcelain and stoneware. Mostly hand-built with slabs, these pieces exhibit strong colours and metallic lustre glazes. The artist's inquisitive nature and technical brilliance are also apparent in his unglazed terracotta sculptures.

Popovits has extended his repertoire to include materials such as wood, metal, stone, glass and plastic. He is simultaneously known as a jewelry designer and the creator of several monumental sculptures in central Helsinki. His works have been acquired by the Arabia Museum, the Design Museum in Helsinki, the International Museum of Ceramics in Faenza, the Finnish Government and the Wäinö Aaltonen Museum of Art, among other prominent collections.

Designs for a Water Tower, porcelain statues by Zoltan Popovits, 1969. Height 70 cm. Photo: Yrjö Sotamaa.

Liisa Tarna

- Born in Simo 1940

- University of Art and Design Helsinki, art teaching and ceramics dept., 1960–64

- Arabia: traineeship under the direction of Kaj Franck

- Staatliche Ingenieur und Werkschule für Keramik, Germany, 1965–66

Between 1966 and 1971 Liisa Tarna (née Tahvanainen) had a studio in Tikkurila, near Helsinki, based on small family workshops she had observed in Germany, where she studied under the direction of master ceramist Hubert Griemert. Tarna specialized in thrown functional ware and also made some decorative items such as wall plaques in vitrified stoneware. She favoured thick, fluid glazes. Her work was sold in design showrooms and she also exhibited in Finland, Sweden and Norway.

Details of pots with thick, runny glazes by Liisa Tarna, 1968. Photo: Antti Bengts.

Ritva Tulonen

Earth, clay and silence

- Born in Kotka 1941

- University of Art and Design Helsinki: art dept. 1962–66, ceramics dept. 1966–67

- Studios in Helsinki, Hämeenlinna, Hyvinkää and Vehkalahti 1968–94, Tuusula 1994 onwards

- Public works at Helsinki Energy, Elimäki Institute of Social Studies, Vehkalahtitalo and Rovaniemen säästöpankki

- Works in the Design Museum, Helsinki, Lappeenranta Art Museum, Hetjens Museum, Düsseldorf, the Museum of Applied Arts, Frankfurt, and the Finnish Government collection

- National Design Award, 1987

Ritva Tulonen's work is characterized by a continuous quest for nature and the peace of the deep forests of the eastern Finnish lake district. She was one of the first Finnish ceramists to attempt salt glazing in wood-fired kilns, a technique rarely used in Finland. In her work she pursues 'earth, water, forest spirits, darkness and silence'. She now fires some of her sculptures in her colleague Elina Sorainen's large, wood-burning Noborigama kiln, where ash, smoke and flames cause interesting surface effects, creating a kind of living skin on the clay.

Apart from nature, Ritva Tulonen is inspired by primitive civilizations, ancient ritual artefacts and age-old relics. A trip to Japanese ceramics centres in 1978 gave her new key stimuli. Tulonen builds her sculptures by hand using coil and slab techniques, sometimes with the help of plaster moulds. Her material is usually grogged stoneware clay and her formats are large. Ritva Tulonen's works are frequently composed of several parts joined together with untreated hemp or tarred rope. She has also used silver-grey tree trunks gnawed by beavers and found on the lakeside.

Jatuli, wood-fired stoneware sculpture by Ritva Tulonen, 1997. 15 x 41 x 30 cm. Photo: Simo Salmi.

Peter Winquist

Activist and organizer

Peter Winquist has left his mark on ceramics in various regions of Finland. While living in Helsinki he was active in the Finnish Association of Designers Ornamo, at the same time working as a designer at Arabia. During his time as artistic director for Pentik in Lapland he spearheaded an international ceramics symposium in 1974. Resident since 1988 in the Åland archipelago, Winquist has with unremitting energy created, organized and actively participated in cultural events on an international as well as a local scale. In addition to this work for the common good, he has been a teacher, visited faraway countries and also had time to create ceramics in his workshop, Peters Studio on the island of Eckerö.

Peter Winquist worked for several years in the ceramic industry, but as an independent artist he has applied craft techniques to the creation of unique works. He works in both stoneware and earthenware clays, using several firing methods, including raku. One of his most important artworks is a large wall composition entitled *Alfa Beta: Literary History*, now in Mariehamn Library. It is made of stoneware, steel and concrete.

■ Born in Tenhola 1941

■ School of Crafts and Design, Gothenburg, industrial design, 1963–67

■ Arabia, designer, 1967–74

■ Pentik, artistic director and designer, 1974–83

■ Founder of the Finnish School of Ceramics in Posio, 1985

■ Åland Folk High School, art teacher, 1988–99

■ Works in the Victoria & Albert Museum, Design House Seoul, Korea, NAPA, Greenland, and the Design Museum, Helsinki

■ Gold medal, Faenza 1971; National Design Award 1976; Åland cultural award 1994

Zapatistas, earthenware by Peter Winquist, 1995.
Photo: Peter Winquist.

Teemu Luoto

■ Born in Helsinki 1941

■ University of Art and Design Helsinki: ceramics dept. 1958–61, evening school 1957–58

■ Studio in Helsinki 1961–71, at Kuhmalahden Taidepappila 1971 onwards

■ Pirkanmaa medal, 1990

Teemu Luoto creates ceramic sculptures in a narrative, often Naive style. His materials are a rough raku body and coloured glazes and engobes. Teemu Luoto also taught art at several schools. His animal sculptures enliven many children's nurseries, and he is represented in several collections, including those belonging to the Finnish Government and several cities.

Animals on Ships by Teemu Luoto, 1996.
Photo: Teemu Luoto.

Leena Liljeström-Puntanen

■ Born in Kotka 1941

■ University of Art and Design Helsinki ceramics dept.: studies 1961–65; assistant and teacher 1965–68; postgraduate studies 1982–93

■ Staatliche Hochschule für Bildende Künste Ab.West-Berlin, 1970–71

■ Traineeships, Arabia 1961–62 and Rosenthal AG 1964

Since 1973 Leena Liljeström-Puntanen has had a studio in Kouvola, where she creates functional as well as decorative items. She prepares her own clay bodies and often combines ceramics with materials such as glass and concrete. In addition to her creative work, she has been an art teacher at Kymenlaakso Polytechnic for some twenty years. Various institutions in Finland and abroad, notably the International Museum of Ceramics in Bechyne (Czech Republic), the Centre del Vidre in Barcelona and Kouvola Art Museum, have acquired work by Liljeström-Puntanen.[1]

Kaija-Riitta Iivonen

Sculptor, graphic artist and painter Kaija-Riitta Iivonen is described as a true Naive artist. She depicts narrative, often droll scenes in coarse stoneware clay to which she adds colourful patinas before and after firing. Her subjects are inspired by everyday life, fairy stories and occasionally Biblical tales. Between 1971 and 1973 Iivonen worked as a visiting artist at Arabia's art department and has since exhibited her work in Finland and abroad. Her work can be found in several ecclesiastical buildings, including Malmi cemetery chapel and Itä-Hakkila church. She lives in Porvoo and has a studio at Taidetehdas.

■ Born in Kangasala 1942

■ University of Art and Design Helsinki, graphic art department, 1961–67

■ Works in the Arabia Museum, the Design Museum, Helsinki, the Atheneum Art Museum, the Röhss Museum, Gothenburg, and Jönköping County Museum, Sweden

■ Sculptures at Brinell School, Nässjö, Sweden, and the SAS Terminal, Oslo

■ First and second prize, Suomen Mitalitaiteen Kilta competition, 1972 and 1973; Wäinö Aaltonen award, 1976

Angel and Devil: A Priest in a Quandary, stoneware sculpture by Kaija-Riitta Iivonen from the 1970s. Photo: Pietinen/Arabia Museum.

Margareta Långhjelm

Margareta Långhjelm departed from the rustic style of her contemporaries by using white clay bodies and light pastel colours. Her debut exhibition in 1971 showed wheel-thrown artefacts as well as wall plaques in faience with lace-like patterns. Långhjelm's work often presents symmetrical relief impressions from organic fragments such as apple halves, slices of onion and sea shells.

■ Born in Tammela 1942

■ University of Art and Design Helsinki, ceramics dept., 1963–67

■ Stoke-on-Trent College of Art, 1968

■ Arabia art department, 1968–74

Airi Hortling
Teacher, researcher and ceramist

- Born in Tampere 1943

- University of Art and Design Helsinki: ceramics 1965–69, head teacher 1970–73, teacher 1982–89, lecturer 1989 onwards

- Keramikboden Östersundom 1981–96

- Works in the International Ceramics Museum in Faenza, the Arabia Museum and the Craft Museum of Finland, Jyväskylä

- Third prize, Faenza 1970; first prize, Faenza 1973; 'Taikon Kehut' recognition, TAIKO 1996; Teacher of the Year, University of Art and Design Helsinki, 1996

Airi Hortling is a skilled thrower, known for her teapots and large platters made with a variety of clay bodies and firing techniques. The beautiful but capricious Finnish red clay has a special place in Hortling's work; she uses it for forms reminiscent of traditional pottery, decorated with free brushstrokes in an Expressionist style. Bright slips applied in layers create an effective contrast to the earthenware surface. A confident feel for materials is the bedrock of Hortling's artistry.

Airi Hortling has also made a significant contribution to Finnish ceramics as a teacher and researcher in materials. She has published several articles on ceramic material science in conjunction with international conferences and is often consulted as an expert on the subject.

Earthenware bowl with brushed engobe and wax-resist decoration by Airi Hortling, 1990s. Diameter 45 cm. Photo: Johnny Korkman.

Ritva Grunberg

Having lived in the United States for sixteen years, Ritva Grunberg returned to Finland in 1997 and set up a studio in an old building in the historic fortress area of Lappeenranta, joining the local community of artists and craftsmen. She uses low-fired white clay for sculptures and unique objects as well as small series of artefacts, each given an individual appearance with vigorous ornaments in vivid underglazes. Grunberg's decoration techniques include wax-resist and sgraffito, and she handles ceramics in a fresh and bold way that is clearly influenced by American artists.

Grunberg has participated in exhibitions in a number of countries and contributed works to the Finnish Government collection, the Finnair office in New York and the Art School for Children and Youth in Lappeenranta.

■ Born in Imatra 1943

■ University of Helsinki, pharmacy degree, 1965

■ Earthworks & Artisans, New York, 1982–84, Houston Potter's Guild Shop & Gallery, member, 1986–97

■ Glassell School of Art, Houston, 1987, University of Houston, Texas, 1994

Colourful sunflowers with underglaze decoration on a faience body by Ritva Grunberg *c.* 1990. Photo: Starfoto Oy.

Raija Cammarano

- Born in Helsinki 1943

- Septaria Ceramics Centre: studies, 1994–98

Raija Cammarano has spent most of her life overseas, including Venezuela where she lived for over twenty years. Her interest in ceramics was aroused by primitive South American pottery. Between 1994 and 1998 she was tutored privately by Irma Weckman, whose assistant she would later become.

Cammarano has exhibited together with colleagues but had her first solo exhibition in 1999, at Galleria Laterna Magica in Helsinki. She specializes in a steel netting technique that is unusual in Finland, used to build impressive sculptures, such as huge ceramic kimonos.

Kimono by Raija Cammarano, 1999. Ceramics on steel mesh. 150 x 160 cm. Photo: Julia Weckman.

Risto Paatero

Technical accomplishment

Risto Paatero is technically accomplished and has built a considerable number of gas and wood-burning kilns to order in Finland, Sweden and the Philippines. He built a salt-glazing kiln in 1972 and was the first ceramist in Finland to fire work in this type of kiln. He now specializes in porcelain fired in a reducing atmosphere at 1,320 °C, using traditional tenmoku, celadon and oxblood glazes. He has also created pliable porcelain bodies for fellow ceramists.

Paatero's work is composed of thrown functional ceramics such as tea sets, pots and mugs which he makes with his wife Anneli. He also creates unique pieces, including a large relief for Heinävesi health centre. Hannu Siren's large outdoor sculpture *Stoa* at Helsinki's Itäkeskus shopping centre, made of dyed concrete, incorporates a cobalt blue porcelain aggregate prepared by Paatero.

■ Born in Helsinki 1943

■ University of Helsinki, political history, 1965–70

■ Studio in Karjalohja 1970–73, Kuopio 1978–80, Somero 1980–89 and Fiskars 1996 onwards

■ Pentik and Kermansavi Oy: founder of the factories' ceramic departments, 1973–78

Ceramic samovar with copper red glaze by Risto Paatero. Height 20 cm. Photo: Johnny Korkman.

Tuula & Erkka Auermaa

Death, wall plaque by Tuula Auermaa, 1987. 65 x 90 cm. Photo: Kristian Runeberg.

Tuula and Erkka Auermaa, both ceramists, share a studio in Halikko, south-western Finland. Tuula was born in Helsinki in 1943 and studied at the ceramics department of the University of Art and Design Helsinki between 1960 and 1963 and again in 1969. Erkka, born in Salo in 1943, is mainly self-taught but studied briefly at Keramikmuseum Westerwald in Germany.

Tuula Auermaa makes plaques that incorporate figurative, occasionally romantic motifs and tends to depict female figures, which appear as graphical drawings against a background of stoneware clay. Keramikmuseum Westerwald, the Miina Sillanpää Foundation and the City of Innsbruck have works by Tuula Auermaa in their collections.

Erkka Auermaa hand-builds sculptures of animals, angels, boats and human figures, depicting them in a stylized but humorous and playful way. His work is in Keramikmuseum Westerwald and the collections of the SOL company and various banks.

Both artists have exhibited independently and in groups, also outside Finland, and have received several commissions for public spaces – notably a joint wall relief for Halikko hospital.

Elina Sorainen

Oriental inspiration

■ Born in Hauho 1943

■ University of Denver, ceramics, 1965–72, College of Decorative Arts, Tehran: teacher, 1974–78, Tama Art University, Tokyo, 1980

■ Studio in Pernå, 1981 onwards

■ National Institute of Design, Ahmedabad, India: ceramics teacher, 1987

■ Works in the Design Museum, Helsinki, the Museum of Decorative Applied Arts, Riga, the Art Museum of Estonia, Tallinn, the Museum of Decorative Arts, Prague, and the Römhild Ceramics Museum, Germany

■ Pernå cultural award, 1999

Elina Sorainen creates functional items and sculptures. Her utilitarian ceramics include transparent porcelain lamps, cast in several layers with slips in different colours. She also makes thrown ovenware, jugs and beakers, often using mixed techniques. Thrown elements are combined with press-moulded clay slabs. Among her notable sculptures are stoneware horses, around fifty centimetres in height, inspired by Chinese Tang-dynasty ceramics.

For long periods of time Elina Sorainen studied and worked in foreign countries including Japan, which shows in her artwork. Close to the old school which is her home and studio, she has a large, wood-burning Noborigama kiln, a rarity in Finland. This traditional Japanese kiln nurtures the firing with natural ash glazes that would be impossible to achieve in electric kilns. Sorainen also uses the Japanese nerikomi decoration technique, creating a marbled effect by mixing clays in different colours.

In addition to her ceramic work, Sorainen has recently conducted research for her doctoral thesis on a group of women who create traditional pottery in a small Iranian village. About her own attachment to clay, Sorainen says: 'Nothing can be taken for granted. That is how the relationship remains alive!'[1]

Heppa, terrine by Elina Sorainen in nerikomi technique with ash glaze, fired in a Japanese-type noborigama kiln, 1996. Photo: Tuomo-Juhani Vuorenmaa.

Sinikka Ahla

Sinikka Ahla was active at the Keramiikkakellari group workshop between 1977 and 1980, moving on to independent studio work in Helsinki until 1992. She created wheel-thrown boxes with geometric sgraffito designs as well as sculptures and reliefs. Her work can be seen at the Design Museum in Helsinki, Musée de Carouge in Switzerland and the collection of the Finnish delegation to the United Nations.

■ Born in Helsinki 1942

■ University of Art and Design Helsinki, ceramics dept., 1963–68

■ Honorary mention, World Triennial Exhibition of Small Ceramics, Zagreb 1984; second prize, City of Carouge award, Geneva 1987

Inkeri Leivo

Ceramist Inkeri Leivo is known for her designs for Arabia, including the *Arctica* dinner set. Since the 1980s she has also been making unique ceramic pieces. Initially she worked with dyed feldspar porcelain bodies fired in a reducing atmosphere at around 1,400 °C. She made hand-built vases, plates and other objects. In later years she has produced lanterns in bone china, cast in layers of varying thickness to achieve translucency. Leivo's work has been exhibited in Finland and elsewhere.

■ Born in Helsinki 1944

■ University of Art and Design Helsinki, ceramics dept., 1966–70

■ Arabia: product planning 1971 onwards; art dept. *c.* 1975 onwards

■ Works in the Arabia Museum, the Design Museum, Helsinki, the Victoria & Albert Museum and the City of Helsinki collection

■ Formland design award 1988; National Design Award 1992

Lea Klemola

Lea Klemola co-founded group workshop Seenat in 1976.[1] Since 1981 she has had a studio in Helsinki, where she mainly creates utilitarian ceramics in stoneware, with glazes in multiple colours. In 1992 she mounted a solo exhibition at Design Forum, showing unique, geometric sculptures executed in a variety of techniques. Since then she has reverted to making functional ware.

■ Born in Pälkäne 1944

■ University of Art and Design Helsinki: ceramics dept. 1966–71, teaching dept. 1980–81, teacher 1971–89

■ Premio Minestrone Publica Instruzione, Faenza 1973 (to work group); National Design Award 1978 (to Seenat)

Paul Envalds

Approaching stone

- Born in Helsinki 1945

- University of Art and Design Helsinki, ceramics dept.: studies 1966–71, teacher 1989–94

- Arabia art dept.: assistant 1965–70, artist 1970–74

- Studio in Vantaa, 1975 onwards

- Helsinki University of Technology, lecturer in plastic composition, 1977–91

- Works in the National Museum, Stockholm, Musée Municipal de Céramique Vallauris, the Design Museum, Helsinki, the Arabia Museum and the City of Helsinki collections

- Grand Prix Vallauris 1972 (with A. Hovisaari and R. Bryk); National Design Award 1988

Arabia artist Paul Envalds has come a long and winding way in his career. He began at the factory's plaster department, then went on to assist Birger Kaipiainen and Toini Muona at the art department. As an independent artist at Arabia he became known for his rounded, stone-like sculptures. They are well-adapted to a variety of glazes, from metallic, browny-black tenmoku to orange-peel salt glazes. In addition he made plates and wide bowls with rich red-clay glazes in earthy tones.

In his workshop, Keramiikkastudio Envalds, Paul Envalds and his wife Sinikka generally work on thrown stoneware. They fire in oil-burning and gas kilns to achieve reducing effects on glazes and clays. In autumn 2003 the Arabia Museum gallery held a retrospective exhibition of work by Envalds, ranging over four decades: this collection bore witness to the artist's faithfulness to his personal style. Paul Envalds's ceramics tend to have simple, soft forms and surface treatments reminiscent of ancient, wind-swept granite rocks.[1]

Paul Envalds working on a slip-cast sculpture at Arabia, 1972. Photo: Arabia Museum.

Terhi Juurinen
Seenat group workshop

The Seenat workshop was established in 1976 by ceramists Terhi Juurinen, Lea Klemola and Riitta Siira (née Pensanen), all graduates of the University of Art and Design Helsinki.[1] Their goal was to create limited series of high-quality functional ware mainly by slip-casting and press-moulding. Their production includes Japanese-inspired square plates and tea sets.

Terhi Juurinen is now the sole member of Seenat and continues to create high-quality ceramics with an emphasis on beauty and functionality. Since 2000 she has fired some work in a wood-burning kiln, giving each item specific colours and structural effects by the reduction process. She uses classic oxblood and celadon glazes. In the last few years Juurinen has been working with carpenter Markku Tonttila, who provides her ceramics with wooden bases, boxes and other parts.

■ Born in Helsinki 1945

■ University of Art and Design Helsinki, ceramics dept.: studies 1967–72, postgraduate studies 1993–96

■ Seenat group workshop, Palojoki, 1976 onwards

■ Exhibitions in Finland and abroad

■ Ceramic tile walls, Helsinki railway station, 1982

■ National Design Award for Seenat 1978; first prize, Paulig teapot competition 1991; art award of the Arts Council of Uusimaa 1993; second prize, Posio design competition 1996

Wood-fired pots by Terhi Juurinen, 2001.
Photo: Ana Pullinen.

Catharina Kajander

Giant terracotta

■ Born in Helsinki 1945

■ University of Art and Design Helsinki, ceramics dept.: studies 1962–66, part-time teacher 1966–68

■ Franzén's Pottery, Täkter, 1965–71 and 1980

■ Ceramics expert, Tanzania 1972–74 and Guinea 1977

■ Organizer of clay symposia in Somero, 1998–2001

■ Works in the Design Museum, Helsinki, the Craft Museum of Finland, Jyväskylä, the Troya National Museum, Bulgaria, and the Pécs international ceramics collection, Hungary

■ National Design Award, 1969; Stina Krook Foundation award, 2001

Catharina Kajander is one of the few Finnish ceramists to have worked consistently with domestic earthenware clay, which is well-suited to ceramic sculpture. Kajander has a solid background and experience in its use, having trained with Finnish country potters, organized seminars on the topic at brick-manufacturing plants and created low-fired clay items with local women's groups in Africa.

Catharina Kajander's own production consists of large pots and sculptures which she hand-builds using the coil technique. Her pots are often enlarged, giant versions of everyday items such as teacups and jugs – some of them so huge that the artist herself can crawl into them. Quirky details and ornamentation give these objects additional character.

Kajander creates stylized patterns with the engobes and sgraffito; sometimes she polishes the leather hard surfaces, achieving distinct contrasts between glossy and matte textures. Her pieces are fired in a wood-burning, gas or electric kiln; some are then smoke-fired. The finished objects bring to mind archaeological finds from ancient South-American Indian cultures.

Kajander's big sculptures of female torsos bear witness to a strong personality, an artist who expresses her emotions through clay. In her imagery we meet woman as lover and mother but also as intellectual artist and professional. Kajander also pays homage to artists whom she admires, including dancer Jorma Uotinen, poet Leif Färdig and the Leningrad Cowboys rock band. With her own, strongly individual way with Finnish clay, Catharina Kajander has made important advances in her field.

> *Kiss by the maker,* Catharina Kajander and her pot in 1968. Photo: Ilmari Kostiainen.

>> Large earthenware torsos by Catharina Kajander, 2003. Photo: Katja Hagelstam.

v Earthenware by Catharina Kajander, 2000. Photo: Catharina Kajander.

Marjukka Pietiäinen

■ Born in Kuusankoski 1945

■ University of Art and Design Helsinki, ceramics 1964–68, fashion design 1971–74

■ Group workshop Keramiikkakellari 1973–80, Pot Viapori 1980–88

■ Studio in Helsinki 1988 onwards

Marjukka Pietiäinen prefers hand-building with the slab technique to wheel-throwing. She shapes thin clay slabs into platters, goblets and sculptures, decorating them with engobes or pigments. With different techniques she creates free-form ornaments full of rhythm and movement. In later years her work has leaned towards more geometric and austere forms. For over ten years, Marjukka Pietiäinen has also been a teacher at the Helsinki Swedish Adult Education Centre, and has exhibited her work widely.

Letters from Suraya I–III, sculptures in slab technique by Marjukka Pietiäinen for the thirtieth anniversary exhibition of Pot Viapori at the Arabia Museum Gallery, 2002. Photo: Johnny Korkman.

Ulla Fogelholm

In her student days Ulla Fogelholm was one of the founders of group workshop Keramiikkakellari.[1] In the intervening thirty years, Finnish ceramic art has undergone tremendous developments; similarly, Fogelholm's own production has evolved towards a marked individuality. Her utilitarian stoneware has simple, purposeful forms and a focus on opulent, richly structured glazes.

Fogelholm's recent work has increasingly absorbed Japanese aesthetics. Her rectangular plates complement the round dishes created on the wheel. She has cooperated with a Japanese tea ceremony association in Finland and made tableware for a Japanese restaurant in Helsinki. Her ceramics have been shown at regional exhibitions as well as in foreign galleries.

■ Born in Helsinki 1945

■ University of Art and Design Helsinki: evening school 1967–68, ceramics dept. 1968–72

■ Group workshop Keramiikkakellari 1971–*c.* 1984

■ Studio in Helsinki 1984 onwards

■ Works in the Design Museum, Helsinki, the Ostrobothnian Museum, Vaasa, the Finnish Ministry for Foreign Affairs and the Craft Museum of Finland, Jyväskylä

Stoneware by Ulla Fogelholm, 2002.
Photo: Johnny Korkman.

Karin Widnäs

Studio design

- Born in Helsinki 1946

- University of Art and Design Helsinki, ceramics dept., 1970–76

- Studio in Helsinki 1978–94, Fiskars 1995 onwards

- Swedish Adult Education Centre of Helsinki, head teacher in art 1989–2003

- Works in the Design Museum, Helsinki, the Finnish Government collection, the Craft Museum of Finland, Jyväskylä, the Höganäs Ceramics Museum and Baker University, USA

- First prize, Pukkila tile decoration competition 1975; honorary mentions: Zagreb Ceramics Triennial 1993, 'Orton Cone Box Show', USA 1994 and Miyagi, Japan 1995

Karin Widnäs's long career has gone through many stages: she has made cast functional items and hand-built unique sculptures, experimenting with various materials and firing techniques. She has fired work in electric, raku and wood-burning kilns, using pure-white casting clay as well as Finnish red clay. For many years she has shared her knowledge of materials and techniques in her capacity as a much appreciated teacher. In later years Widnäs has concentrated on studio work and product design.

Since moving to the craft and cultural centre of Fiskars in 1995, Widnäs has successfully collaborated with craftsmen in the village. Among designs that show influences from trips to the Far East is a tea set with handles made of hazel. She has also created oil lamps and eco-friendly storage jars. In addition to purely functional objects, Widnäs has designed small decorative boxes. Nature, particularly the sea and the archipelago, has always been a major source of inspiration for her. Lately Karin Widnäs has increasingly cooperated with architects and designed ceramic tiles for use in private and public interiors. Her solo exhibition in 2000 in the Arabia Museum Gallery presented bricks and shaped tiles using various techniques.

Stoneware tea set by Karin Widnäs with handles in hazelwood from Fiskars. Photo: Ture Westberg.

A wall of handmade terracotta bricks at Karin Widnäs's home and studio, 1994. Photo: Winfrid Zakowski.

Kerttu Horila

Powerful emotion

- Born in Iisalmi 1946

- University of Art and Design Helsinki: evening school 1965–68, ceramics dept., 1968–72

- Studio in Rauma, 1972 onwards

- Reliefs at Rauma health centre, Laitila Town Hall and Merikarvia Municipal Building

- Works in Kiasma, the Wäinö Aaltonen Museum of Art, the Oulu City Art Museum, the Design Museum, Helsinki, and the Finnish Government collection

- Third prize, Biennial of the Gulf of Bothnia 1983; first prize, Raisio sculpture competition 1986; Western Finland medal 1987

Although trained as a ceramist, Kerttu Horila has participated more actively in events organized by the Finnish Sculptors' Association than in design exhibitions. From the outset she made thrown jugs and plates, but soon turned her focus to ceramic sculpture. Her imposing human figures, hand-built in red earthenware or stoneware, immediately aroused the interest of both the public and art critics. Hers was a powerfully feminist standpoint, carried out with manly authority, self-confidence and impressive technical virtuosity.

Kerttu Horila's ceramic sculptures have woman as their central motif, analysed from a personal viewpoint.[1] Her large, realistic female figures communicate with each other, with their mirror images and with paintings inspired by famous portraits of women from the past. Horila is also a painter and often combines her sculptures with variations on works by artists such as Georges de la Tour or Caravaggio.

Viewers seldom remain unaffected by the powerful emotional charge conveyed by Horila's work. With a liberating, ironic sense of humour and a pinch of the absurd she portrays the joys and pains of being a woman, always avoiding the excessively grotesque. Horila's sculptures are not idealized: they represent the heroines of everyday life, warts and all. Her creative flow has engendered over twenty solo exhibitions and several commissions for large public pieces.

Women's Room, an installation by Kerttu Horila, 1998. Private collection. Photo: Kerttu Horila.

Marja-Riitta Salama
The warmth of red clay

Marja-Riitta Salama (née Huhtalo) has worked with diverse types of clay, but her principal choice is earthenware. Fresh out of university, she made wheel-thrown functional ware inspired by traditional pottery: jugs and mugs with a shiny, transparent glaze applied to their ochre surface. However, her solo exhibitions in Helsinki have mostly consisted of large, hand-built sculptures in domestic red clay. They often display geometric slip ornamentation in blue-grey and browny black, contrasting with the terracotta-coloured clay. Salama's works have been exhibited in Sweden, Britain, Russia and France, and she has been a ceramics teacher since the 1970s.

■ Born in Helsinki 1946

■ University of Art and Design Helsinki: ceramics dept. 1970–74, textile dept. 1973–75, teacher 1985–95

■ Studio in Helsinki, 1975 onwards

Second Encounter, coiled earthenware sculptures by Marja-Riitta Salama, 1998. Height 69–77 cm. Photo: Jukka Mäntynen.

Irma Weckman

- Born in Nurmijärvi 1946

- University of Art and Design Helsinki, ceramics dept., 1979–84

- Arabia art dept., traineeship, 1984–85

- Reliefs at Nurmijärvi Secondary School, Koulumäki School and Karakallio Activity Centre, Espoo

- Works in the Arabia Museum, the Applied Art Museum, Tallinn, and the collections of the City of Espoo, the University of Art and Design Helsinki and the Finnish Ministry for Foreign Affairs

Many of today's ceramists in Finland master several materials and techniques. One of these versatile artists is Irma Weckman, who is equally comfortable with stoneware or earthenware. She fires her work using both electric and wood-burning kilns, sometimes even in a primitive earth pit. The public knows her best for thrown onion-shaped vessels as well as plates and pots with impressive copper-red oxblood glazes. Urns fired in an earth pit have played an important part in large installations used by the artist to investigate the fragility of the medium and the boundaries of life.

In addition to her own creative work, Irma Weckman is in charge of directing operations at Septaria Ceramics Centre, founded in 1990 at the Cable Factory in Helsinki. The centre offers ceramics courses at various levels, sale of materials and a ceramics gallery. When the TAIKO association named Irma Weckman Craftsman of the Year in 1999, it was not only for her work as a ceramist but also to acknowledge her contributions for the benefit of Finnish ceramic art.

Homesick, installation by Irma Weckman for Galleria Septaria, 1997. Photo: Ulla Paakkunainen.

Suku Park

The Finnish public has had many occasions to enjoy Suku Park's ceramics exhibitions. The ceramist's talents encompass a broad range, from industrial design to ceramic art, and consequently his works include everything from utilitarian china to unique stoneware sculptures. They are all remarkable for their technical execution and artistic confidence.

Suku Park was already well known as a ceramist in Sweden when he moved to Finland to take up the post of artistic director at Pentik Novus in Lapland. Later he became an independent studio ceramist who actively participated in Finnish design exhibitions. Born and bred in a country with a long tradition in ceramics, he was a welcome addition to the Finnish art arena. Suku Park remained in Finland until 2002, when he was appointed Professor at Sangmyung University in Seoul

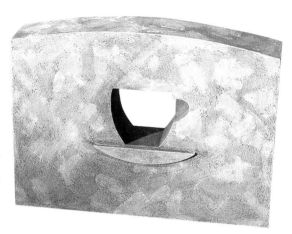

■ Born in Seoul, Korea, 1947

■ College of Fine Arts, Seoul National University, 1966–70, International Art School, Stockholm, 1974–76

■ Studio in Stockholm 1977–84, Espoo 1987–95, Fiskars 1995–2002

■ Works in the National Museum, Stockholm, the National Museum of Contemporary Art, Seoul, the Röhss Museum, Gothenburg and the Ariana Museum, Geneva

■ Prime Minister's Prize, 2nd National Arts & Crafts Exhibition, Seoul; Special Honorable Prize, Korean National Fine Arts Exhibition, Seoul

Stoneware sculpture by Suku Park.
Photo: Suku Park.

Anri Tenhunen

Since 1981 Anri Tenhunen has had a studio in Lahti, where she makes wheel-thrown domestic earthenware fired in an electric kiln. Her undecorated works take functional forms and have been exhibited on several occasions in Finland and elsewhere.

■ Born in Lahti 1947

■ Reino Tamminen's studio, Hollola: traineeship, 1977–81

Riitta Alho

Riitta Alho's work methods include wheel-throwing, slab technique and press-moulding. She favours the use of stoneware, onto which she often applies matte green and blue glazes. Her exhibitions in Finland have attracted critical attention – for her geometric, slab-built cactus vases, for instance. In the late 1990s she also made prominent smoke-fired sculptures inspired by mountains.

■ Born in Tampere 1947

■ University of Art and Design Helsinki, 1969–74

■ Studio in Lisbon, 1981–85, Pot Viapori group workshop, 1988–99

Åsa Hellman

Mediterranean breezes

- Born in Porvoo 1947

- University of Helsinki, art history, 1967–69

- University of Art and Design Helsinki, ceramics dept.: studies 1969–73, teacher 1983–87

- University of Belgrade, Faculty of Applied Arts, 1974–75

- Royal College of Art, London, ceramics dept., 1978–79

- Reliefs on cruiser Birka Princess and at Kårböle primary school

- Works in the Victoria & Albert Museum, the National Museum, Stockholm, the Norwegian National Museum of Decorative Arts, Trondheim, the Röhss Museum, Gothenburg , and the Design Museum, Helsinki

- National Design Award 1982; City of Porvoo cultural award 1997; Stina Krook Foundation award 2002

Since her early childhood, Åsa Hellman has spent her summers in southern Europe, mostly in Provence. Her interests include the ancient Mediterranean, encompassing Egyptian, Islamic and Grecian art, and museum visits provide important sources of inspiration. The Mediterranean influence in Hellman's work distinguishes it from other contemporary trends and typically Finnish ceramics.

Hellman is drawn to large formats and uses robust colours and lustre accents on her sculptures, reliefs, floor vases and plates. Her works frequently combine throwing and hand and slab-building techniques. Hellman achieves varied surface structures with the use of tools and creates decorative patterns by applying colourful engobes. Transparent glazes fired at around 1,200 °C bring out the intensity of the colours, whilst a third lustre-firing process at around 750 °C achieves impressive effects akin to mother-of-pearl and metallic copper. The artist consciously ignores the limitations of the medium, choosing instead to see the infinite possibilities within ceramics.

Two of Hellman's most recent exhibitions presented large, figurative ceramic sculptures with motifs taken from Greek

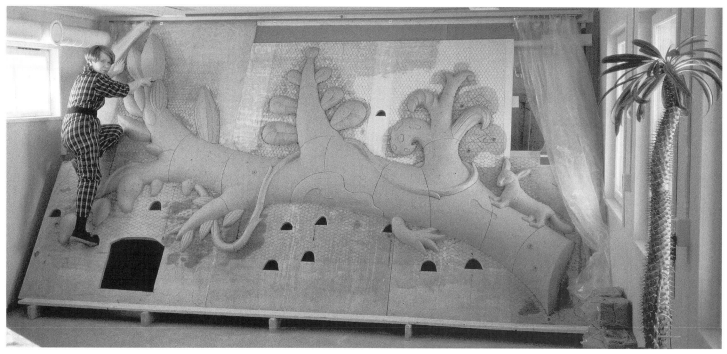

mythology. About the exhibition 'Greek Gods in Clay' (*Grekiska gudar i lera*), critic Carla Enbom wrote: 'Åsa Hellman captures the vitality of a world unknown to us and presents it with a natural self-evidence.'[1]

While living in Helsinki, Hellman worked with the Pot Viapori group between 1973 and 1993. She now lives in Porvoo and works in a garden studio. Since 1968 she has also been a freelance art writer.

<< *Two Fish*, relief on a pitcher with engobes and lustre by Åsa Hellman, mid-1990s. Private collection. Photo: Johnny Korkman.

∠ Åsa Hellman working on *The Traveller*, a relief commissioned by the Helsinki City Arts Council for Kårböle Primary School in 1995. Photo courtesy of Åsa Hellman.

< *Siren I,* a stoneware sculpture by Åsa Hellman, 1997. Height 75 cm. Saastamoinen Foundation. Photo: Johnny Korkman.

Kati Tuominen-Niittylä

From concept to form

- Born in Helsinki 1947

- University of Art and Design Helsinki, ceramics dept., 1972–76

- Studio in Helsinki, 1977–80

- Arabia, 1980 onwards

- Works in Hetjens Museum, Düsseldorf, the Arabia Museum, the Victoria & Albert Museum, the Röhss Museum, Gothenburg, and the New Ceramic Museum, Tajimi, Japan

- National Design Award 1984; Design Plus award, 'Ambiente Frankfurt' 1994; Formland Prize, Denmark 1994; Grand Prix and honorary mention, Mino 1998; gold medal and honorary mention Mino 2002

Kati Tuominen-Niittylä has been a designer for Arabia since 1980. Although her studio is located in the factory, she actively pursues an independent career and organizes her own exhibitions.

Tuominen-Niittylä makes thrown and hand-built objects. Her material – high-fired, often coarse stoneware clay – has a strong presence in her work. The vitrified stoneware appears almost geological with earthy, natural colours ranging from terracotta to metallic black. Her shapes are simple and solid, with beaks and strong handles creating angles and curves that give character to each piece. A slight degree of asymmetry makes tall jugs appear to flex their spines, bow down, bend or stretch. Their surfaces are often patinated with colouring oxides or carved with tools.

The artist's thrown plates display a powerful centrifugal force in the form of spiralling traces in the soft clay. Her solid, wide-bottomed, handled pots, however, are hand-built using the coil technique and have a more static feel.

Within the ceramics profession, Tuominen-Niittylä strikes an exciting balance between industrial design and independent artwork. The former requires visual planning, observing the strictures set by the industry, whereas the latter allows for spontaneity and individual realization. This dualism creates a stimulating interaction that makes up the foundation of Tuominen-Niittylä's art. It is also evident that her works, in spite of their contemporary character, in many ways lean on traditions of the golden age of Finnish design and Arabia's art department.

∧ Hand-built jar by Kati Tuominen-Niittylä, 2001. Height 30 cm. Private collection. Photo: Timo Kauppila.

< Plate by Kati Tuominen-Niittylä, 1999. Diameter 50 cm. Private collection. Photo: Timo Kauppila.

>> 'Perspective II' exhibition by Kati Tuominen-Niittylä at the Arabia Museum Gallery in 2001. Photo: Timo Kauppila/ Arabia Museum.

Hannu Matilainen

- Born in Kemi 1947

- University of Art and Design Helsinki, ceramics dept., 1968–72

- Art award of the Arts Council of Kymi, 2001

Since 1975 Hannu Matilainen has shared a studio in Hamina with his wife Raila Vainonen. He creates unique sculptures with clay, steel and brass. His work also incorporates glass, and his sculptures resemble poles or slender bars. Hannu Matilainen's work can be found at the Design Museum in Helsinki, the Finnish Ministry for Foreign Affairs and the collections of the cities of Hamina, Kotka and Porvoo.

Henrik Gröhn

- Born in Helsinki 1947

- University of Art and Design Helsinki, ceramics dept.: studies 1969–73, head teacher 1982–87

- Media Centre Lume, director, 1998–2001

As head of the ceramics department at the University of Art and Design Helsinki, Henrik Gröhn brought in teaching reforms that sharpened the focus on free artistic creation. He invited foreign artists to the faculty, opening new perspectives for his students, and improved degree curricula and the adoption of information technology. Under his direction the department moved twice to progressively larger premises. Since 1970 Gröhn has worked in a studio in Ylike, near Porvoo, slab-building individual ceramic objects. Since 2001, he has held an important post at the Swedish-language programme section of the Finnish Broadcasting Company.

Tapio Yli-Viikari

- Born in Polvijärvi 1948

- University of Art and Design Helsinki, ceramics dept.: studies 1970–74, Professor 1987 onwards

- Arabia: designer 1976–78, director of art and design departments 1978–87

- Works in the Arabia Museum, the Design Museum, Helsinki, the Museum of Modern Art, New York, Northern Arizona University Art Museum and Shiwan Ceramic Museum, Guangdong, China

- National Design Award for *Kokki* pan series, 1978

Tapio Yli-Viikari has held several important professional positions in Finnish ceramics. As the head of the glass and ceramics department of the University of Art and Design Helsinki, he sought to deepen the education offered in ceramic art and product planning through extensive research. He has stressed the importance of international contacts and initiated several international ceramics symposia, including Clay Az Art 1986, Interaction in Ceramics 1992 and Networks in Ceramics 1996. In addition, Yli-Viikari has created unique ceramics, which have been widely exhibited.[1]

Olavi Marttila

In his student days in the early 1970s, Olavi (Olli) Marttila was one of the founders of group workshop Keramiikkakellari in Helsinki. Between 1979 and 1982 he made functional ware and small sculptures in earthenware clay at his studio in Laihia. Marttila is best known as a painter, with several pieces in Finnish museums. He has taught painting at Orivesi College since 1983.

- Born in Jalasjärvi 1948
- University of Oulu, architecture dept., 1967–69
- University of Art and Design Helsinki, ceramics dept., 1969–73

Earthenware bowl with painted slip ornamentation by Olavi Marttila, 1970s. Diameter 34 cm.
Private collection.
Photo: Johnny Korkman.

Meri Saarnio

Since 1977 Meri Saarnio has been working in Porvoo, in a workshop in the heart of the old town. She rolls out clay for rectangular and square plates in red clay and stoneware. She also creates brightly decorated bird sculptures and serially produced, thrown traditional wares in red clay.

- Born in Helsinki 1949
- University of Art and Design Helsinki, ceramics dept., 1968–72

Maila Klemettinen

■ Born in Saari 1948

■ University of Art and Design Helsinki: evening school 1967–70, ceramics dept. 1970–72

■ University of Helsinki, political science, 1974

■ Croydon College of Art and Design, 1984–85

■ First prize, Stockmann Design competition, functional ware series 1986; honorary mention, Church of Finland grave monument competition, 1989; third prize, Hackman design competition 1993

Maila Klemettinen creates hand-built works using a variety of techniques. Her sculptural pieces, including large reliefs, are often carried out in smoke-fired earthenware or raku clay. She has participated in exhibitions in Finland and abroad, and her work can be found in collections including those of the Design Museum in Helsinki, the Craft Museum of Finland, the City of Kotka, the Shigaraki Ceramic Cultural Park Museum in Japan, the International Museum of Ceramics in Faenza and the Association AIR-Vallauris in France.

Unnamed, sculpture consisting of 36 raku-fired pieces by Maila Klemettinen, 1998. Each piece c. 40 x 30 x 10 cm. Photo: Maila Klemettinen.

Riitta Siira

■ Born in Hausjärvi 1948

■ University of Art and Design Helsinki, ceramics dept.: studies 1970–73, teacher 1973–89

■ Group workshop Seenat in Palojoki, 1976–96

■ Art award of the Arts Council of Uusimaa (for Seenat), 1993

In 1976 Riitta Siira (née Pensanen) established group workshop Seenat together with Terhi Juurinen and Lea Klemola.[1] For many years she has been a part-time teacher and lecturer at the University of Art and Design Helsinki ceramics department. She has had a studio in Tuusula since 1997.

Maija Vainonen-Gryta

Maija Vainonen-Gryta works with several materials, including bronze, stone, wood and paper clay. Her ceramic work consists of sculptures, reliefs and installations, and she has also participated in theatrical and performance projects. As a member of the Finnish Sculptors' Association she is more readily associated with art than design. Her work can be seen in the Design Museum, Helsinki, the Finnish Government collection, the City of Riihimäki, Eläke-Fennia and the Kuopio Lutheran congregation. She has also exhibited her works internationally.

■ Born in Kuusankoski 1948

■ University of Art and Design Helsinki, ceramics dept., 1972–76

■ Group workshop Pot Viapori, 1975–76

■ Moscow School of Industrial and Applied Art, ceramics dept., 1976–77

■ Studio in Riihimäki, 1980 onwards

■ Academy of Fine Arts, teacher, 1986 onwards

More White than Black Nodes, a series of twelve paper clay items by Maija Vainonen-Gryta, 2003. Height 4–5 cm. Photo: Johnny Korkman.

Heikki Rahikainen

Having worked in Lahti for several years, Heikki Rahikainen moved to Verkkosaari in Helsinki, where he has had a studio since 2003. Experiments with most types of materials, techniques and firing methods led to a preference for throwing and wood firing. His creative work is based on the study of form through series of teapots in varied shapes as well as vases, bowls and platters, some of them unique pieces. Rahikainen has had commissions for Lahti city library and the Mukkula underpass, and received the Pro Arte Tawastica award in 1997.

■ Born in Sippola 1948

■ University of Art and Design Helsinki, ceramics dept., 1969–75

■ Ruukkumaakari Oy, Messilä, product director, 1975–78, studio in Lahti, 1985–2000

■ Works in the Design Museum, Helsinki, the Arabia Museum, the Finnish Government collection, Lahti Art Museum and Lahti City Museum

Raila Vainonen

■ Born in Vehkalahti 1948

■ University of Art and Design Helsinki: studies 1970–74, postgraduate studies 1995–98

■ Studio Vainonen-Matilainen in Hamina, 1975 onwards

Raila Vainonen works in various materials, combining for instance stoneware with light steel elements and ceramic serigraphy in her sculptural work. A fanciful multimedia piece includes serigraphy and musical animation. Vainonen's work has been purchased by the Design Museum in Helsinki, the Finnish Ministry for Foreign Affairs and the cities of Kotka, Hamina and Kouvola.

Raila Vainonen's 1998 multimedia animation *Evidence* transfers the outlaw technique of graffiti to ceramic stone, to the sounds of the guitar piece *Adelita*.
Photo: Raila Vainonen.

Eeva Turunen

Eeva Turunen's sculptures evoke a bygone age: rural Finland in the 1950s. Her red-clay statuettes, thirty to forty centimetres tall, depict the everyday lives of women, often revealing a warm, witty undertone. Animals, especially cats, also appear in her work. Lately she has been occupied with miniature figures, four to five centimetres in height, formed in a non-pliable clay that vitrifies, creating a natural glaze during firing. Turunen has had several solo exhibitions in Finland and participated in shows abroad. Since 1978 she has been working at her studio in Artjärvi.

■ Born in Joensuu 1948

■ University of Art and Design Helsinki: evening school 1968–71, ceramics dept. 1972–77

∧ *Woman with Book* by Eeva Turunen, 2003.
Height 35 cm. Photo: Nanna Salmi.

> *Diver*, miniature sculpture by Eeva Turunen, 2003.
Porcelain and glass. Height 5 cm. Photo: Nanna Salmi.

Pirkko Räsänen-Borgers

■ Born in Lahti 1949

■ University of Art and Design Helsinki, ceramics dept., 1970–74

■ Studio in Helsinki, 1972–88

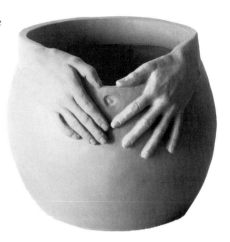

Pirkko ('Pike') Räsänen(-Borgers) co-founded the Keramiikkakellari group workshop when she was a student. For almost ten summers between 1982 and 1991, she also worked at the Gamla Mejeriet workshop in Fagervik, western Uusimaa, where she made thrown functional ceramics in stoneware as well as a number of unique pieces. She now lives in the Netherlands all year round, where her own studio, Pottenbakkerij De Witte Driehoek, has been operating in Schoorl since 1992. She has participated in exhibitions in Finland and the Netherlands.

Expectation, earthenware pot by Pirkko Räsänen-Borgers, 1978. Photo: HS-Lehtikuva.

Pauli Partanen

■ Born in Helsinki 1949

■ University of Art and Design Helsinki, ceramics dept., 1971–77

■ École Nationale Superieure Des Arts Décoratifs, Paris, 1977–79

■ Paris American Academy, 1978

■ Arabia art dept., 1979–84

Pauli Partanen dedicates himself exclusively to unique objects, principally stoneware sculptures made of clay slabs. He builds pieces from soft, undulating clay slabs that combine to form free compositions. Powerful female figures follow the shape of the sculptures, covering a large part of their surfaces. He carves into the clay, accentuating lines in black; bright glazes and metallic lustres in various shades cover the images. His work relies on marked contrasts and material effects.

Since 1980 Pauli Partanen has had a studio in central Helsinki. He has shown work in Finland and abroad and organized over twenty solo exhibitions. His work can be found at the Arabia Museum, the Porvoo Museum, the Design Museum in Helsinki, the Finnish Glass Museum and Paulon säätiö foundation.

Slab-built vase with lustre glaze by Pauli Partanen, 2000. Photo: Pauli Partanen.

Erkki Stenius

Lush oxblood glazes

In contrast to most workshops, Erkki Stenius's studio has been accessible and open to the public right from the beginning. Several ceramics students have completed traineeships there, and Stenius has welcomed qualified ceramists needing a place to work. The studio consists of a spacious area with three wheels and four electric kilns allowing several people to work simultaneously. It also houses a shop and an exhibition gallery. The heart of the workshop is a wood-burning kiln located in the garden, where each firing requires around twelve hours' teamwork, making it an enjoyable social event. In addition to administrative work for his company, Stenius finds time for the ongoing production of thrown domestic ware. As an artist he is best known for his unique wood-fired vases and plates with spectacular oxblood glazes.

■ Born in Helsinki 1949

■ University of Art and Design Helsinki, ceramics dept.: studies 1971–75, teacher 1978–83

■ Savitorppa enterprise, 1972–86

■ Studio in Tapanila, 1978 onwards

■ Helsinki Association for Handicraft and Industry award, 2002

Wheel-thrown, wood-fired pot with copper red glaze by Erkki Stenius, 2002. Height 30 cm. Private collection. Photo: Johnny Korkman.

Outi Leinonen

Sensitive observer

- Born in Helsinki 1950

- University of Art and Design Helsinki, ceramics dept., 1969–75

- Group workshop Pot Viapori, 1975–76; studio in Helsinki, 1976 onwards

- Arabia and Pentik: freelance work, 1980s

- Group and solo exhibitions in Finland and abroad

- Works in the Design Museum, Helsinki, the Arabia Museum and the collections of the Finnish government and the cities of Helsinki and Espoo

- Wall reliefs at Käpylä Elementary School

Outi Leinonen can be singled out as a sensitive observer and analyst of nature and the environment. After graduation she joined Pot Viapori, a workshop on the island of Suomenlinna outside Helsinki. There she created miniature sculptures in stoneware portraying life on the island: the ferries, the shipyard, workers in the forgery and the shipyard's canteen. She also made animal sculptures, including commissioned dog portraits in clay.

In her studio in Herttoniemi, Helsinki, Leinonen continues to create works of art based on observations of her immediate surroundings. She favours stoneware but will also use paper clay and occasionally smoke-fired red clay. She replicates details from nature: seeds, seashells, fossils and objects found on beaches. A leitmotif is the tortoise shell, scarred with evidence of a lived life. In addition she reproduces everyday domestic objects, such as a pair of worn-out slippers or a sun-bleached cotton hat. She pays special attention to surface structures and colours in order to mirror materials such as textiles, wood or leather faithfully. Leinonen achieves such bewildering realism that viewers may easily think that they are looking at the original objects. Thanks to her perceptive modelling and exquisite surface treatments, Outi Leinonen's sculptures often seem to be animate, with a soul of their own.

v Ceramic slippers by Outi Leinonen, 1999.
Photo: Johnny Korkman.

> *Cooking for the Crew*, miniature stoneware
sculpture by Outi Leinonen, 1976.
Photo: Johnny Korkman.

>> Outi Leinonen in her studio, surrounded by seeds,
watermelons and tortoises, 2001. Photo: Ilari Järvinen.

Erna Aaltonen

Weight and weightlessness

- Born in Loimaa 1951

- Kuopio Academy of Design, 1981–87

- Arabia, Pro Arte ceramist, 1987–88

- Studio Arteos in Tervakoski with Howard Smith, 1988–95; studio in Fiskars, 1996 onwards

- Works in the Arabia Museum, the Hämeenlinna Art Museum, the Höganäs Ceramics Museum, Sweden, Museum Keramik International, Römhild, Germany, and the Finnish and Swedish government collections

Erna Aaltonen works slowly, building up her pieces by hand from tiny coils. Through this tedious process she creates symmetrical, closed shapes which could be completed far faster on a wheel, but which – thanks to this technique – acquire a static peace and timelessness. At the same time Aaltonen's work can be described as truly earth-bound, like Egyptian burial urns, and weightless and otherworldly, resembling planets in space. Despite their weight, Aaltonen's pots appear to soar like upside-down balloons.

Aaltonen is best known for her spherical vases with narrow openings and rounded bottoms. Slight variations transform each vessel into a unique piece of art. These vases lack a functional use: they are in fact sculptures that borrow their shapes from pots, reflecting the cultural heritage of past millennia. The exclusive nature of these vessels is heightened with fascinating colours and structures; powerful blue, turquoise, ochre, pink and black glazes burst forth in grainy, mossy patterns reminiscent of geological strata and various minerals.

In addition to series of vases, Erna Aaltonen creates unique sculptures and reliefs in geometric shapes built up into larger compositions. A winding ribbon motif appears time and again in these works, bringing to mind prehistoric spiral ornaments and labyrinths. These pieces bear testament to the artist's profound knowledge of her field.

Erna Aaltonen outside her studio in Fiskars in 2003. Photo: Katja Hagelstam.

v *River*, wall relief by Erna Aaltonen, 1997. Length 150cm. Photo: Winfrid Zakowski.

>> Meticulously finished and glazed work by Erna Aaltonen, 2003. Photo: Johnny Korkman.

Savitorppa 1951–86

The Oy Atelier Nordquist Ab ceramic workshop was established in Nurmijärvi in 1951. In 1967 the name changed to Keramiikka-ateljee Savitorppa. As its products found buyers among opera-goers during the summer season at the Savonlinna Opera Festival in the 1970s, the studio experienced a marked increase in popularity and became known to a wide audience. The company was set up by Saul Nordqvist (1911–2003) and Holger Granbäck (1927–85); the former mainly did decoration work while the latter designed and threw the products. In its heyday Savitorppa employed five people in addition to its two founders.

The production consisted of wheel-thrown pots in red clay and faience, but slip-cast and press-moulded series were also made. Most products were decorative in a manner uncharacteristic of Finnish design, with brush-painted patterns and gold lustres. Saul Nordqvist and Holger Granbäck were self-taught and technical improvements were introduced in the 1970s by ceramist Erkki Stenius, a graduate of the University of Art and Design Helsinki. Several skilled, professional throwers were periodically employed by Savitorppa, including Garizim Hansen, Åke Kjellberg and Kauko Forsvik. Noteworthy among the studio's decorators are Lisbeth Holmström (employed 1951–55) and Eira Savolainen (employed 1955–58 and 1976–86). For a long time Savitorppa was popular with tourists, and its products were also sold at Artek and Stockmann in Helsinki.

Saul Nordqvist decorating a pot at Savitorppa. *c.* 1975.
Photo: Erkki Stenius.

Nina Karpov

Stylized forms

Three solo exhibitions arranged at the Design Forum gallery in Helsinki in 1995, 1997 and 2000 established Nina Karpov's renown as a purposeful and imaginative artist. She hand-builds unique items and small ceramic series with clays in various colours, including black, grey, terracotta and eggshell. Her shapes are simple, often geometric, and the austere execution coupled with natural tones brings to mind Japanese architecture. Karpov also transforms functional items into abstract objects, retaining their original nature. In addition to pieces planned for tables and walls, Karpov has created intricate sculptural installations – hanging 'swings' made of ceramic plates suspended at different levels.

■ Born in Pielavesi 1952

■ University of Art and Design Helsinki, ceramics dept., 1974–79

■ Studio in Helsinki, 1980 onwards

■ Espoo Adult Education Centre and Finnish Adult Education Centre of the City of Helsinki, teacher

■ Works in the Finnish Government collection

■ Exhibitions in Finland, Korea, Japan, Venezuela, Denmark and Iceland

■ Honorary mention, 'Suomi Muotoilee' 1991

The Beginning, coil-built object by Nina Karpov, 2000. Photo: Rauno Träskelin.

Swings by Nina Karpov, 1997. Photo: Rauno Träskelin.

Hilkka Niemi

- Born in Nokia 1952

- Tampere University of Technology, 1972–75; University of Helsinki, 1975–81

- University of Art and Design Helsinki, ceramics dept., 1981–87

- Works in Janakkalan Osuuspankki bank and the Pohjola Group

- Third prize, Kemira Oy tile relief competition 1986; second prize Posio Pot ceramic art series 1991

Hilkka Niemi is a member of the Kuuma Linja women artists' group which has been an active organizer of exhibitions in Finnish art museums since 1998. She has worked in three different studios in Helsinki, sharing a workshop with her colleague Kirsi Kivivirta since 1997.

Niemi makes sculptures and reliefs, which often form series with a common theme. She hand-builds pieces with stoneware clay and uses coloured glazes for decoration. Her works frequently consist of serial installations dealing with life's basic questions: human moods, natural forces, the universe. Studies in astronomy have led to the adoption of space and various astral phenomena as subjects, and from figurative motifs depicting people she has lately progressed to more abstract sculpture. Niemi's work has been seen at several exhibitions in Finland and further afield.

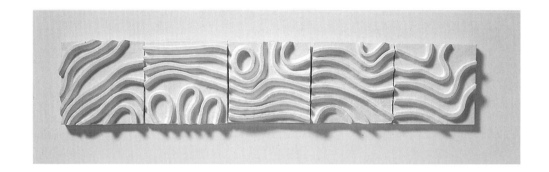

African-inspired relief by Hilkka Niemi, 2002.
Photo: Johnny Korkman.

Riitta Mattila

- Born in Helsinki 1953

- University of Art and Design Helsinki: ceramics 1977–81, art teaching studies 1993–98

- Studio Ronelle Frangoulis, Crete, 1981

- Pot Viapori group workshop, 1981–88

- First prize, 'Jugend Gestaltet', 'Exempla Munich' 1984

Riitta Mattila uses stoneware, raku and smoke-firing techniques to make sculptures in clay and other materials, including glass. In recent years her work has mostly consisted of environmental pieces and outdoor installations in natural and urban surroundings. In 1998 she was one of the founders of the Nomad-ryhmä group, dedicated to environmental art. Mattila has participated in design exhibitions in a number of countries.

Turkish Cemetery, installation by Riitta Mattila at Gjutars, 1998. Photo: Riitta Mattila.

Arja Martikainen

Arja Martikainen's large stoneware sculptures represent abstract imagery from the artist's realm of fantasy, although they are also reminiscent of primitive items such as cult objects or totem poles. Her largest pieces are 170 cm in height, slab-built – like most of her work – in stoneware clay and fired at 1,250 °C. Martikainen has had a studio in the old fortress area of Lappeenranta since 1982.

■ Born in Kuorevesi 1953

■ University of Art and Design Helsinki, evening school 1973–75, ceramics dept. 1975–79

■ Works in the Craft Museum of Finland, Jyväskylä, the Ceramics Museum in Barcelona, Museu de Ceràmica de Manises, Musée de Châteauroux and the Southern Karelia Art Museum

Pirjo Pesonen

Pirjo Pesonen creates abstract stoneware sculptures which she covers with pale underglaze colours. Her 2002 solo exhibition in Helsinki was aptly called 'At the Factory' (*Tehtaalla*) and featured sculptures reminiscent of machinery and tools. The Cable Factory in Helsinki has housed Pirjo Pesonen's studio since 1998.

■ Born in Helsinki 1953

■ University of Art and Design Helsinki, ceramics dept., 1976–81

Anne Virtanen

Anne Virtanen favours utilitarian ware, generally wheel-thrown or built using the slab technique. She uses stoneware, paper and raku clays, often combining ceramics with materials such as metal or wood. Virtanen specializes in sculptural yet functional teapots. She has worked at the Keramiikkakellari group workshop in Helsinki (1980–87) and at a studio in Karkkila (1987–99).

■ Born in Helsinki 1953

■ Lausanne University, psychology, 1973–76

■ Atélier de Céramique Testuz, Lausanne, 1976–80

■ Awards from annual Finnish household product competition, 1987 and 1990; honorary mention, Lappeenranta national teapot competition 1991

Merja Pohjonen

Merja Pohjonen focuses on thrown domestic earthenware pots with simple shapes based on traditional pottery. She decorates her pieces with slips and fires in both electric and wood-burning kilns. In 1987 she contributed a wall relief to Kirkonmäki day-care centre in Kokkola, and her work can also be found at K. H. Renlunds Museum and the Pohjola Group's offices.

■ Born in Helsinki 1955

■ University of Art and Design Helsinki: ceramics dept. 1976–80, teaching dept. 1988

■ Studio in Kokkola, 1985 onwards

Anneli Sainio

Contemplative presence

- Born in Helsinki 1953

- University of Art and Design Helsinki, ceramics, 1974–79

- Studio in Helsinki 1982–93, Fiskars 1994 onwards

- Works in the Finnish Government collection, the Finnish President's residence (Mäntyniemi), the Finnish Embassy, Warsaw, Neste Oy, Moscow, and the Wihuri Fund

- Suomi Award, 1998; Kaj Franck design award, 2002

Anneli Sainio began to work full-time as a ceramist in 1994, having been a teacher of the subject for almost twenty years. She moved from the capital to the Fiskars craft centre, which brings together an active group of artists, craftsmen and designers, and in a few years became an important name in Finnish ceramics.

Sainio's ceramics are based on simple, geometric forms created in a variety of materials, including porcelain, stoneware, raku, paper and earthenware clays. Her minimalist dinner sets derive from circles and squares, with round bowls on square bases. Her point of departure is always the functional purpose of the object, but her finished pieces give the impression of being simultaneously figurative and abstract.

Sainio works 'alone, calmly and without hurry'.¹ This is evident in her work, which is generally described as typically Finnish, but has also been strongly influenced by Japan. The artist has never visited Japan but her serene forms and natural surface treatments exude a contemplative presence reminiscent of Zen tea ceremonies. Nature is present in colours and structures, which also reflect the changing of the seasons. Thick white glazes shrink and create irregular, intricate patterns reminiscent of snow melting in early spring, while browny-black, metallic surfaces suggest deep woodland marshes. The foundations of Sainio's artistry lie in a natural feel for and knowledge of the material.

<< Anneli Sainio at work in her studio in 2003.
Photo: Katja Hagelstam.

Porcelain and raku pots by Anneli Sainio,
2003. Photo: Katja Hagelstam.

Pirkko & Timo Pajunen

Pirkko Pajunen was born in the town of Nokia in 1953 and studied at the University of Art and Design Helsinki ceramics department (1974–79). In addition to ceramics, she paints and shows her work at visual arts exhibitions and has also organized large ceramics events, including the 'Ceramega' exhibition at Voipaala art centre in 1996.

Timo Pajunen was born in Helsinki in 1953. He studied at the University of Art and Design Helsinki ceramics department (1975–79), where he also worked as a teacher (1981–89). Lately he has been involved with ceramics, graphic art and oil painting, and has participated in several exhibitions. Pirkko and Timo Pajunen are well known as teachers of ceramics and painting.

Satu Syrjänen

■ Born in Tampere 1953

■ Kankaanpää Art Institute, 1972–74

■ University of Art and Design Helsinki: ceramics 1978–82, teaching studies 1993–96

■ Studio in Tampere, 1975 onwards

Satu Syrjänen generally uses grogged stoneware clays and avails herself of several techniques, including throwing, coil- and slab-building and casting. Her versatility enables her both to design functional ware for serial production and to build unique sculptures. Satu Syrjänen's sculptural work reveals a geometric and constructivist approach to materials, and the spiral is a frequently recurring symbol. The Design Museum in Helsinki, the Archie Bray Foundation, USA, the Tampere Museum of Contemporary Art, the Finnish Ministry for Foreign Affairs and the Finnish Government collection have all acquired sculptures by Syrjänen.

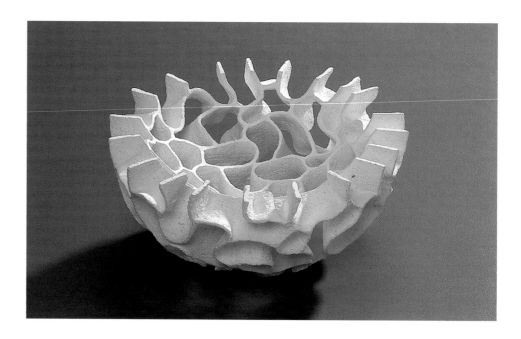

Sculpture by Satu Syrjänen in her *GEO* series, 2002.
Photo: Jukka-Pekka Juvonen.

Meeri Hiltunen

Meeri Hiltunen is an interior designer who has been active as a sculptor since the mid-1990s, with a focus on clay. She is attracted to larger units and architectural installations in the form of sculptures, reliefs and installations consisting of small, suspended ceramic elements. She uses a variety of clays and has experimented with mixing organic substances into the clay prior to firing. Her works are often composed of fragments depicting the passing of time, erosion and decomposition. Meeri Hiltunen is an experimenting and investigating artist who continuously stretches the boundaries of Finnish ceramics.

■ Born in Kaavi 1953

■ University of Art and Design Helsinki, interior design dept., 1974–81

■ Academy of Fine Arts, 1994–95

■ Finnish School of Ceramics, Posio, 1996

■ Works in Musée de Bertrand, France, Craft Space Mokkumto, Seoul and the collections of the Finnish Government and the universities of Helsinki and Turku

< *Fragments of Silence* by Meeri Hiltunen, 2001. Photo: Meeri Hiltunen.

∨ *Each Day is the Best*, smoke-fired earthenware by Meeri Hiltunen, 1999. 40 x 1200 x 3 cm. Photo: Juha Perämäki.

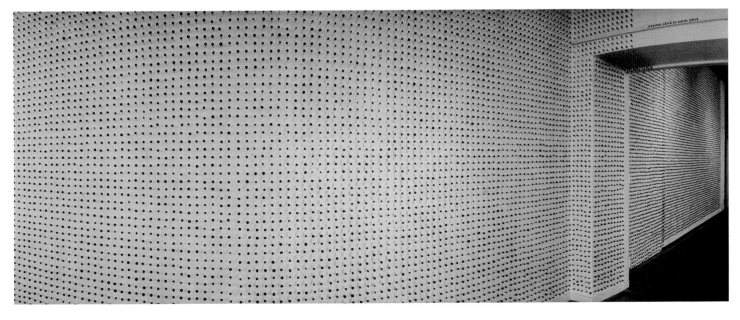

Judy Mäkelä

Delight in decoration

■ Born in Barnet, Hertfordshire, 1954

■ Amersham College of Art, ceramics and history of art, 1971–74

■ 'Workshop', Hackney, 1974–77

■ Studio Krukmejeriet in Mariehamn, 1993 onwards

Visit an old dairy in the centre of Mariehamn, the Åland islands, and you will find ceramist Judy Mäkelä at work. Mäkelä, née Judith Lynden Bradley, came to Finland in 1977 to develop her experience as an artist and now runs a successful ceramics enterprise with two employees.

Mäkelä's production consists of wheel-thrown functional objects decorated with coloured slips under transparent or matte glazes. Commissioned pieces by Mäkelä are found in the homes of many prominent people, including Finnish President Tarja Halonen. Mäkelä often takes part in design exhibitions with unique bowls and plates decorated with her characteristically stylized, original plant and animal motifs.

Wheel-thrown stoneware by Judy Mäkelä, 2003, recalling printed textile patterns of the 1950s. Photo: Rita Jokiranta.

Outi Särkikoski

Outi Särkikoski was an apprentice at two ceramic workshops before establishing her own studio in 1983. Like so many others, she began by making functional ware before turning to reliefs and sculptural objects, which she hand-builds out of various types of clay. Her vases, as tall as a man, are identical in form but have different colours and varied relief-like structures. Her works have been acquired by the Shigaraki Institute of Ceramic Studies, the City of Helsinki and the Posio International Coffee Cup Museum. Her ceramic reliefs can be seen at the North Karelia Central Hospital as well as Marjala day-care centre and Noljakka church, both in Joensuu, where Outi Särkikoski has worked since 1987.

■ Born in Kuusjärvi 1954

■ University of Art and Design Helsinki, graphic art dept., 1973–78

■ National Sculpture Factory, Cork, Ireland, 1998

■ Shigaraki Institute of Ceramic Studies, Japan, 2001

■ Second prize, Ornamo miniature artwork competition 1991; Veikko Jalava recognition award 2000; first prize, Northern Karelia regional hospital visual arts competition 2000; Northern Karelia Arts Council award 2002

Hand-built, low-fired *Winter Pots* by Outi Särkikoski, 1999. Height 120 cm. Photo: Outi Särkikoski.

The Berglöf Company

Tor Berglöf (born in Porvoo, 1921) studied at the Academy of Fine Arts between 1942 and 1944 but was more interested in interior design and ceramics. He returned to Porvoo in 1945 to manage his father's stonecutting and cement-casting business, and was married the same year to Ilma Berglöf (born in Jyväskylä, 1925). She had learnt glazing and firing techniques at a private ceramics studio in Helsinki and by attending various courses.

Family Celebration, tile arrangement by Tor Berglöf, 1975. 60 x 155 cm. Photo: Pasi Hornamo.

Tor and Ilma Berglöf began to manufacture ceramic items in the 1950s, initially as a hobby. They bought a small kiln in 1954. As the stonecutting company's office was located in the historic part of Porvoo they had good opportunities to sell souvenirs to passers-by and their operations grew. They began with small figurines but from the 1960s onwards Tor Berglöf also threw vases, bowls and jars. Tor produced while Ilma finished and decorated the work. Their company grew with the move of the actual workshop to larger premises by the Berglöfs' home and the installation of more kilns. Their production consisted mainly of earthenware but they also used stoneware clay, firing in electric as well as gas or wood-burning kilns. Some of the output was exported to Europe and the USA. In addition to small retail products, Tor Berglöf created large sculptures and wall plaques for private homes and cafés.

The couple's son, Kai Berglöf, born in Porvoo in 1946, was trained between 1967 and 1971 at the ceramics department of the University of Art and Design Helsinki, where he later worked as a teacher. Through his contact with the school, several of its students trained at Berglöf's in Porvoo, later to become ceramic artists. Kai's daughter Minna Sola has studied ceramics, so the future of the Berglöf family enterprise appears to be in safe hands.

Risto Hämäläinen

Risto Hämäläinen lives and works in the middle of a forest, far from any neighbours, where he strives for a stress-free existence in harmony with nature. He uses stoneware clay and fires in a large wood-burning kiln built to French ceramist Bernard Dejongh's design. Hämäläinen creates sculptural vases measuring up to 170 cm in height, with wheel-thrown bases and the rest built from coils. Their exciting patina is achieved through the use of copper-based glazes, which in a reducing atmosphere will create powerful blue and turquoise flambé effects. Risto Hämäläinen has had several solo exhibitions and has shown his ceramics in France, Germany, Spain and Denmark.

■ Born in Savitaipale 1954

■ Kuopio Academy of Design, 1980–85

■ Studio in Savitaipale, 1985 onwards

■ Works in the Ceramics Museum in Barcelona and the City of Chateauroux collections

Thrown and coiled, wood-fired sculptural vases by Risto Hämäläinen, 2001. Heights 160–170 cm. Photo: Pertti Rikkilä.

Johanna Rytkölä
Musical abstractions

■ Born in Helsinki 1956

■ University of Art and Design Helsinki: art teaching and ceramics, 1977–86

■ Studio in Vantaa, 1999 onwards

■ Works in the Arabia Museum, the Taipei Fine Arts Museum, Taiwan, the Northern Arizona University Art Museum and Galleries, the Finnish Government collection and the Youngone Corporation, Seoul

■ Arts Council of Uusimaa award for Esineitä group 1983; Award of Merit, Kutani International Decorative Ceramics Competition, Japan 1997; Medaglia d'argento del Presidente della Republica, Faenza 1995

When Johanna Rytkölä began to exhibit her work in the 1980s, she attracted immediate attention. The Finnish public had grown accustomed to associating sculpture with stone, bronze, plaster or wood. Even though Finnish ceramic artists frequently created clay sculptures, their works were generally seen in terms of design or decorative arts. Rytkölä's abstract works displayed a language of form more akin to traditional sculpture, while her grasp of ceramic techniques was clear.

The large-format sculptures of Johanna Rytkölä are especially appropriate for public spaces, but on a smaller scale her reliefs and plaques are, like paintings, well suited to domestic interiors. The abstract, hollow works are slab-built. Although she eschews the figurative, organic associations are evident – for example in the form of acanthus leaves. Other elements appear to have been gleaned from architecture; we glimpse arches, bridges and vaults. Further details echo the shapes of musical instruments.

Rytkölä's palette is deliciously tropical. She layers rose pink, lilac and yellow glazes, alternating matte and glossy surfaces. The glazes are allowed to flow freely into each other achieving unexpected and seemingly uncontrolled effects. Expressing graceful movement, her sculptures hint at music and dance. As an artist her identity is twofold: her Association of Finnish Sculptors colleagues embrace her as one of their own, whereas fellow members of the Finnish Association of Designers Ornamo see her as a ceramic artist.

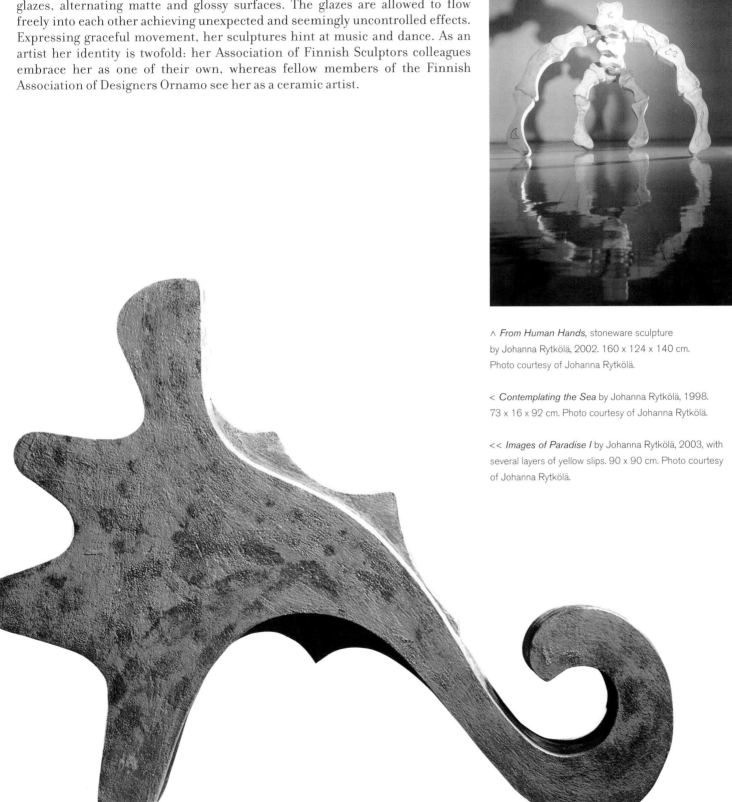

∧ *From Human Hands,* stoneware sculpture by Johanna Rytkölä, 2002. 160 x 124 x 140 cm. Photo courtesy of Johanna Rytkölä.

< *Contemplating the Sea* by Johanna Rytkölä, 1998. 73 x 16 x 92 cm. Photo courtesy of Johanna Rytkölä.

<< *Images of Paradise I* by Johanna Rytkölä, 2003, with several layers of yellow slips. 90 x 90 cm. Photo courtesy of Johanna Rytkölä.

Beni Juslin

■ Born in Porvoo 1957

■ Umeå ABF Art School, 1977–78; Capellagården School of Craft and Design, Sweden, ceramics dept. 1979–81

Bengt (Beni) Juslin worked as a full-time studio ceramist between 1981 and 2001. His first workshop on the island of Vessö was equipped with a wood-burning kiln; then, from 1997 to 2002, he ran a studio, shop and art gallery in the historic part of Porvoo together with his wife, ceramist Teija Laine. Juslin concentrated on utilitarian ware in light clay, richly decorated with bright pigments using the Majolica technique. Juslin has recently left ceramics to pursue a career in painting.

Eeva-Liisa Mölsä

■ Born in Nakkila 1957

■ Drawing School of the Turku Art Association, 1977–80

■ Kopijyvä Award, Jyväskylä Artists' Association annual exhibition, 1998

Sculptor Eeva-Liisa Mölsä alternates between the use of clay and wood. She learnt ceramic techniques by attending professional courses in the 1990s. She now works in a studio equipped with an electric kiln, though some of her sculptures are wood-fired. The artist's style is characterized by realistic animal and human motifs. Mölsä works and lives in Konnevesi and her work can be found at the Central Finland Hospital in Jyväskylä and the collections of the cities of Helsinki, Porvoo, Kemi and Jyväskylä.

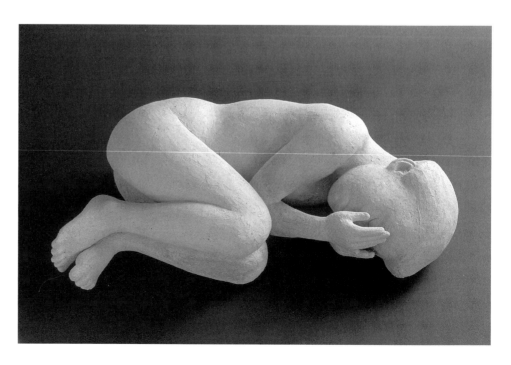

The Wicked World, stoneware sculpture by Eeva-Liisa Mölsä, 1996. 30 x 60 cm. Photo: Martti Kapanen.

Srba Lukić

Ceramist Srba Lukić creates stoneware sculptures and reliefs, which he decorates with ceramic stains with the brush technique and fires in an electric kiln at 1,270 °C. First he used dark, contrasting colours but in recent years he has developed a softer style with pastel shades. His ceramic reliefs can be seen in Lundi shopping centre in Porvoo and Oy Snacky Ab in Helsinki, among other places, and he has exhibited his work at several exhibitions in Finland and abroad.

Lukić lives and works in Porvoo, an important town in the history of Finnish ceramic art.[1] With his wife Tuula he organized five ceramics seminars between 1988 and 1996, with participants from more than thirty countries. These international meetings inspired Finnish ceramists and helped to create beneficial professional networks. Also, as a result, the city of Porvoo owns an excellent collection of modern ceramics donated by artists from over twenty countries, called the Iris Collection in remembrance of the Iris ceramics factory.[2]

■ Born in Vranje, former Yugoslavia, 1957

■ University of Belgrade, Faculty of Applied Arts: glass and ceramics, 1976–81

■ Kerman Savi, Heinävesi 1982–84; Sibbo 1984–86

■ Studio KASL-keramiikka, Porvoo, 1987 onwards; Savilinna Yhtiö, 1998 onwards

■ Organizer of international Iris seminars

■ Works in Muzej Moderne Jugoslovenske Keramike in Subotica, Yugoslavia

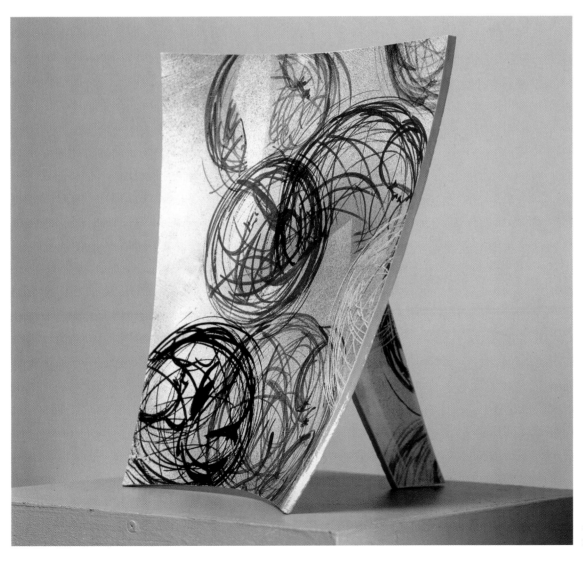

Prisoners of Time by Srba Lukić, 2000. Photo: Srba Lukić.

Jarmo Vellonen

- Born in Sääminki 1958

- Liminka Art School, 1978–79

- Academy of Fine Arts, sculpture, 1979–84

- Works in the collections of the Finnish Government and the City of Porvoo

- Second prize, international stone sculpture competition, Nanto, Italy, 1989

Sculptor Jarmo Vellonen favours stone but also uses glass, metal and clay. His large ceramic sculptures are often spatial installations, executed in coarse stoneware or terracotta clay, in an abstract style influenced by architecture. Jarmo Vellonen has several works in public spaces, including a sculpture at Porvoo city library. He works in a studio at Taidetehdas in Porvoo.

Impressio I, installation by Jarmo Vellonen, 1995. 12 x 250 x 240 cm.
Photo: Sakari Viika.

Paul Bradley

Åland-based ceramist Paul Bradley was born in Barnet, England, in 1958 and studied ceramics at Middlesex University. He moved to Finland in 1980 and now works at his sister Judy Mäkelä's enterprise, Krukmejeriet in Mariehamn. Bradley's own production consists of paper-clay sculptures built with the slab technique.

Merja Haapala
Dynamic artist

The eyes of the Finnish public were opened to the talents of Merja Haapala in 2000 when the Tampere-based ceramist was awarded the first prize in a large international ceramics competition held in Lappeenranta. One year later she exhibited in Helsinki on the themes of snow, sleep and sleeplessness. Her show consisted of sculptural compositions of stoneware 'snowballs' dyed with colourful pigments. She also displayed abstract reliefs created from small, cast elements.

Haapala's ceramics express her particular individuality, though influences from contemporary Western ceramic art can occasionally be seen. Her openness to current styles makes Haapala appear a more dynamic personality than most contemporary Finnish ceramists. She approaches her medium – stoneware clay – in an unprejudiced fashion and creates expressive ceramic pieces with varied techniques.

■ Born in Kankaanpää 1958

■ Kuopio Academy of Design, 1982–87

■ Studio in Tampere, 1987 onwards

■ Works in the Finnish Government collection, Nokia Telecommunications, the city of Tampere, the Posio International Coffee Cup Museum and the Villa Urpo Museum

■ Wall relief at Koivisto Primary School; altar set at Aitolahti church, Tampere

■ First prize for technique, Finnish throwing championships 1997; honorary mention, Mino, Japan 1998; first prize, Lappeenranta international pottery competition K'2000

Yellow Snow, sculpture by Merja Haapala, 2001. 34 x 38 x 33 cm. Photo: Jouko Järvinen.

Black Spots, stoneware teapot by Merja Haapala, 1999. Photo: Jouko Järvinen.

Kirsi Kivivirta
Bricks, tiles and architectural elements

■ Born in Turku 1959

■ University of Art and Design Helsinki, ceramics
dept.: studies 1980–85, teacher 1987–98

■ Studio in Helsinki, 1988 onwards

■ Member of Kuuma Linja women artists' group

■ Works in the Design Museum and the
collections of the Finnish Government, the
Finnish Ministry for Foreign Affairs, the Tapiola
group and Arabianranta

■ Arts Council of Uusimaa award to Esineitä group
1983; honorary mention, 'Finndesignnow' Design
Forum 2002

When it comes to colour and form, Kirsi Kivivirta gives an impression of restraint.
She lets her materials – various stoneware and porcelain clays – speak for themselves,
without assistance from glazes or bright pigments. Her forms are based on simple,
basic elements: rectangular and square bricks and variations on architectonic
supporting components or constructions. Calm, natural colours such as sand, ochre,
grey and eggshell contribute to the low-key look.

Kivivirta creates ceramic surfaces and walls. Some works centre around unique
sculptures and installations, others on serially manufactured tiles. These are
designed to be used in kitchens, bathrooms or public interiors such as restaurants
and cafes. Small variations in colour, shape and structure form interesting details
which distinguish Kivivirta's ceramic elements from their mass-produced, industrial
counterparts.

The Builder, a series of cut clay blocks
representing buildings by Kirsi Kivivirta, 1999.
Photo: Malla Hukkanen.

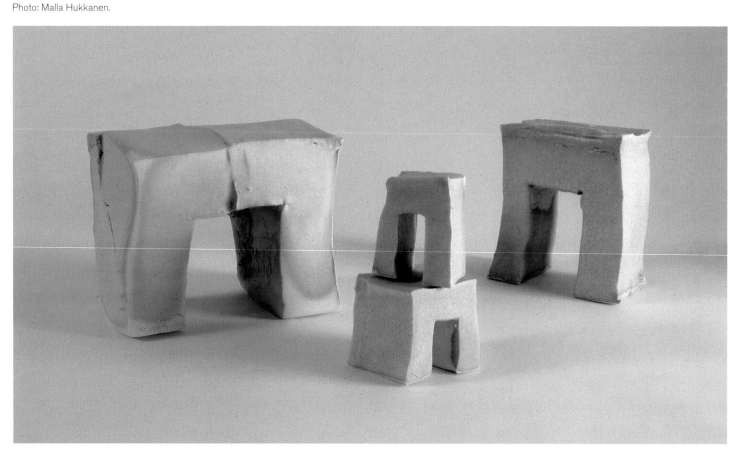

Tiina Veräjänkorva

Environment art

Tiina Veräjänkorva's environment art often combines ceramics with photographs or natural elements such as sand, grass, hay or soil. Her outdoor sculptures live and change together with the seasons, acquiring a blanket of snow in winter and leaves in autumn. Some of her work is reminiscent of garden paths, winding through nature; other pieces represent more austere architectural elements.

The materials in Veräjänkorva's sculptures and installations are earthenware and stoneware clays. She favours large formats and hand-builds simple base components which are then combined, adapting forms to their environments. Lately she has examined man's relationship with nature by contemplating gardens, which has led to exhibitions of ceramics related to gardens, landscape art and man's environment. Tiina Veräjänkorva also works as a freelance art and design writer.

■ Born in Pyhäjärvi 1959

■ Free Art School, Helsinki, 1984–86

■ University of Helsinki, degree in teaching and art history, 1987

■ University of Art and Design Helsinki, ceramics dept.: studies 1987–93, teacher and researcher 1995–2001

■ Studio in Vihti, 2003 onwards

■ Reliefs at Metsätalo and Taitotalo, Pitäjänmäki Vocational Institute, environmental artwork at Arabianranta

■ Member of Kuuma Linja women artists' group

∨ *The Garden* by Tiina Veräjänkorva from her series *Traces of Summer*, 1997.
Photo: Lasse Wallenius.

⌐ A work from the series *Garden Excerpts* by Tiina Veräjänkorva, 1998.
Photo: Raija Siikamäki.

Paula Blåfield

Whimsical Surrealism

■ Born in Vaasa 1960

■ University of Art and Design Helsinki, ceramics dept., 1980–85

■ Stundars ceramics studio, Korsholm 1985–2000

■ Studio in Vaasa 2000 onwards

■ Works in the Norwegian National Museum of Decorative Arts, Trondheim, the Ostrobothnian Museum, Vaasa, the Pro Artibus Collection and the cities of Nykarleby and Vaasa

■ Arts Council of Uusimaa award to Esineitä group, 1983

Paula Blåfield found her individual, simple technique early, avoiding the common pitfalls of frustrating material experiments and technical digressions. She uses stoneware clays and colourful engobes, glazing objects sparingly, if at all. She treats bisque fired surfaces with oxides, achieving dark, graphic-style effects in a final firing carried out at around 1,200 °C.

Blåfield is known for her whimsical, sometimes ambiguous sculptures, which appeal to people of all ages. Her subjects include wolves, horses and rabbits in period costume, but she also makes abstract pieces. In 2000 she arranged a solo exhibition of Surrealist houses that depicted various moods and two years later she organized a large retrospective exhibition. In 2004 she is to complete a big wall relief for Pietarsaari swimming pool.

The House of the Old Owl, sculpture by Paula Blåfield, 2000. 23 x 23 x 36 cm. Photo: Paula Blåfield.

Eliisa Isoniemi
Ceramic monotypes

Eliisa Isoniemi's ceramics bear witness to her graphic arts education. She rolls out clay containing thirty per cent paper into thin sheets, onto which she presses unique images: monotypes. She lays on ceramic pigments and oil colours containing metallic oxides, which change – partly burning off – in the firing. The kiln also burns away the paper content, resulting in porous and hard, yet fragile clay sheets.

The motifs in Isoniemi's ceramic monotypes consist of human figures – often female – which suggest various emotions, such as love, fear or longing. Human identity and development are also perceptively depicted. Eliisa Isoniemi is a rare ceramist in that she hardly ever creates three-dimensional work; instead her pictorial style makes use of graphic as well as ceramic techniques.

■ Born in Seinäjoki 1960

■ MA in theology, 1986

■ University of Art and Design Helsinki, 1988–94

■ Academy of Fine Arts, graphic art dept., 1992–93

■ Group workshop at Cable Factory, Helsinki, 2001 onwards

■ Member of Kuuma Linja women artists' group

■ Works in the Arabia Museum, Keuruu Art Museum, Paulon säätiö and the Finnish Government collection

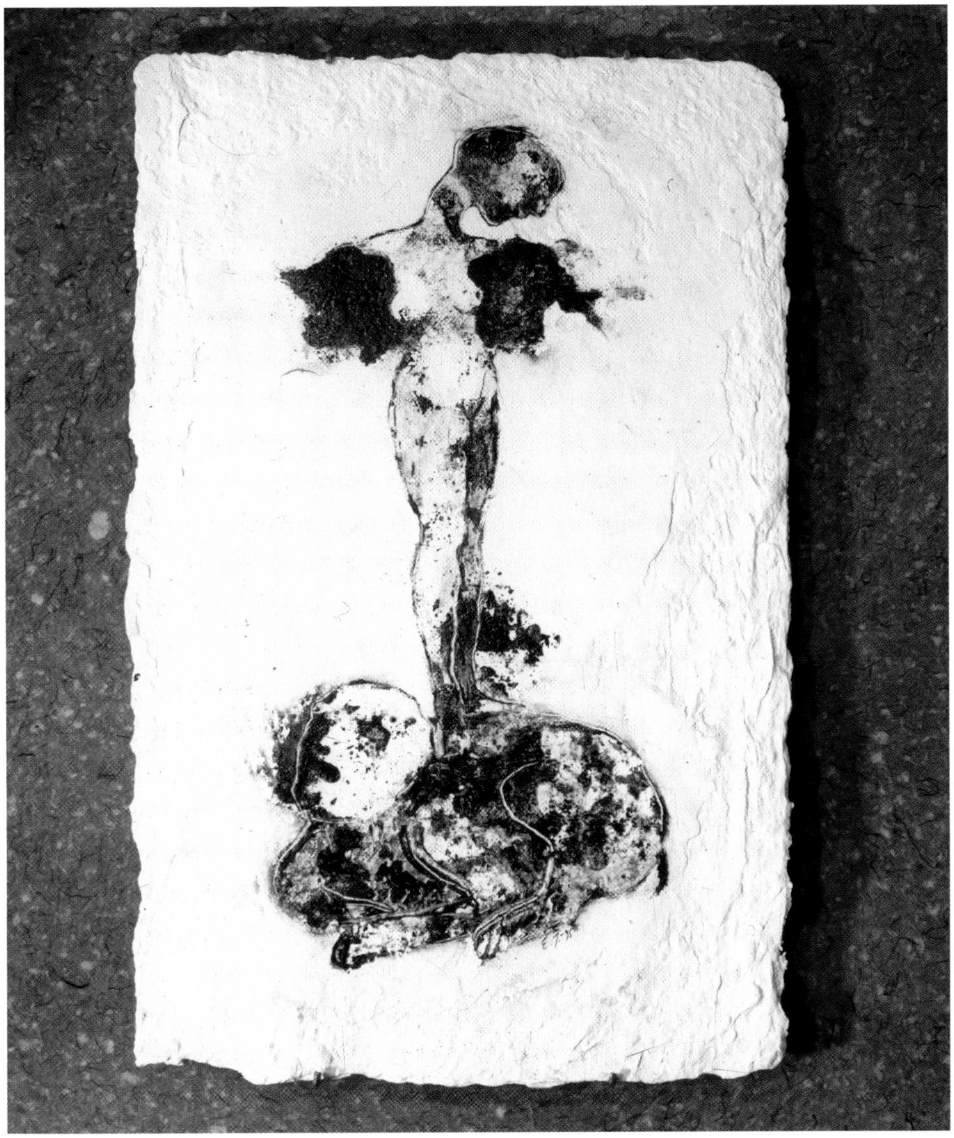

The Pursuit of Happiness, clay monotype by Eliisa Isoniemi, 1995, depicting the life and identity of a woman. Photo: Eliisa Isoniemi.

Pekka Paikkari

Fire and clay

■ Born in Orivesi 1960

■ Orivesi Institute, art studies, 1977–78

■ Kuopio Academy of Design, 1978–83

■ Humanities Polytechnic, Turku, 2000–3

■ Arabia: artist and designer, 1985 onwards

■ Works in the Arabia Museum, the Victoria & Albert Museum, the Shigaraki Ceramic Cultural Park Museum, the International Ceramics Museum in Faenza and the Höganäs Ceramics Museum

■ Third prize, Pasila courthouse art competition 1989; Fondazione Cassa di Risparmo di Ravenna, Faenza 1993

The material and the firing process are strongly present in Pekka Paikkari's work. He handles the malleable clay powerfully and intuitively, eschewing glazes and traditional ornamentation. Marks left by hands and tools in the wet and soft medium are sufficient for him. Firing in a reducing atmosphere contributes further, as the flames and smoke produce unexpected effects. Pekka Paikkari's insight into different reduction techniques has deepened through working trips to Japan and Korea.

Paikkari's ceramic production is notably sculptural, although some of his shapes seem to originate in vessels. Since 1985 his production has focused on large bottle-shaped sculptures, brick installations and collections of thousands of pieces of clay. The importance of the firing process is often emphasized as a conceptual point of departure. Paikkari's work makes use of aluminium oxide, bricks and other materials used in the production of ceramics. As a designer at Arabia, he has contributed to the company's Pro Arte collection.

⌐ *The Ice Breaks Up* by Pekka Paikkari, 1992. 500 x 300 cm. Photo: Timo Kauppila/ Arabia Museum.

> *The House of the Brick-Maker,* installation by Pekka Paikkari, 1999. Photo: Timo Kauppila.

Anna Hackman

Anna Hackman makes stoneware sculptures and wall plaques in shapes inspired by submarine creatures such as jellyfish and octopi. Lately another important theme of hers has been seeds and seed husks. She also applies serigraphy to ceramic wall plaques. Blue-green, off-white and beige are recurring colours in Hackman's work, which has been purchased by the Arabia Museum, the Pro Artibus Collection and Sanitech Oyj Abp.

■ Born in Leppävirta 1961

■ University of Art and Design Helsinki, ceramics dept., 1983–89

■ Studio in Helsinki 1995–2000, Espoo 2000 onwards

Tiina Harjola

Tiina Harjola has worked at her studio in Kisko since 1990. Her production consists of ceramic sculptures, reliefs, functional ware and gift items. In 2000 she built a wood-burning kiln, and since then her work has increasingly been directed towards its use. Tiina Harjola's work has been acquired by the Municipality of Halikko and in 2001 she was awarded an honorary mention at the 'Cheongju International Craft Biennial' in Korea.

■ Born in Imatra 1962

■ Savilintu Oy and Ateljee KASL, apprenticeship contracts, 1987–90

■ University of Art and Design Helsinki and the Open University in Finland, 1999–2000

Helena Sarvela

Helena Sarvela founded Udumbara Ceramics in Helsinki in 1994. She makes wheel-thrown utilitarian ware, with a focus on specialist kitchen crockery such as fermentation pots and moulds for cheese, pasha and tofu. Her materials are stoneware and earthenware and thus she proves that traditional crafts can successfully be united with modern living.

■ Born in Espoo 1962

■ Finnish School of Ceramics, Posio 1985–87, Kuopio Academy of Design 1987–90

■ Studio Arla, Helsinki 1990–97; own studio 1997 onwards

Kristina Riska

Matter versus spirit

■ Born in Helsinki 1960

■ University of Art and Design Helsinki: ceramics dept. 1979–84, teacher 1988–97

■ Studio at Cable Factory, Helsinki, 1989–92; at Arabia 1992 onwards

■ Works in the Ulster Museum, Belfast, Gifu Museum, Japan, the Finnish Embassy in Washington DC, Wayne State College, USA, and the Swedish Government collection

■ Gold medal, Faenza 1995; Suomi award 1995; Stina Krook Foundation award 1999; honorary mention from Finnish Government, 2001; silver medal, Mino 2002

From the beginning, Kristina Riska chose her own genre within the vast field of ceramics and she has developed it consistently. She favours large-scale work, building big, abstract forms of thin clay coils. This technique leaves barely perceptible traces of the artist's hands on the finished work. Despite the solid material and the age-old method, the result is unexpectedly light. The surfaces gleam with patinas of metallic oxides and pigments, and play a decisive role in adding expression to these ceramics.

Riska's work has multiple connotations in intellectual as well as emotional terms. It is reminiscent of primitive clay huts found south of the Atlas Mountains in northern Africa, but it also brings to mind skyscrapers or the remaining steel skeletons of bombed-out buildings. Some of Riska's forms echo storage vessels and her tall, asymmetrical cylinders bring to mind old tree trunks or prehistoric boats hollowed out of single logs.

We see a development from vessel-like shapes towards more architectural ones. Riska's language of form has become more open: this is expressed by small perforations in the clay walls, like rows of small widows that let in light. Her latest series of architectural-spatial sculptures are to a great extent based on contrasts of light and shade and the perpetually changing shadow patterns caused by the sun's progress across the sky. Attempts at increasing simplification and focus are evident: the dynamism of the material has overtaken the significance of intricately patinated surfaces. In Kristina Riska's work, the material and the immaterial meet in a new, fascinating synthesis.

∨ *Crossroads* by Kristina Riska, 1998. Finnish Government Collections. Photo: Museokuva.

⊿ Sculptures in Kristina Riska's studio in 1996. Photo: Kari Holopainen.

Meandra by Kristina Riska, constructed *in situ* at her
exhibition in the Kluuvi Gallery, Helsinki, 1991.
Photo: Kari Holopainen.

Maarit Mäkelä

Transparent bone china

■ Born in Helsinki 1961

■ University of Helsinki, degree in teaching, 1984

■ Kuopio Academy of Design, 1984–86

■ National College of Art and Design, Dublin, 1992–93

■ University of Art and Design Helsinki, ceramics dept.: Doctor of Art, 2003

■ Member of the Kuuma Linja women artists' group

■ Works in the Finnish Government collections, Sodankylä municipality, the Niilo Helander Foundation and Arabianranta, Helsinki

■ First prize, Opettajien Kulttuuripäivät event, Helsinki 1992; honorary mention, Lappeenranta international pottery competition K'2000

Maarit Mäkelä's ceramic serigraphy depicts three generations of women based on her own maternal family tree. She transfers photographic images onto thin, wet clay sheets using serigraphy techniques. To keep the fragile clay sheets from breaking prior to firing, she adds paper pulp to strengthen the clay. With photographs from her own family album and heavily symbolic female archetypes from art history, she examines different aspects of womanhood.

Mäkelä initially worked with red earthenware, but she has since changed to white porcelain clay, especially bone china made of reindeer bones from Lapland. The transparency of the material is emphasized with small lights placed behind the paper-thin porcelain sheets. Occasionally Mäkelä will combine the sheets to create large hanging 'lanterns' with transparent images. Her work reflects the interaction of material, image and light.

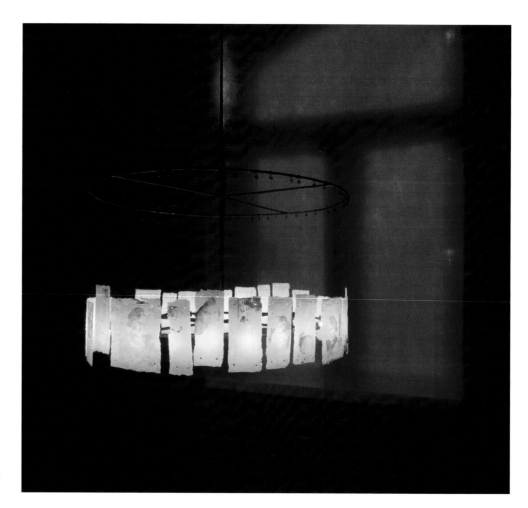

The Holy Family, a series describing five generations of mothers and daughters by Maarit Mäkelä, 1999. Silk-screen on reindeer bone china. Photo: Erkki Valli-Jaakkola.

Jyrki Valkola

Jyrki Valkola initially created hand-built sculptures and reliefs in earthenware clay, and arranged a solo exhibition of simple, vessel-like press-moulded sculptures at the Cable Factory in 1996. He gradually progressed to lighter clay bodies, leading to his current preference for bone china. In 2001 he established Kola Design Oy Ltd, which manufactures limited series of slip-cast lamps in transparent bone china. The Finnish Government collection contains works by this artist.

■ Born in Joensuu 1961

■ University of Art and Design Helsinki, ceramics dept.: studies 1982–88, teacher 1991–2000

■ Studio at Cable Factory, Helsinki 1993–2001, Tuusula 2001 onwards

Pirjo Eronen

The Italian village of Tolfa, located around seventy kilometres north-west of Rome, has been home to Pirjo Eronen's studio since 1997. There the artist hand-builds unique sculptural pieces, occasionally with the help of plaster moulds. She also makes slip-cast porcelain items fired in a gas kiln, and sells her work in galleries and showrooms in Rome. In 1997 she built a large ceramic wall relief for a church in Faenza; other places containing Pirjo Eronen's work include Taipei County Yingko Ceramic Museum, Taiwan, and the International Museum of Ceramics in Faenza.

■ Born in Pielisjärvi 1958

■ Helsinki University of Technology, University of Art and Design Helsinki: graphic art, 1978–86

■ Istituto Statale d'Arte per la Ceramica, Faenza, 1996–98

■ First prize, 'Third Annual International Pottery Show', Laramie, USA 1999; Premio Ceramica e Sport, Faenza 1998

Riitta Talonpoika

A broad spectrum

■ Born in Lappeenranta 1961

■ University of Art and Design Helsinki, ceramics dept.: studies 1984–89, teacher 1990–96

■ University of Colorado, Boulder, USA, 1992–93

■ University of Western Sydney, Milperra, Australia, 1990

■ Group workshop Pot Viapori, 1994–2002; studio in Fiskars, 2003 onwards

■ Works in the Finnish Ministry for Foreign Affairs, the Finnish Government collection, the University of Western Sydney, the Shuvalovo Collection, St Petersburg, and Nordea Bank

■ Three gold medals in Finnish throwing competitions

Riitta Talonpoika belongs to a generation of ceramists who have had the whole world as their playing field. Talonpoika has studied and worked on three continents and passed on her international experience to students at the University of Art and Design Helsinki. Since 1996 she has worked full-time as a ceramic artist.

The broad register of Talonpoika's work stems from her solid knowledge of ceramic materials and firing techniques. Her sizeable portfolio ranges from purely functional items such as teacups and jugs to large abstract sculptures and wall reliefs. She uses both red clay and stoneware, and is a master of many decorative techniques. An accomplished thrower, she also hand-builds unique items by coiling or joining clay slabs. Riitta Talonpoika is a productive ceramist always in search of new challenges. In recent years she has created suspended room partitions and chandeliers made of small ceramic pearls.

⌄ Sculpture in dark clay with vitrified black slip by Riitta Talonpoika, 2000. Height *c.* 100 cm.
Photo: Riitta Talonpoika.

⌄ *Eenie-Meenie*, patinated wall plaques by Riitta Talonpoika, 2002. 20 x 20 x 3 cm.
Photo: Katja Hagelstam.

Pii-Pot

Marjaleena Piippo was born in Kiuruvesi in 1963 and graduated in 1987 from the ceramics department at the University of Art and Design Helsinki. In addition to working with clay she creates interiors and textiles and works as a graphic designer. Like her husband Markku she has participated in several ceramics exhibitions in Finland and abroad. Her work can be found at the Arabia Museum and the Icelandic Museum of Design and Applied Art.

Markku Piippo was born in Vieremä in 1960. He too graduated from the University of Art and Design Helsinki at the age of twenty-eight. Between 1987 and 1997 he worked as a lecturer in ceramics at Kuopio Design Academy. In 1985 he shared second place in Stockmann's Design competition and in 1999 he won first prize for interior decoration and table setting at the 'Forma' fair in Helsinki.

Marjaleena and Markku Piippo both favour porcelain. In 1996 they established the Pii-Pot workshop in Maaninka, where they create limited slip-cast series of domestic ware as well as unique ceramic art.

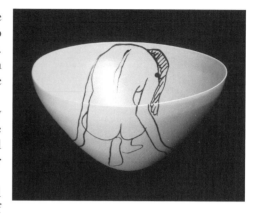

Illusion of the Two-Dimensional, a porcelain vase by Marjaleena Piippo, 1987. Diameter 30 cm. Photo courtesy Marjaleena Piippo.

Heli Valaja
Salt-glazing specialist

Heli Valaja is one of a handful of Finnish ceramists with a particular attachment to wood-firing. She specializes in salt glazing at temperatures ranging from 1,250 to 1,300 °C. She often hand-builds her unique pieces out of thin clay slabs extruded from a vacuum press, paying special attention to seams and the execution of details. She uses stoneware clays and glass-like, transparent porcelain bodies. Some of her production consists of small series of slip-cast artefacts. In 2003 Heli Valaja received the art award of the Arts Council of Häme.

■ Born in Nurmes 1963

■ University of Art and Design Helsinki, ceramics dept., 1987–93

■ Studio in Renko, 1994 onwards

■ Works in the Design Museum, Helsinki, and the collections of the Nelimarkka foundation, the City of Nurmes and the Association of Finnish Local and Regional Authorities

Wood-fired, shino-glazed *Shino Fly* by Heli Valaja, 2000. Photo: Terho Aalto.

Soile Paasonen

Ceramics in a historical environment

■ Born in Ristiina 1961

■ Kuopio Academy of Design, 1981–86

■ Visual arts and ceramics teacher, 1986 onwards

■ Group workshop Pot Viapori, 1988 onwards

■ Works in the Tokoname Collection, Japan, and the Shah Alam Collection, Malaysia

■ Ceramic Communion ware and candleholders for Suomenlinna church

Soile Lyydia Paasonen lives and works in the historic environment of Suomenlinna, an island near Helsinki. Her workspace at the Pot Viapori group workshop is close to nature and the ever-present seascape. There she transforms clay on the potter's wheel, models it or casts it in plaster moulds, creating small series of functional items and larger sculptures. Her emphasis is on the material itself, which is often left wholly or partially unglazed. The decoration of the plain forms is often limited to a few brushstrokes in wax-resist.

Paasonen has worked at international ceramics workshops in Malaysia and Japan. Her interest in Japanese culture is evident, and impressions from Ikebana flower arrangements and traditional tea-ceremony vessels are reflected in her work. She develops her production methodically, apparently free from any stress. Soile Paasonen has participated in exhibitions in Finland and abroad. Recently her rectangular earthenware plates, cut and unfolded from cylinders, have received critical acclaim.

The Engagement, coiled sculpture by Soile Paasonen, 2002. Photo: Johnny Korkman.

Earthenware dishes by Soile Paasonen, 2000. Photo: Matti Järvi.

Jenni Linnove

Since 1999 Jenni Linnove has had a studio at the Cable Factory in Helsinki, where she makes small sets of slip-cast functional ware, which complement or even offer alternatives to industrial mass-produced items. She also makes sculptures and reliefs in grogged stoneware, favouring sparkling yellow, orange or green glazes.

■ Born in Siilijärvi 1963

■ Kuopio Academy of Design, ceramics dept., 1982–87

■ Works owned by the Craft Museum of Finland, Jyväskylä, the Arts Council of Northern Karelia and the Municipality of Lapinlahti

Tiina Wallius

Tiina Wallius has had a studio in Pukkila since 1993, where she creates stoneware reliefs and sculptures decorated with acrylic paints. Her work brings to mind comic strips, graffiti and other forms of popular culture. She has made several reliefs for public spaces, including Warkaus-sali hall in Varkaus, Pukkila municipal building and School no. 25 in Pihkova, Russia.

■ Born in Varkaus 1961

■ Kuopio Academy of Design, ceramics dept., 1989–92

■ First prize, City of Kuopio mural competition, 1991

A work from the *Crazy Lollipops* series by Tiina Wallius. Acrylic paint. Height 50 cm. Photo courtesy of Tiina Wallius.

Kirsi Kaarna

Kirsi Kaarna principally creates small series of cast stoneware. Interesting glaze effects achieved with crystal glazes, for instance, give each item its particular character. Kaarna's products include the *Pebble* series of asymmetric, stackable bowls. Since 1996 she has worked as a freelance product designer for a number of companies. Kirsi Kaarna's work is included in the collection of the Arabia Museum.

■ Born in Hämeenlinna 1963

■ Hackman Designor, visiting artist, 1996

■ University of Art and Design Helsinki, ceramics dept., 1991–98

■ Studio in Helsinki, 1999 onwards

Rozalia Janovic

- Born in Sombor, former Yugoslavia, 1964

- University of Belgrade, Faculty of Applied Arts, 1983–88

- University of Art and Design Helsinki, ceramics dept., 1988–89

- Arabia, Pro Arte ceramist, 1988–90

- Kuopio Academy of Design, lecturer in ceramics and visual arts, 1990 onwards

Rozalia Janovic's porcelain and stoneware sculptures express a free and casual language of form. Her large unique pieces serve as room dividers with suspended ceramic elements attached to stable steel constructions. Janovic has worked in her own studio since 1991 and has successfully exhibited her ceramics. Some of her works are in the Finnish Government collection and the Posio International Coffee Cup Museum. Janovic has recently been experimenting with the use of parchment in her art.

Summer's Night and *First Raindrops*, screens in glazed porcelain and coloured paper clay by Rozalia Janovic, 1994. Photo: Kari Hakli.

Jatta Lavi

Since 1997 Jatta Lavi has been working at the Työhuone 62 group workshop at Vallila industrial estate in Helsinki. She uses press-moulding and casting techniques with porcelain clay to create lanterns, teacups, bowls and saltshakers. She has also worked as a teacher in ceramics at Septaria Ceramics Centre.

■ Born in Espoo 1966

■ University of Art and Design Helsinki, ceramics dept., 1991–97

■ Exhibitions in Finland and abroad

Leena Juvonen
Paper clay

Since the 1980s, in the paper-manufacturing country of Finland ceramists have been turning their attention to paper clay, a combination of clay and cellulose fibres. One of them is Leena Juvonen who makes use of the specific characteristics of this material: its capacity to support large, thin-walled objects without cracking.

Juvonen belongs to a young generation of ceramists, but she has already made her name through some large solo exhibitions, establishing her standing as a highly individual artist who uses paper clay as her point of departure. Juvonen favours large formats, pressing the clay by hand into plaster moulds. Her exhibition in the Arabia Museum Gallery in 1991 revealed plates with diameters of up to 70 cm. They were decorated in bright colours applied in bold strokes of the brush.

Leena Juvonen's 2002 exhibition in Helsinki, called 'The Forgotten Spa' (*Unohdettu kylpylä*), consisted of ceramic fountains, springs and water tubs. The patina of these pieces is suggestive of mossy stone ruins, worn down by centuries of running water. Juvonen often applies images on the clay in the form of ceramic transfers and has developed a way of transferring digital pictures onto ceramics. The themes of her latest work have included distance and measuring time and space.

■ Born in Helsinki 1966

■ University of Art and Design Helsinki: studies 1986–91, postgraduate 1992–96

■ Arabia art department, 1991–92

■ Studio in Helsinki, 1998 onwards

■ Works in the Arabia Museum, the Finnish Government collection and the Finnish Ministry of Education

■ Honorary mention, 'Talentbörse Hantwerk', Munich, 1993

Forgotten spa, ceramic transfers on stoneware by Leena Juvonen, 2002. Photo: Kari Hakli.

Johanna Ojanen

■ Born in Jyväskylä 1967

■ Oulu College of Culture and Technology, degree in carpentry, 1991

■ Kuopio Academy of Design, degree in ceramics, 1997

Johanna Ojanen has belonged to the Pot Viapori group workshop in Suomenlinna since 2002. She uses many ceramic techniques and is intent on examining form itself. She has been a freelance designer for the glass and ceramic industries, including the company IDO Kylpyhuone Oy, and designed the highly acclaimed *Eclipse* porcelain lamp together with ceramist Iiro Ahokas. Ojanen's works are frequently included in ceramics exhibitions.

Terhi Vähäsalo

■ Born in Kokkola 1969

■ University of Art and Design Helsinki, ceramics dept.: studies 1990–97, teacher 1998–2001

■ First prize, Sievi Municipality Library planning competition 1995, Sievi cultural award 1999

Terhi Vähäsalo comes from a long line of ceramists: her great-grandfather manufactured bricks and her mother founded Sievin Savi Oy in 1979. Since 1994 Terhi Vähäsalo has worked as a designer for the family enterprise, creating original porcelain dinner sets and other goods. The main library in the municipality of Sievi contains a hand-built earthenware brick mural made by Vähäsalo.

Nathalie Lahdenmäki

■ Born in Jämsänkoski 1974

■ University of Art and Design Helsinki, ceramics dept.: studies 1993–99, part-time teacher 1999–2001, lecturer 2001 onwards

■ Honorary mention, Mino 1998; Design Plus award, 'Ambiente Frankfurt' 2002; Maire Gullichsen Jubilee fund award 2002

Nathalie Lahdenmäki decorates the insides of her round, light bowls with glazes in various colours, often leaving the outside bare. She creates press-moulded earthenware using plaster moulds, but she casts her porcelain items. Since 1999 Lahdenmäki has participated in the Työhuone 62 group workshop in Helsinki. She has also been a freelance designer for Arabia from 1997.

Ulla Kujansuu

Plaited clay

Ulla Kujansuu forms soft chamotted clay into long coils, which she then plaits and weaves into larger compositions. Open plaster moulds help to support the resulting baskets and bowls which, once bone dry, can stand independently. Firing transforms the material further into hard, vitrified stoneware.

With this technique, Ulla Kujansuu's pieces come out airy and light, comparable to wicker, knitted or woven textiles. With different clay bodies and construction patterns, Ulla Kujansuu creates variations on her theme. In addition to bowls and plates she makes transparent, hanging partitions and wall compositions of plaited clay. The shadow patterns cast by these works when lit give Ulla Kujansuu's ceramics a great deal of charm.

■ Born in Pori 1967

■ Kuopio Academy of Design, 1986–91

■ University of Turku, humanities with major in art history, 2003 onwards

■ Studio in Turku, 1996 onwards

■ Works in the International Museum of Ceramics in Faenza and the Finnish Government collection

■ First prize in Animal Design Factory drawing competition, 2000

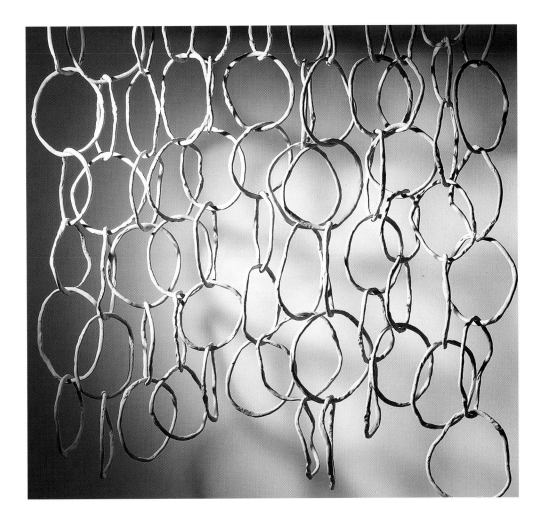

Suspended screen by Ulla Kujansuu exhibited at Design Forum, Helsinki, 2002.
Photo: Seilo Ristimäki.

246

Sarita Koivukoski

■ Born in Tampere 1968

■ University of Art and Design Helsinki, ceramics dept., 1991–97

■ National College of Art and Design, Dublin, 1996

■ Works in the Finnish Ministry for Foreign Affairs, Keijärvi hospital, Ylöjärvi, and Korven koti, Tampere

Sarita Koivukoski has participated in the Työhuone 62 group workshop in Helsinki since 1997. Her chosen material is stoneware, in which she creates sculptures and press-moulded functional ware. Her *Ruutu* series consists of small square plates with gaily coloured glazes, intensified by contrasting dots. Koivukoski has achieved recognition at national and international exhibitions alike.

Flat bowls by Sarita Koivukoski from her *Square* series, 2001. 15 x 15 x 8 cm. Photo: Sarita Koivukoski.

Johanna Sarparanta

■ Born in Helsinki 1968

■ Mikkeli Institute of Crafts and Design, metalworking, 1988–89

■ Kuopio Academy of Design, ceramics degree, 1994

■ Company in Halikko, 1995 onwards

■ Works owned by the cities of Kuopio and Salo, the Municipality of Halikko and the Finnish Ministry for Foreign Affairs

Johanna Sarparanta creates unique, amply decorated vases, jars, plates and wall reliefs in hand-built stoneware, applying colourful patterns with industrial pigments and an airbrush. Her vessels are thin-walled with finely executed details, often in the form of three-dimensional Art Nouveau motifs: plants, insects, frogs and peacocks. Her artefacts are generally partly or wholly unglazed. Johanna Sarparanta's work embellishes the walls of several public spaces.

Frog Pot by Johanna Sarparanta, 1998. Height 45 cm. Photo: Jorma Marstio.

Camilla Groth

Camilla Groth's wide-ranging education has included practical work at ceramics and glass workshops in Finland and Sweden. Between 1994 and 1996 she had her own workshop in Helsinki; since 2001 she has lived in London, working as a freelance designer with a variety of clients, among them Japanese, Italian, Swiss and Finnish companies. Most of her work is carried out in slip-cast porcelain. In 2001 she received the Wedgwood Travel Award of the Royal Society of Arts in London.

■ Born in Stockholm 1973

■ University of Art and Design Helsinki, ceramics dept., 1996–99

■ Gerrit Rietveld Art Academy, Amsterdam, ceramics dept., 1998

■ Royal College of Art, London, ceramics dept., 1999–2001

■ Central Saint Martins College of Art and Design, London, ceramics teacher, 2001

Porcelain installation by Camilla Groth at Galleria Naistenhuone, Helsinki, 1999. Photo courtesy of Camilla Groth.

Iiro Ahokas

Iiro Ahokas established an experimental workshop in 2003 on an island off the Porkkala peninsula in southern Finland, where he creates both industrial designs and individual artwork in glass and clay. The artist's preferred material is high-firing stoneware combined with deep, lustrous glazes. His unique pieces can be wheel-thrown, hand-built, cast or extruded. Commissioned works include a relief for the SOK consortium's headquarters.

■ Born in Nurmijärvi 1976

■ University of Art and Design Helsinki, ceramics dept., 1995–2001

■ Freelance design for Arabia, Design House Stockholm and Anouska Hempel Ltd

Connections, a necklace by Iiro Ahokas, 2003. Photo: Iiro Ahokas.

Kim Simonsson
Brutal innocence

■ Born in Helsinki 1974

■ University of Art and Design Helsinki, ceramics dept., 1995–2000

■ Exhibitions in Finland and abroad

■ Works in the Helsinki City Museum, the Pro Artibus collection, the city of Châteauroux and the Art Museum of Tampere

■ Best in Show, 'Toronto Outdoor Art Exhibition', 2003; Young Artist of the Year, 2004

Kim Simonsson's large figurative porcelain sculptures bring to mind romantic statues in nineteenth-century palace interiors but also nightmarish scenes from horror films. The clinically white porcelain used for his racing greyhounds emphasizes the animals' muscles and tendons, but the dogs are captured in motion and fully alive. They provoke strong emotions of horror and compassion for animals manipulated by human beings for their selfish goals.

Japanese *manga* comics are another source of inspiration for Kim Simonsson. He builds human figures with forms derived from absurd, stylized cartoon drawings and creates innocent-looking narratives in white porcelain, where sexuality and violence hide under the surface. Simonsson hand-builds his works from white porcelain clay, occasionally with the help of plaster casts, joining up the pieces after glaze-firing. The tension in these contemporary sculptures arises from the contrast between a sophisticated technique and themes acquired from commercial popular culture. Simonsson, who lives and works in Toronto, is the first ceramist to have been appointed Young Artist of the Year in Finland.

>> Porcelain figures by Kim Simonsson.
Photo: Kim Simonsson.

Caroline Slotte

■ Born in Helsinki 1975

■ Design School Kolding, Denmark, 1995–98; Open University at Åbo Akademi, art history, 1998–99; Norwegian National School of Art and Design, Bergen, 2001–3

■ Works in Vestlandske Kunstindustrimuseum in Norway

Bouquet with recycled pieces of broken china by Caroline Slotte, 2003. Photo: Caroline Slotte.

Caroline Slotte has studied ceramics in Finland, Denmark and Norway. She reflects the past through found or purchased ceramic arte-facts, which she reworks to endow them with new meaning. Mass-produced, industrial ware such as floral every-day plates is transformed in this artist's hands into heavily sym-bolic, unique artwork. Two of her themes are imperfection and dashed hopes, represented by cracks.

Caroline Slotte's quest to elimi-nate boundaries may be rooted in her international experience. Since 1999 Slotte has had a studio at the Cable Factory in Helsinki.

TERMINOLOGY

SCHOOLS AND INSTITUTIONS

The University of Art and Design Helsinki has evolved from institutions with a distinguished history. The School of Sculpture, founded in 1871, became the Central School of Arts and Crafts in 1886 and the Industrial School of Art in 1949. In 1973, the institution gained academic status and acquired its current name. It is the alma mater of many of the artists included in this volume whose education spanned years of renaming. For consistency, the artist presentations refer to the University of Art and Design Helsinki throughout, regardless of year of attendance.

The names of the **Academy of Fine Arts** and the **Kuopio Academy of Design** have undergone similar transformations and only their current versions are quoted.

GLOSSARY

Biscuit firing – The first firing, which causes the clay body to mature and turn into ceramics. Biscuit-fired (bisque) items are usually then glazed and re-fired.

Celadon – Classic Chinese semi-translucent, high-fired, greyish green glaze. The green hue is obtained during reduction firing in gas or wood-burning kilns when iron oxide is present in either the clay body or the glaze.

Chamotte (grog) – High-fired, crushed ceramic material mixed into the clay body for the purpose of making it less disposed to shrinkage and cracking during firing.

Engobe (slip) – Liquid mixture of clay and water normally applied to a pot's surface at the leather-hard stage. Coloured engobes can be brushed or trailed, as in Iris ceramics, and are integral to the sgraffito technique.

Faience – Light, porous clay body fired to between c. 1,050 and 1,150 °C. Mediterranean majolica is made of faience.

Flambé (flame effects) – The occurrence of random colour variations in glazed surfaces during reduction firing in gas or wood-burning kilns. Flambé effects are unpredictable and frequently surprising.

Glaze – Glossy or matte coating applied to the surface of ceramics, usually composed of quartz, feldspar and other minerals. Coloured glazes have additions of metallic oxides or stains.

High firing – Firing that reaches temperatures of up to 1,400 °C, suitable for some stoneware and porcelain bodies.

Low firing – Firing suitable for bodies such as the Finnish red clay, which can tolerate 700–1000 °C. Low-fired ceramics remain porous unless glazed.

Majolica – Traditional Mediterranean ware with brush decorations applied over a white tin glaze.

Oxblood (*sang de boeuf*) – Classic Chinese copper red glaze. Depending on the glaze formula, the presence of copper usually brings up green or turquoise hues. During reduction firing, however, a deep red colour emerges. Some Arabia ceramists, notably Toini Muona and Friedl Kjellberg, are famous for their expert use of oxblood glazes.

Paper clay – Made by mixing paper or cellulose fibres into the clay body. The fibres are incinerated during firing, resulting in strong but extremely lightweight ceramics. Paper clay is considered one of the most versatile inventions in today's ceramics.

Porcelain – White clay body fired to 1,300–1,400 °C, when it vitrifies and becomes translucent. Traditional porcelain bodies consist of 50 % kaolin, 25 % feldspar and 25 % quartz.

Raku – Firing method from the Far East, lately adopted by Western ceramists. Raku requires a coarse clay able to withstand abrupt changes in temperature. Raku pots are removed with metal tongs from the firing chamber at about 1,000 °C and plunged into a chamber filled with straw, sawdust or a similar combustible material. Unpredictable lustre effects occur during cooling.

Red clay – Finnish red (earthenware) clay, high in iron content, is grey in its natural state and turns terracotta-coloured during firing. It can withstand 1,000 to 1,050 °C but melts and collapses at higher temperatures.

Reduction firing – The presence of flames in gas and wood-burning kilns requires a certain amount of oxygen; if the oxygen content is reduced by limiting the air intake, it is drawn from the metallic oxides present in the clay or glazes, thus altering their colour compositions. Celadon and copper red effects, among many others, are obtained during reduction firing.

Salt glaze – Stoneware glaze obtained by throwing salt into the chamber of a gas or wood-burning kiln during firing. The sodium in the salt adheres to the clay, producing a glaze with an orange-peel surface. Toxic fumes are emitted in the process. The early pharmaceutical industry and liqueur producers favoured flasks with a hard and impervious salt glaze for their potions.

Sgraffito (engraving technique) – Decorations scratched through a layer of slip or glaze to expose the clay surface. The sgraffito technique enables sharp and clearly delineated ornamentation.

Smoke firing – Firing biscuit ware in containers or pits filled with straw or sawdust, for example, resulting in charcoal grey or black surface effects.

Stoneware – Non-porous ceramics fired to a temperature of c. 1,200–1,300 °C, when the clay body vitrifies.

Vitrification – Firing a clay body to the point when the clay particles fuse together, resulting in compact and non-porous ceramics.

St Petersburg, centrepiece
by Åsa Hellman. Height 43 cm.
Photo: Johnny Korkman.

We wish to thank our partners:

Alfred Kordelin Foundation

Arts Council of Finland

City of Porvoo

Committee for Public Information

Ensto

Finnish Cultural Foundation

Fiskars Oyj Abp

Foundation for Swedish Culture in Finland

Hackman Pro Design Foundation

Hagelstam Auctions

IDO Kylpyhuone Oy

Konstsamfundet Association

Kyösti Kakkonen

Ministry for Foreign Affairs of Finland

***Taitaja* magazine**

Yvonne Tigerstedt-Suonne

SIGNATURES

This key contains the signatures of ceramic artists who work or have worked studios in connection with, in private workshops or in factories. Most of these ceramists both designed and produced their unique pieces; we have left out most decorators at Kupittaan Savi and Arabia. The key includes stamped, engraved and painted signatures. Question marks next to artists' names indicate that there are doubts as to the author of the signature.

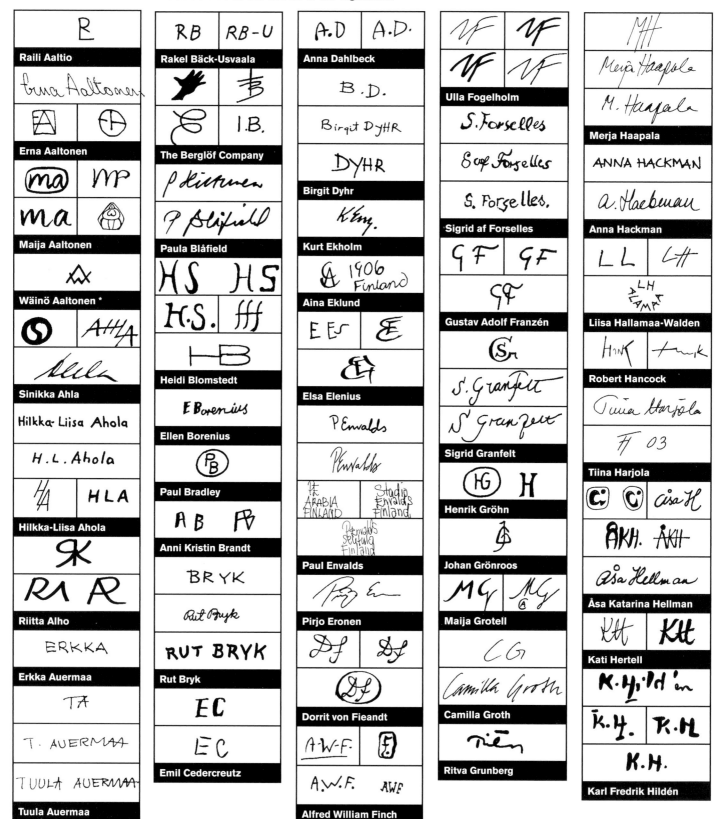

* Wäinö Aaltonen did not throw his own work, so any thrown pieces
with his signature are forgeries.

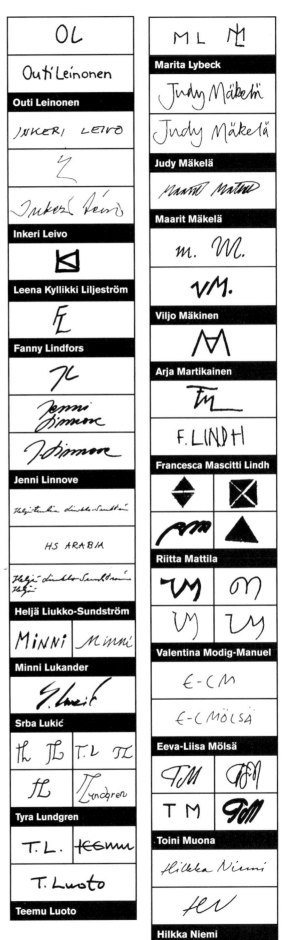

Meeri Hiltunen

K. HORILA

Kerttu Horila

Airi Hortling

Annikki Hovisaari

Kaija-Riitta Iivonen

Kaija-Riitta Iivonen

ISHIMOTO ISHIMOTO

Fujiwo Ishimoto

Eliisa Isoniemi

G-L-JÄDERHOLM.

Greta L. Jäderholm-Snellman

Rozalia Janovic

Hilkka Jarva

RUUKKUPAJA TURKU

Jack Johnsson

EJ

Elin Juselius

Beni

Beni Juslin

Leena Juvonen

Kirsi Kaarna

T. KAASINEN

Taisto Kaasinen

BIRGER KAIPIAINEN

KAIPIAINEN

Birger Kaipiaine

Birger Kaipiainen

Catharina Kajander

Eija Karivirta

Nina Karpov

RR RR

RK

Ritva Kaukoranta

Kirsi Kivivirta

—F.H.K.—

FH HOLZER

Friedl Kjellberg

Maila Klemettinen

Lea Klemola

UK

Ulla Kujansuu

LS LIISA₃

Liisa Kurki

Taina Kurtze

Elsa Kyander-Elenius

Okki Laine

Margareta Långhjelm

Tamara Laurén

OL

Outi Leinonen

Outi Leinonen

INKERI LEIVO

Inkeri Leivo

Leena Kyllikki Liljeström

Fanny Lindfors

Jenni Linnove

HS ARABIA

Heljä Liukko-Sundström

MINNI Minni

Minni Lukander

Srba Lukić

T.L TL

Tyra Lundgren

T.L.

T. Luoto

Teemu Luoto

ML

Marita Lybeck

Judy Mäkelä

Judy Mäkelä

Judy Mäkelä

Maarit Mäkelä

m. M.

VM.

Viljo Mäkinen

Arja Martikainen

F.LINDH

Francesca Mascitti Lindh

Riitta Mattila

Valentina Modig-Manuel

E-CM

E-C MÖLSÄ

Eeva-Liisa Mölsä

TM T M

Toini Muona

Hilkka Niemi

Hilkka Niemi

254

Thure Öberg

Johanna Ojanen

Gunvor Olin-Grönqvist

Anna-Maria Osipow

Marjukka Pääkkönen-Paasivirta

Soile Paasonen

Risto Paatero

Pekka Paikkari

Pirkko Pajunen

Timo Pajunen

Ulla Parkkinen

Pauli Partanen

Marri Penna

Pirjo Pesonen

Marjukka Pietiäinen

Merja Pohjonen

Zoltan Popovits

Heikki Rahikainen

Pirkko Räsänen

Emil Rekola

Johanna Rytkölä

Anneli Sainio

Marja-Riitta Salama

Kyllikki Salmenhaara

Outi Särkikoski

Johanna Sarparanta

Helena Sarvela

Eira Savolainen

Michael Schilkin

Karl-Heinz Schultz-Köln

Seenat

Aune Siimes

Howard Smith

Elina Sorainen

Mirjam Stäuber-Wessman

Erkki Stenius

Satu Syrjänen

Riitta Talonpoika

Liisa Tarna

Anri Tenhunen

Gerda Thesleff

Gregori Tigerstedt

Oiva Toikka

Ritva Tulonen

Kati Tuominen-Niittylä

Eeva Turunen

Raija Tuumi

Terhi Vähäsalo

Maija Vainonen-Gryta

Ville Vallgren

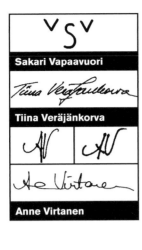

Sakari Vapaavuori

Tiina Veräjänkorva

Anne Virtanen

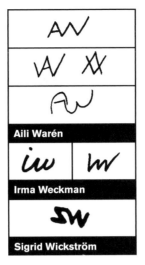

Aili Warén

Irma Weckman

Sigrid Wickström

Karin Widnäs

Sigrid Wiljomaa

Peter Winquist

Tapio Yli-Viikari

THE FOLLOWING ARTISTS ARE NOT DESCRIBED IN MORE DETAIL IN THE ARTIST PRESENTATION SECTION:

Kaarina Aho 1925–90

Tarja Ahokainen (b. 1959)

Aino Anttila (b. 1923)

Göran Bäck 1923–2003

Margareta Carlberg (b. 1945)

Eva Corander

Frans Richard Franzén 1898–1978

Georg Alexander Franzén ? 1896–1953

Gustaf Alexander Franzén ? 1867–1922

Gösta Alfons Franzén 1911–86

Elmar Granlund (d. 1936)

Svea Granlund 1901–86

Brita Heilimo (b. 1928)

Sussi Henrikson (b. 1952)

Anja Juurikkala (b. 1923)

Else Kangasniemi (b. 1943)

Ritva Karpio (b. 1922)

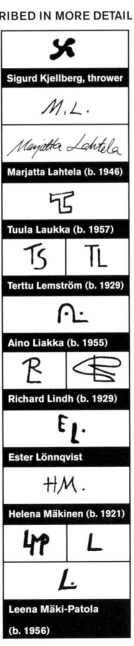

Sigurd Kjellberg, thrower

Marjatta Lahtela (b. 1946)

Tuula Laukka (b. 1957)

Terttu Lemström (b. 1929)

Aino Liakka (b. 1955)

Richard Lindh (b. 1929)

Ester Lönnqvist

Helena Mäkinen (b. 1921)

Leena Mäki-Patola (b. 1956)

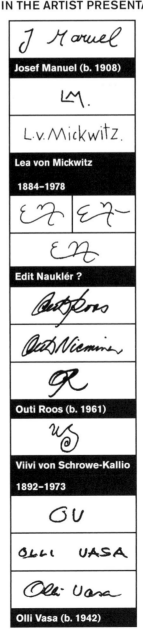

Josef Manuel (b. 1908)

Lea von Mickwitz 1884–1978

Edit Nauklér ?

Outi Roos (b. 1961)

Viivi von Schrowe-Kallio 1892–1973

Olli Vasa (b. 1942)

Pauli Vuorisalo (b. 1944)

Maaria Wirkkala (b. 1954)

Laila Zink 1915–99

NOTES AND SOURCES FOR ARTICLES

JENNIFER OPIE

I am indebted to Marketta Tamminen, Director of the Porvoo Museum, for answering my questions so patiently and for supplying so much information. Marjut Kumela, Director of the Arabia Museum, has also been immensely helpful.

Notes

1 Brussels, Musées Royaux des Beaux-Arts de Belgique: *A.W. Finch 1854–1930*, p. 201, cat. no. 116. This catalogue also reproduces a photograph of 1892 of a ceramic panel by Finch first illustrated in *Association pour l'Art*, Anvers, (1892), p. 56. The exhibition was a joint project with the Atheneum, Helsinki, where it was shown first, in 1991.

2 The Iris company opened its first shop in Helsinki in 1897 at Läntinen Heikinkatu (present-day Mannerheimintie); it moved to Fabianinkatu 29 in 1898 (by which time it was stocking goods from Liberty) and in 1899 to a building owned by businessman Julius Tallberg in Aleksanterinkatu. Tallberg was a shareholder in AB Iris.

3 There is a bulb pot in the collections of the Design Museum, Helsinki, with this motif, made in the more usual carved slip-and-painted-dot style. See Supinen, M.: *A.B. Iris Suuri Yritys*, p. 39.

4 Ibid. p. 75 etc.

5 Clark, Garth and Margie Hughto: *A Century of Ceramics in the United States*, p. 294.

6 Formerly known as the American Craft Museum. Inv. No. 1967.12

7 Schlanger, J etc.: *Works Which Grow From Belief*, p. 87.

8 Expressionism in ceramics and direct interventionist engagement with clay was also being explored in Japan in the early 1950s. Isamu Noguchi was the most celebrated exponent and was given his first major exhibition in 1950.

9 Zilliacus, Benedict: 'Ceramic Art in Finland', *The Studio*, November 1955 p. 139.

10 Marguerite Wildenhain, was born Marguerite Friedlander. With her husband, Franz Wildenhain, after a long experience of designing for the national porcelain factory in Berlin as well as running their own workshop-pottery, she emigrated to the USA to escape the rise of Nazism.

11 In 1967 Salmenhaara made a number of designs for industrial production for the Iron Mountain Stoneware company, Tennessee. See Helsinki, Aav: *Kyllikki Salmenhaara*, no page numbers.

12 Parker-Fairbanks, Dixie: *Essential Passions, Fairbanks-Salmenhaara Letters*, various pages throughout.

13 Ibid. '…it had become stronger, gutsy-er, simpler: just expressive volumetric form and spectacularly textured and colored glazes,' p. 41.

14 She was often scathing about Rut Bryk, Francesca Lindh and Birger Kaipiainen, for instance.

15 Ibid. Although she makes no accusations, it has been whispered since that these jealousies perhaps overspilled into action, and that the blade was left in the clay deliberately. Richard Fairbanks's diary suggests that her hand was damaged twice; p. 34, entry for 6 April 1960. On 2 December she wrote that she could only just hold a pen. p. 81.

16 Helsinki, Aav: *Kyllikki Salmenhaara*, – letter from Henrik Gröhn, no page numbers.

17 Parker-Fairbanks: p. 29, illustration and entry for 9 January 1960.

18 Helsinki, Aav: *Kyllikki Salmenhaara*, etc: description from Timo Pajunen.

19 Parker-Fairbanks: p. 84, letter of March 1962. 'From Arabia has written to me only Tuumi, Aarin (*sic*) Aho and Margit Knues… of course they are angry of my Gold-medal… and PRO FINLANDIA medal… so silly…'

20 Nyman, Hannele: 'Raija Tuumi – Uncompromising Ceramist', *Form Function* no. 87, p. 50.

21 Seen in the exhibition Raija Tuumi, Arabia Foundation Gallery, June, 2002

22 Parker-Fairbanks: p. 83, letter of 9 March 1961.

23 *The Sunday Times*, (no page nos) 1962.

24 Rytkölä website text, http://www.kolumbus.fi/johanna.rytkola/index.html

25 Lehtonen, Susanna: 'Expressions of strength'; in *Hot Line*, *Six touches of clay*; Keuruu Art Museum, 1998. (no page nos.)

Sources

Bodelsen, Merete: *Gauguin's Ceramics: A Study in the Development of His Art*; London, Faber & Faber, 1964.

Brussels, Musées Royaux des Beaux-Arts de Belgique: *A.W. Finch 1854–1930*; 1992.

Clark, Garth and Margie Hughto: *A Century of Ceramics in the United States*; Dutton with Everson Museum of Art, NY, 1979.

Helsinki, Design Museum; Marianne Aav: *Kyllikki Salmenhaara, 1915–1981*; publication no. 18, 1986.

Lehtonen, Susanna: 'Expressions of strength' in *Hot Line*, *Six touches of clay*; Keuruu Art Museum, 1998.

Nyman, Hannele: 'Raija Tuumi – Uncompromising Ceramist'; *Form Function* no. 87, 3/2002.

Parker-Fairbanks, Dixie: *Essential Passions, Fairbanks-Salmenhaara Letters*; University of Washington Press, 1999.

Schlanger, J, *et al.*: *Maija Grotell: Works Which Grow From Belief*; Goffstown, NH, Studio Potter Books, 1996.

Supinen, Marja: *A.B. Iris Suuri Yritys*; Sulkuva, 1993

MARJUT KUMELA

Notes

1 Kumela 1987.

2 Kälviäinen 1989.

3 Kumela 1993.

4 Franck 1973, Kumela 1987

5 Carring 1955.

6 Franck 1973, Kumela 1987.

7 Franck 1973, Kumela 1987.

8 Nyman 1996.

9 Kumela 1987.

10 Baltscheffskij 1981.

11 Kumela 1983.

12 Savinen 1985.

13 Slotte 1987.

14 Eskelinen 1985.

15 Pauloff 1986.

16 Kalin 1987.

17 Slotte 1986a.

18 Slotte 1986b.

19 Pauloff 1986a.

20 Pallasmaa 1986.

21 Maunula 1988.

22 Maunula 1988, Pauloff 1988.

23 Charter of the Arabia Foundation, 1989.

24 Pauloff 1990.

25 Blomster 1990.

26 Hiltunen 1992.

27 Annual Report of the Art Department, 1992.

Sources

Archive of the Arabia Foundation, Helsinki.

Charter of the Arabia Foundation, 1989.

Annual Report of the Art Department, 1992.

Archive of the Arabia Museum:

Baltscheffskij, Greta: Rudy Autio. *Saviseppo* 3/81. Oy Arabia Ab, Helsinki 1981.

Blomster, Harry: Wärtsilän kausi päättyi – Arabia siirtyi Hackman-konserniin. *Saviseppo* 3/1990. Oy Arabia Ab, Helsinki 1990.

Carring, Holger: *Memorandum on arrangements agreed upon with the artists Friedl Kjellberg, Lea von Mickwitz, Toini Muona, Kyllikki Salmenhaara, Aune Siimes, Raija Tuumi and Sakari Vapaavuori*, 20.8.1955.

Eskelinen, Uuno: Uurna on muistutus elämää ja kuolemaa varten. *Saviseppo* 3/85. Oy Arabia Ab, Helsinki 1985.

Franck, Kaj: Arabian taideosasto in *Keramiikka ja Lasi* 1973. Oy Wärtsilä Ab Arabia, Helsinki 1973.

Hiltunen, Hilkka: Yhteisellä tuotesuunnitteluorganisaatiolla parempaan tulokseen. *Tabletop* 1/1992. Oy Hackman Ab. Helsinki 1992.

Kalin, Kaj: *Hauras aika – Skör tid. Kristina Riska*. Arabia Cultural Foundation, Helsinki 1987.

Kumela, Marjut: *Rohkeat kokeilijat*. Oy Wärtsilä Ab. Helsinki 1983.

Kumela Marjut: *Taideosasto in Arabia*. Oy Arabia Ab. Helsinki 1987.

Kumela, Marjut: *Kurt Ekholm Arabia 1931–1948*. Arabia Foundation, Helsinki 1993.

Kälviäinen, Mirja: *Greta-Lisa Jäderholm-Snellman. Arabian aika 1921–1937*. Master's degree dissertation, University of Jyväskylä, Faculty of Arts, Department of Art History, 1989.

Maunula, Leena: *Astiat ja taide osaksi uuden ajan elämäntyyliä. Helsingin Sanomat* 17.4.1988.

Nyman, Hannele: *Arabia-Rörstrand 1975–1977. Yhteistyösopimuksen tausta, synty ja vaikutukset Arabian tuotantoon*. Keramos, Helsinki 1996.

Pallasmaa, Juhani (Ed.): *Rut Bryk*. Exhibition catalogue. Amos Anderson Art Museum, Helsinki 1986.

Pauloff, Marjatta: Dorrit von Fieandt vierailevana taiteilijana. *Saviseppo* 4/86. Oy Arabia Ab, Helsinki 1986a.

Pauloff, Marjatta: Francesca Lindhin näyttely Brondassa "Valon tie". *Saviseppo* 4/86. Oy Arabia Ab, Helsinki 1986b.

Pauloff, Marjatta: Pro Arte Arabia – Yhteistyön vahva näyttö. *Saviseppo* 2/88. Oy Arabia Ab, Helsinki 1988.

Pauloff, Marjatta: Fujiwo Ishimoton seurana savi. *Saviseppo* 5/1990. Oy Arabia Ab, Helsinki 1990.

Savinen, Merja: Taiteilija Howard Smith ja uuvuttavan ihana keramiikka. *Saviseppo* 5/85. Oy Arabia Ab, Helsinki 1985.

Slotte, Tove: Maata ja ilmaa. *Saviseppo* 4/86. Oy Arabia Ab, Helsinki 1986a.

Slotte, Tove: II Clay Az Art –konferenssi. *Saviseppo* 4/86. Oy Arabia Ab, Helsinki 1986b.

Slotte, Tove: Jun Kaneko. Sirpale tämän päivän keramiikkahistoriaa. *Saviseppo* 4/1987. Oy Arabia Ab, Helsinki 1987.

HARRI KALHA

Notes

1 On Lundgren's work in Finland, see Kalha 1996a, 85–100.

2 See Är vi egentligen så bra? Interview med Tyra Lundgren, *Form. Svenska Slöjdföreningens tidskrift* 3/1947, 54; ibid.

3 Cixous 1985, 255.

4 The European studio ceramicists (Chaplet, Carriès, Delaherche, Dalpayrat; Martinit, Wells, Leach, Staite Murray...), like their more outstanding Scandinavian counterparts (Nordström, Salto, Kåge, Friberg, Finch...), have almost without exception been men.

5 See also Kalha 1996b, 111–116; Kalha 1997, 236–246; Kalha 2000, 37–41

6 I refer here to *modern* training in industrial art. Teaching in 'artistic pottery' began at the Atheneum's Central School of Industrial Arts in 1902, as part of the new curriculum drawn up by Armas Lindgren. See Kalha 1996c, 12–15, 19–20; Kalha 1993a, 137–156; Kalha 1998, 150–157; on Thesleff, see also Kalha 1988, 16–19.

7 One of Finch's early pupils to graduate was Maija Grotell, in 1919, but aptly enough, she qualified in model design rather than ceramics. Of those who began their studies during the first ten years of the ceramics course, Edit Nauklér graduated in 1912 and Gustaf Alfred Franzén in 1915, but they too may have had some other main subject rather than ceramics. See the annual reports of the Industrial Arts Association.

8 Blomstedt 1927, 642.

9 *Suomen sosiaalidemokraatti* 10.2.1927.

10 Finch wrote: 'All ornamentation mostly just covers up faults in the proportions of the article and expresses a lack of imagination. Excessive ornamentation and decoration ... is the greatest error in modern arts and crafts.' Finch A.W. 1901, 471.

11 Brummer, Arttu, Suomen keraaminen taide, undated manuscript [*c. 1935; transcript by Markus Brummer–Korvenkontio 5.8.1990*], Brummer archives.

12 Ibid. At the same time Finch showed his students the way back to their own roots, as it were, since folk traditions in clay pots had been his inspiration in the 1890s.

13 I am not aware of any signed objects with landscape decorations prior to 1914, although several earthenware items with Italian landscapes are known from that year

14 Gerda Thesleff was evidently inspired to try these techniques by her travels in Italy, which introduced her to various craft traditions, including intarsia and basket weaving.

15 Thesleff's vase was exceptionally expensive, but studio ceramics in general were more costly than Arabia's products, even if the latter had been decorated by artists who had attended the School of Industrial Art. *Konstflitföreningens lotterivinst – och konstindustriutställning 1923* (Catalogue).

16 Finch made a statement in 1928 deploring the way his students were treated at the Arabia factory, where it was said that these ceramic artists were expected to 'spend long periods of time painting stripes on teacups for wages of a few marks an hour'; 'My conclusion after ten years' experience in factories is that they have no need of artists...' Finch was commenting on a report of the Vocational Schools Committee which cast doubts on the value of teaching in ceramics and wondered at the lack of cooperation with industry. Finch 10.10.1928; see also Kalha 1993a; 1996c.

17 Nils 1921.

18 Kalha 1996c, 20–22.

19 Blomstedt 1927, 627.

20 Tamara Lauren berättar för Kaj Franck, 1981(?).

21 Linssi (1930).

22 See Kalha 1996b, 114.

23 Uusi Suomi 30.8.1938.

24 Okkonen 19.4.1934.

25 Lindström 1934, 93–94.

26 Lundgren 1946, 117–118.

27 On developments in firing techniques and working conditions at the Atheneum, see Kalha 1996b, 20, 28, 41, 50–52.

28 Urrila–Stenbäck.

29 Kalha 8.12.1989.

30 Kupittaan Savi Oy, advertisement, November 1937.

31 Suvanto designed about 40 models for Kupittaa, which were produced in numerous variations, with different glazes or painted ornamentations. These have remained anonymous, as very few carry the signature KS, but they can be attributed to her on the basis of stylistic similarities revealed in comparisons. Some of the models remained in production for a considerable time after her death and were painted in a manner that did not match her 'monumentalizing' style. These hybrids nevertheless have an interesting tale to tell about the stylistic preferences of their times.

32 Kalha, interview with Valentina Modig-Manuel.

33 *Uusi Aura* 1.1.1938.

34 Poulsen 1946, 233–236.

35 Kalha 1997, 202–216, 270–271.

36 Blomstedt 1946, 107.

37 Kalha 2003, 66–81.

38 Møller 1947, 123.

39 Krebs 1945.

40 Blomstedt 1946, 107.

41 The Scandinavian modification of the Chinese ideal in ceramics was regarded as entailing a danger of phlegmatic imitation and dry 'historicism'. As Signe Tandefelt wrote: 'The form that is usually seen in Sweden is too perfect. It is so even and faultless that it could have been cast, and it will undoubtedly become boring in time and kill the material that it is made of. (*Hufvudstadsbladet* 9.12.1940, pencil notes 1941). See also Kalha 1993b, 130–136.

42 Middleton 25.12.1953.

43 The earlier sgraffito decoration was replaced by a technique in which the pictures were first engraved on the gypsum sheets of which the moulds were made, so that they could be duplicated rather in the manner of graphics (Bryk had been trained as a graphic artist), although the glazes would make the individual items unique.

44 Rislakki 1951, 10.

45 In his discussion of the status of the still life, Norman Bryson considers its nature as

a representation of femininity. It should be emphasized that even everyday topics can gain a strong expressive potential by virtue of their content. Bryson 1990, 61, 136–137, 157–159. See also Kalha 2002.

46 Susanna 1948, 17.

47 'This occurred in any case by such modest means that the whole space took on virtually an air of sanctity. At the core of this atmosphere lay a feeling of humility before nature and before the spirit, and there is something holy about its inviting sweetness.' Erdös 1951.

48 See Kalha 2002.

49 Her works in the 1940s were still mostly bowls or table tiles, and it was only at the end of the decade that her plaques began to break free of their utilitarian or decorative functions. An attempt to defend these boundaries is evident from Sigrid Schauman's (in itself comprehensive and positive) article of 1943 in which she shied at Bryk's 'naturalism', i.e. *visual* aspirations, which she claimed were unable to compete with 'pure art'. On the other hand, she was ready to praise the jug that Bryk had decorated as being a real utility object. Schauman 1943.

SOURCES

Bibliography

Blomstedt, Rafael: Arabia ja sen taiteilijat. *Arkkitehti* 1946.

Blomstedt, Rafael: Taideteollisuus, in *Suomen taide* (Ed. L. Wennervirta). Helsinki 1927.

Brummer, Arttu: *Suomen keraaminen taide.* Undated manuscript [c. 1935; transcribed by Markus Brummer-Korvenkontio 5.8.1990]. Brummer archives.

Bryson, Norman: *Looking at the Overlooked. Four Essays on Still Life Painting.* London 1990.

Cixous, Hélène: The Laugh of the Medusa [Le Rire de la Méduse, 1975], transl. K. & P. Cohen, in *New French Feminism* (Ed. E. Marks & I. de Courtivron). Schocken, New York 1985.

Erdös, Stephan: Die Keramik auf der 9. triennale zu Mailand. *Keramische Zeitschrift.* Lübeck, December 1951.

Finch, A. W.: *Utvecklingen af smaken för dekorativ konst i hemmen.* Ateneum 1901.

Finch, A. W.: *Mietteitä ammattikoulukomitean mietinnön johdosta.* 10.10.1928.

Hufvudstadsbladet 9.12.1940.

Industrial Arts Association, annual reports.

Kalha, Harri: Gerda Thesleff – Keramiikkataiteemme unohdettu ekspressionisti. *Muoto* 3/1988.

Kalha, Harri: *Modernin suomalaisen keramiikkataiteen juurilla. Alfred William Finch – opettaja, esikuva, suunnannäyttäjä.* Taidehistoriallisia tutkimuksia 13. Helsinki 1993a.

Kalha, Harri: Modernismin klassinen kieli, in *Kultaa, mirhamia. 10 kirjoitusta taidehistoriasta* (Ed. Jukka Ervamaa). Helsingin yliopiston taidehistorian laitoksen julkaisuja XII. Helsinki 1993b.

Kalha, Harri: Tyra Lundgren ja Arabia – Näkökulmia taiteilijan työhön teollisuudessa, in *Keramos. Kirjoituksia keramiikasta* (Eds. Hannele Nyman and Harri Kalha), transl. Carla Enbom. Helsinki 1996a.

Kalha, Harri (Ed.): *Ruukuntekijästä multimediataiteilijaan: suomalaisen keraamikon ammatillinen ja taiteellinen identiteetti 1902–1999.* University of Art and Design, Helsinki 1996b.

Kalha, Harri: Johdanto & A. W. Finchin aika, in *Ruukuntekijästä multimediataiteilijaan. Suomalaisen keraamikon ammatillinen ja taiteellinen identiteetti 1902–1995* (Ed. Harri Kalha). Helsinki 1996c.

Kalha, Harri: *Muotopuolen merenneidon pauloissa, Suomen taideteollisuuden kultakausi: mielikuvat, markkinointi, diskurssit.* SHS & Design museum, Helsinki 1997.

Kalha, Harri: Moderni suomalainen keramiikka keräilykohteena, in *Rakkaat vanhat tavarat* (Ed. Leena Nokela). Helsinki 1998.

Kalha, Harri; Franck, Kaj: Gendering the (Aesth)Ethics of Modernism. *Scandinavian Journal of Design History*, Rhodos, Copenhagen 2000.

Kalha, Harri: Myths and Mysteries of Finnish Design. Reading 'Wirkkala' and the National Nature Paradigm. *Scandinavian Journal of Design History.* Rhodos, Copenhagen 2002.

Kalha, Harri: Materiaalin sielua etsimässä. Keramiikan estetiikasta 1930–50-luvuilla, in *Ruukun runoutta ja materiaalin mystiikkaa* (Ed.) Helena Leppänen. University of Art and Design, Helsinki 2003.

Konstflitföreningens lotterivinst- och konstindustriutställning, catalogue. Helsinki 1923.

Krebs, Nathalie: Arabias utställning på NK. *Svenska hem i ord och bilder* 12, Stockholm 1945.

Kupittaan Savi OY, advertisement, November 1937.

Lindström, Aune: Elsa Elenius. Ateneumin kasvatista Ateneumin opettaja. *Suomen nainen* 7/1934.

Linssi: Taidetta ja ammattitaitoa. *Kansan Kuvalehti*, undated (1930), 17 (?), photocopy in the author's possession.

Lundgren, Tyra: *Lera och eld, Ett keramiskt vagabondage i Europa.* Stockholm 1946.

Middleton, M. H.: Modern Art in Finland. *The Spectator.* London 25.12.1953.

Møller, Svend-Erik: Dansk Udstillingsforaar. *Bonytt* 7–8/1947.

Nils W.: Ornamos utställning i Salon Strindberg. Undated newspaper cutting 1921. Ornamo press archives.

Okkonen, Onni: Erikoisnäyttelyjä Taideteollisuusmuseossa. *Uusi Suomi* 19.4.1934.

Poulsen, Christian: Arabia udstillingen i Kunstindustrimuseet. *Nyt Tidskrift for Kunstindustri.* XIX year, 12/1946.

Rislakki, Eero: Levyistä ja laatoista. *Kaunis koti* 3/1951.

Schauman, Sigrid: Konstflitföreningen utställer. *Nya Pressen* 3.12.1943.

Suomen sosiaalidemokraatti 10.2.1927.

Susanna: Rut Bryk. Taideosasto – kukka isä Arabian napinlävessä. *Saviseppo* 3/1948.

Uusi Aura 1.1.1938: Keramiikka on kaunein kukka savenvalajan kädessä.

Uusi Suomi 30.8.1938.

Interviews

Kaipiainen, Birger, interview/Auli Urrila-Stenbäck

Karpio, Ritva, interview 8.12.1989/Kalha.

Modig-Manuel, Valentina, interview/ Kalha

Tamara Lauren berättar för Kaj Franck, photocopy of manuscript (1981?), Keramiikka- ja lasitaiteen laitos, TaiK.

Är vi egentligen så bra? Interview with Tyra Lundgren, *Form. Svenska Slöjdföreningens tidskrift* 3/1947.

ESA LAAKSONEN
Sources

Archive of the Arabia Museum.

Tervo, Tuija & Kalha, Harri & Ahtola-Moorhouse, Leena: *Michael Schilkin.* Kustannus W. Hagelstam, Helsinki 1996

Kalin, Kaj: *Hauras aika – Skör tid.* Exhibition at the Arabia Museum Gallery, Helsinki 1987

Pallasmaa, Juhani (toim.): *Rut Bryk.* Retrospective exhibition at the Amos Anderson Art Museum and Rovaniemi City Art Gallery, 1986.

Kristina Riska, interview 24.2.2003

Karin Widnäs, interview 26.2.2003

Tiina Veräjänkorva, interview 27.5.2003

HANNELE NYMAN
Notes

1 The Suotniemi earthenware works did not employ designers, only mould makers. The first work done there was by the sculptor Fredrik Heinonen, who may well have moulded and designed figurines. The Turku Tile Works and Rakkolanjoki used german glazes to a large extend. Hyvönen 1993, 44.

2 "As in the making of the pot, so in its surface ornament, the hand of the workman must always be visible on it...", Morris 1882/Clark 1978, 15; see also Clark 1995, 104; the studio work of William de Morgan came closest to Morris' ideals in England.

3 Finch 1901/1991.

4 Clark 1978, viii–ix; Gauguin wrote on the artist's relation to his clay in his account of the 1889 World Exhibition in *Le Moderniste*.

5 Finland also supported the industrial arts when the great expansion of industry took

place in the 1920s and 1930s, and a good example of this was Arabia with its artists, cf.eg. Hård af Segerstad 1982, 32–34.

6 Finch 1898/1991.

7 Aav 1991, 68; A.W. Finch, Mietteitä ammattikoulukomitean mietinnön johdosta 10.10. 1928.

8 See Kenyon 1982, 153–173 and Leppänen 2003.

9 See Hellman, manuscript 2003.

10 Nottelman 2000, 95, 105.

11 See Rasmussen 2002, 69–74 and Busk Laursen 1996.

12 Finch 1898/1991.

13 Key 1899 and before that, 1897 Iduns julnummer; Nyström 1982, 14.

14 Both were active within Svenska Slöjdföreningen (the Swedish Handicrafts Association), nowadays Föreningen Svensk Form (the Association for Swedish Design); Nyström 1982, 16, 24–26.

15 Paulsson 1919/1995.

16 The title of Edvard Elenius' book *Kotiemme Kauneus – Asuinrakennukset, huoneidensisustus, puutarha*, Kansanvalistusseura, 1915, was quoted by Elias Härö in his article Viiden vuosikymmenen takaa: *Kaunis Koti* 2/1964).

17 Nyman, lecture 1996.

18 Ekholm, *Saviseppo* 3/1948.

19 Blomstedt 1927.

20 Brummer 1927.

21 Ekholm, *Saviseppo* 3/1948.

22 Herlitz installed Wethje as manager at Rörstrand, which was owned by Arabia at the time; on Wethje, see Herlitz-Gezelius 1989, 133,139; Arthur Percy had already been taken on in 1923 as a result of Paulsson's pamphlet, in order to revise the forms and ornamentations of the Gefle range, and Wilhelm Kåge, who had been artistic director at Gustavsberg from 1917 onwards, began in the 1920s to put the *vackrare vardagsvara* ideal into practice in the factory's production, Hald 1991, 46,50; the division of responsibilities between the art and the technical staff was not always a clearcut matter, and some tension began to be passed onto sales at times – in the sense of who should decide what is to be produced. This is an eternal question that has surpassed all boundaries between factories and countries.

23 Ekholm, *Arkitekten* 7–8/1946.

24 Herlitz 1935.

25 Herlitz 1945.

26 As in his speech to the Arabia employees, Herlitz 1937, 6.

27 Lundgren 1946,120, 122–123; Kurt Ekholm also thanked Herlitz personally for his support and ceramic expertise on his departure from Arabia in 1947, Ekholm, *Saviseppo* 6/1947.

28 Suna 1993, 69–70.

29 See the albums of photographs and newspaper cuttings kept by his daughter Yvonne; also an article about Tigerstedt in *Helsingfors Journalen* 1939.

30 Septima, *Taiteen Maailma* 3–4 1946.

31 Aaltonen, interview 2003.

32 Pfäffli 1994, 94, 258–259.

33 Leach 1940/1976, xxii; on different types of ceramics, see also Leppänen 1998, 92–93 and Kalha & Leppänen 1996.

34 Leach 1940/1976, 1,13; Herbert Read had already considered the same question, Read 1936; see also Cardew 1942.

35 Brummer 1933.

36 See Kalha's doctoral thesis, 1997, which deals at length with the status of Finnish industrial arts in the 1940s and 1950s.

37 Kaufmann Jr. 1949; in the USA the country's own designers began to come to the fore only in the 1920s and 1930s – all in all, the relation between the artist and industry is very much a European issue.

38 Taideteollisuus, *Keramiikka ja Lasi* 2/1953.

39 Other experiences have also been documented, however. Ritva Karpio, who was a trainee at Kera in summer 1943, recounts that 'I was the only student at that time who had applied for a trainee position with a factory, and I was regarded as slightly "crazy" by my confederates.' She maintains that the factories did not want trainees from the Atheneum, because they were afraid that these people would steal their ideas and ways of working. She reckons that she was only accepted because her father had good relations with the company, Karpio, letter to Hellman, 2002.

40 Blomstedt 1941; Brummer 1949.

41 Rislakki, *Kaunis Koti* 4/1949.

42 Häme Provincial Museum 1984; Kalha 1993, 55–56; Young People's Christmas 1953.

43 Mattsson, *Turun Sanomat* 22.2.2003.

44 Lindgren 1996, 136–137.

45 See Korvenmaa 1999, 172–201; Frick 1986, 10.

46 Nurmesniemi, *Kaunis Koti* 4/1963.

47 Pajastie, *Kaunis Koti* 3/1961.

48 Franck, *Keramiikka ja Lasi* 1973.

49 For details of this process and the Arabia-Rörstrand agreement in general, see Nyman 1996.

50 Nyman 2003; discussions and interviews with the Arabia artists 2000–2003.

SOURCES
Published sources and bibliography

Aav, Marianne: *Keramiikan opetuksen uranuurtaja – A.W. Finch Taideteollisuus-keskuskoulun opettajana 1902–1930* in Anneli Lindström & Olli Valkonen (Ed.): *Alfred William Finch 1854–1930*. Atheneum and Museum of Art and Design, Helsinki 1991.

Blomstedt, Rafael: En återblick på 1930–1940. Ornamo Yearbook No.11, 1941, Helsinki 1941.

Brummer, Arttu: Kodin taiteellisesta huolittelusta. Ornamo Yearbook No. II, 1928, Helsinki 1927.

Brummer, Arttu: Aikamme suuntauksia. Ornamo Yearbook No. VI, Helsinki 1933.

Brummer, Arttu: *Taideteollisuutemme taiteilijoita – Finnish Decorative Art*, Ornamo Yearbook No.13, 1949, Helsinki 1949.

Busk Laursen, Bodil (Ed.): *Thorvald Bindesbøll – En dansk pioner*. Det danske Kunstindustrimuseum, Copenhagen 1996.

Cardew, Michael: Industry and the Studio Potter. (*Crafts* 2/1942) – see Clark 1978.

Clark, Garth (Ed.): *Ceramic Art – Comment and Review 1882–1977*. E.P. Dutton, New York 1978.

Clark, Garth: *The Potter's Art – A Complete History of Pottery in Britain*. Phaidon Press, London 1995.

Finch, A.W.: Modernt krukmakeri. Ateneum no 2, 20.3.1898. – *Finch's collected writings 1898–1902* (Ed. Marjatta Levanto). National Art Museum/Publications of the Pedagogical Unit 1, Helsinki 1991.

Finch, A.W.: Utveckling af smaken för dekorativ konst i hemmen. Ateneum no 9–11, Nov. 1901. – *Finch's collected writings 1898–1902* (Ed. Marjatta Levanto). National Art Museum/Publications of the Pedagogical Unit 1, Helsinki 1991.

Frick, Gunilla: *Konstnär i industrin*. Nordiska Museets Handlingar 106, Sweden 1986.

Hald, Arthur: *Gustavsberg, verktyg för en idé – Hjalmar Olsons skildring av 60 års arbete*. Atlantis, Stockholm 1991.

Herlitz-Gezelius, Ann Marie: *Rörstrand*. Signum, Sweden 1989.

Herlitz, C.G.: *Teollisuuden tehtävistä suhdannevaihteluiden tasoittajana*. Helsinki, 1936.

Herlitz, C.G.: *Industrins samhällsuppgift*. Holger Schildts förlag, Helsinki 1945.

Hyvönen, Heikki: *Suotniemi – Suomen ensimmäinen fajanssitehdas*. Publications of Heinola Municipal Museum, No. 2, Heinola 1993 (2nd revised edition).

Hård af Segerstad, Ulf: Unity and diversity in Scandinavian design in David Revere McFadden (ed.), *Scandinavian Modern Design 1880–1980*. Cooper-Hewitt Museum, New York 1982.

Kalha, Harri: Kupittaan saviosakeyhtiön käyttö- ja koristekeramiikka – Tuotannon tyylillisen kehityksen pääpiirteitä in *Aboa 1989–1990*, Yearbook of Turku Provincial Museum, 53-54, Turku 1993.

Kalha, Harri: *Muotopuolen merenneidon pauloissa – Suomen taideteollisuuden kultakausi: mielikuvat, markkinointi, diskurssi*. Apeiron/ Finnish Historical Society and Design Museum, Helsinki 1997.

Kalha, Harri & Leppänen, Helena: *Ruukunteki-jästä multimediataiteilijaan – Suomalaisen keraamikon ammatillinen ja taiteellinen identiteetti 1902–1995*. Publications of the University of Art and Design, B49, Helsinki 1996.

Kaufmann Jr., Edgar J.: *Kirje Suomen taide-teollisuudelle. Finnish Decorative Art*, Ornamo Yearbook No.13, 1949, Helsinki 1949.

Key, Ellen: *Skönhet för alla*. Verdandis små-skrifter nr. 77, Sweden 1899.

Korvenmaa, Pekka: *Tietoisuuden tasot 1960–79. – Ateneum maskerad Taideteollisuuden muo-toja ja murroksia*. Publications of the University of Art and Design, B62, Helsinki 1999.

Leach, Bernard: *A Potters Book*. Faber and Faber Limited, England 1940/1976.

Leppänen, Helena (Ed.): *Ruukun runoutta ja materiaalin mystiikkaa*. Publications of the University of Art and Design, B71. Ilmari, Helsinki 2003.

Lindgren, Liisa: *Elävä muoto – traditio ja modernisuus 1940-50-luvun suomalaisessa kuvanveistossa*. Dimensio 1, Academic publications of the National Museum of Art, Helsinki 1996.

Lundgren, Tyra: *Lera och eld – Ett keramiskt vagabondage i Europa*. Bokförlaget Natur och Kultur, Stockholm 1946.

Morris, William: *The Lesser Arts of Life*, 1882. – See Clark 1978.

Nottelman, Steen: *Det internationale gennem-brud. – Dansk Porcelaen 1775–2000 – Design i 225 år*. Nyt Nordisk Forlag Arnold Busck, Copenhagen 2000.

Nyman, Hannele: *ArabiaRörstrand 1975–1977 – Yhteistyösopimuksen tausta, synty ja vaikutukset Arabian tuotantoon* in Hannele Nyman & Harri Kalha (Ed.), *Keramos – Kir-joituksia keramiikasta*. Keramos, Helsinki 1996.

Nyström, Bengt: *Konsten till industrin – Alf Wal-lander och Gunnar Wennerberg som konstin-dustriella formgivare*. Bokförlaget Signum, Lund 1982.

Paulsson, Gregor: *Vackrare vardagsvara*. Sven-ska Slöjdföreningen, Stockholm 1919. Fac-simile, Rekolid, Stockholm 1995.

Pfäffli, Heidi (Ed.): *Wäinö Aaltonen 1894–1966*. Publications of the Wäinö Aaltonen Museum, No. 10, Turku 1994.

Rasmussen, Peder: *Kählers Værk – Om familien Kähler og deres keramiske værksted i Næstved 1839–1974*. Nyt Nordisk Forlag Arnold Busck & Det Danske Kunstindustrimuseet, Copenhagen 2002.

Read, Herbert: *Art and Industry*. Faber and Faber Limited, London 1936.

Sillanpää-Storsjö, Pirkko: *Kera Oy – 35 vuotta Viherlaaksolaiset ry 1957–1992*. Helsinki n.d.

Suna, Eija: *Keramiikkataiteilija Valentina Modig-Manuel. – Aboa 1989–1990*, Year-

book of Turku Provincial Museum, 53–54, Turku 1993.

Newspaper and magazine articles

Carring, Holger: Myyntiosasto – tehtaamme tuntosarvet. *Saviseppo* 3/1947.

Ekholm, Kurt: Arabia – En keramisk stor-industri. *Arkitekten* 7–8/1946 .

Ekholm, Kurt: Taide suurteollisuudessa. *Savi-seppo* 6/1947.

Ekholm, Kurt: Arabian taiteellisen johtajan puhe museon avajaisissa 22.5.48. *Saviseppo* 3/1948.

Franck, Kaj: Arabian taideosasto. *Keramiikka ja Lasi* 1973.

Mattsson, Ulla: Savesta saatiin leipää lähes 300 vuotta. *Turun Sanomat* 22.2. 2003.

Nurmesniemi, Antti: Onko Suomella varaa elää vain sunnuntaita varten. *Kaunis Koti* 4/1963.

Nyman, Hannele: The Arabia Art Department – A solid group of professionals. *Form Func-tion Finland No 89*, 1/2003.

Pajastie, Eila: Nimettömyyden kausi taideteol-lisuuteen – Kaj Franckilla on puheenvuoro. *Kaunis Koti* 3/1961.

Rislakki, Eero: Kaivataanko kilpailua kera-miikkataiteen alalla?. *Kaunis Koti* 4/1949.

Septima: article on Tigerstedts workshop. *Taiteen Maailma* 3-4/1946.

Taideteollisuus. *Keramiikka ja Lasi* 2/1953.

Viljo Mäkinen – Kiven ja saven runoilija. *Nuo-rison joulu*, Hämeenlinna 1953.

Unpublished sources

Hellman, Åsa: *Early manufacture at Kupittaa*, manuscript 2003.

Herlitz, Carl Gustaf: *wages notebook* (no title) 11.9.1935/archive of the Arabia Museum.

Herlitz, Carl Gustaf: *Puhe Arabian työläisille 2.10.1937*. Helsinki, 1937/archives of the Arabia Museum.

Karpio Ritva: letter to Åsa Hellman, summer 2002.

Kenyon, Richard Allan: *A. W. Finch and the Emergence of Modern Ceramic Design in Fin-land*. Columbia University Teachers College, Columbia 1982.

Leppänen, Helena: *Keraamikko ristiaallokossa – Keraamikon arvot ja identiteetti taideteol-lisessa opetuksessa 1964–1994*. Licentiate thesis for the Department of Ceramic and Glass Design, University of Art and Design, Helsinki 1998.

Nyman, Hannele: *Greta Lisa Jäderholm-Snell-man – Kauniimpaa arkitavaraa ja luksus-esineitä*. Paper presented at the Thure Öberg seminar, Arabia 1996.

Tigerstedt, Yvonne: albums of photographs and newspaper cuttings.

Oral communications and interviews

Aaltonen, Maija 2003/Åsa Hellman

Leivo, Inkeri 2002-2003/Hannele Nyman

Liukko-Sundström, Heljä 2002–2003/Hannele Nyman

Paikkari, Pekka 2002–2003/Hannele Nyman

Riska, Kristina 2002–2003/Hannele Nyman

Tuominen-Niittylä, Kati 2000–2003/Hannele Nyman

Tuumi, Raija/Hannele Nyman

Uosikkinen, Raija 1992/Hannele Nyman

ÅSA HELLMAN

Notes

This article is based on the writer's own subjective experiences. The following individuals have kindly granted interviews and contributed valuable infor-mation: Tor and Ilma Berglöf, Birgit Dyhr, Paul Envalds, Dorrit von Fieandt, Ulla Fogelholm, Liisa Ikävalko, Catharina Kajander, Eija Karivirta, Valentina Modig-Manuel, Anna-Maria Osipow, Marja-Riitta Salama, Yvonne Tigerstedt-Suonne, Piippa Tandefelt, Liisa Tarna, Anne Virtanen, Marita Wilskman and Peter Winquist.

1 Salmenhaara, Kyllikki: 'Unohdettu savi III', *Kotiteollisuus* magazine, issue 1 1972.

2 Cf. the presentations of Willy Finch, Aina Eklund, Anna Dahlbeck and the Grönroos family of potters elsewhere in this book.

3 The material used for ceramics teaching at the Central School of Arts and Crafts was red earthenware, and pieces requiring low firing temperatures were fired there. Some ceramists used the kilns at Arabia for firing faience and light-coloured clays, as described in *Ruukuntekijästä multimedia-taiteilijaan. Suomalaisen keraamikon amma-tillinen ja taiteellinen identiteetti 1902–1995* by Harri Kalha & Helena Leppänen. University of Art and Design, Helsinki 1996. Small studios fitted with kilns did not become standard in Finland until, in the 1970s, much later than in the neighbouring Scan-dinavian countries.

4 Information on Mirjam Stäuber is mainly based on Pirjo Juusela-Sarasmo's research for an exhibition held in 1995 at the Ekenäs Museum.

5 Hellman, Åsa: 'Näkökulma Antakaa taid-ekäsityöläisille tilaisuus', in *Helsingin Sano-mat* 2 July 1978. This article confirms that Arabia stopped selling clay to independent studios in the mid-1970s. This caused a commotion among ceramists but eventually turned out to be in their favour: companies were established for importing ceramic materials and gave artists a choice of clays – including ones suitable for low firing. Arabia has since resumed the sale of clay.

6 Interview with Eija Karivirta on 31 Octo-ber 2002 and telephone interview with Anna-Maria Osipow in autumn 2002. The Töölönkatu workshop was neither long-lived nor of decisive importance, but it is cited as a typical example.

7 In an interview held on 18 July 2002, Paul Envalds gave a detailed description of the atmosphere at Arabia's art department around the time of the great reorganization. In his opinion the news was unexpected, although the production of sanitary porcelain and tiles had already been wound up. The Envalds interview gives the impression, that subconsciously, the artists were expecting something to happen: 'Each looking after his own interests …no solidarity …Raija Tuumi could perhaps have stayed …'

8 Interviews with ceramists who graduated in the 1960s point to inadequacies that still existed in the teaching at the time, making it difficult to succeed later as a practising ceramist.

9 Lundsten, Ritva: 'Savikyläunelma', *Me Naiset* magazine, issue 25, 1967.

10 *Form* magazine, issues 2–3, 1978.

11 This section is largely based on personal recollections, as at the time I was an active member of the Finnish Association of Designers Ornamo and of the first European board in the World Crafts Council. As a board member of both Ornamo and Taiko, I also took part in the Nordic cooperation networks and wrote articles on Finnish industrial art for *Form* magazine. The word *taidekäsityö*, a direct translation of the Swedish *konsthantverk*, seemed a novel concept for defining Finnish handmade ceramic work in the 1970s, so I was surprised to find, in the course of researching this book, that the word was used at least once in an Ornamo yearbook dating from the 1930s.

12 For further information on Pot Viapori, see Helena Leppänen's book *Pot Viapori 1972–1997*. Por Viapori r.y, Helsinki 1997.

AIRI HORTLING

Notes

1 Aav 2003, 44.

2 Inspired by the Finnish ceramic artist Maija Grotell, a pupil of A. W. Finch, many American students wanted to become acquainted with Finnish ceramics production, and it was for this reason that a number of Fullbright scholars came to the Arabia factory and the Atheneum. Howard Tollefson was one of these, in 1962, and he made a return visit in 1992 to be professor of ceramics at the University of Art and Design, with Tapio Yli-Viikari taking his place in the USA.

3 Gröhn 2003.

4 A.W. Finch used pigments because they represented the latest products of 19th century industrialism and they gave the mass-produced Iris products an even coloured surface. It was Kyllikki Salmenhaara who aimed at a material-conscious style of teaching and would not use the department's limited financial resources to buy ready-made pigments when the students could learn to make their own.

5 The coloration potentials of the pigments were tested with various glaze mixtures and types of clay, and the resulting research reports were used for teaching purposes. See Hortling 1991.

6 Mikkilä 2002, 29.

7 EU Leader project, Sodankylä, for the developing of reindeer bone china in Lapland. See Hortling et al. 1999.

8 Hortling 1995.

9 Hortling et al. 1997.

10 The experiments on the applicability of ground soapstone for use with Finnish red clay were carried out by the research assistant Tiia Matikainen as part of the Soapstone Ceramics Centre project in Juuka. A second project, concerned with glazes, took place in 1998.

11 Hortling et al. 2001a.

12 Part of the Finnish Stone Centre at Nunnanlahti, inaugurated on 17.6.2003.

13 The aim nowadays is to achieve entirely lead-free products. Research into the solubility of lead has concentrated on oxide compositions that promote its solubility and on solubility resulting from specific choices of raw materials, see Hortling 2000.

14 Hortling et al. 2001b.

15 Latva-Somppi 1995.

16 Sotamaa 1998.

17 Aav 1996.

18 For example, Tiia Matikainen's statuesque dissertation work 'Pesät' (Nests) 2002, or Pia Backström's research into the concept of Paria marble and the resulting porcelain clay for the purpose of producing statues in her dissertation work, 2003.

19 Ahokas 2001.

20 Launonen 2000.

21 Vähäsalo 1997.

22 Jokinen 2002.

23 The design garden and coffee house TARHA (Garden) existed in the Design Museum in 2001, and a documentary exhibition reflecting its summery atmosphere was held in the permanent coffee bar of the Design Museum on 7.–19.12.2001. This exhibition also included a compilation of opinions on design products gleaned from the Garden project. The initiative for the project came from the students themselves, and many of the colleagues of Terästö and Rissanen.

Sources

Aav, Marianne: *Rudolf Staffel – Searching for Light*; Taideteollisuusmuseon julkaisuja No. 42, Helsinki, 1996.

Aav, Marianne: 'Ruukuntekijä vai taiteilija – kansainvälisiä heijastuksia', in *Ruukun runoutta ja materiaalin mystiikkaa* (Ed. Helena Leppänen); University of Art and Design, Helsinki, Ilmari 2003.

Ahokas, Iiro: *Fenix – tuhka-astia metaforisena siirtymäobjektina aineellisen ja aineettoman välillä*, Master's degree dissertation in fine art. University of Art and Design, Helsinki 2001.

Gröhn, Henrik: *Muutoksen vuodet*, in *Ruukun runoutta ja materiaalin mystiikkaa* (Ed. Helena Leppänen); University of Art and Design, Helsinki, Ilmari 2003.

Hortling, Airi: *The Influence of the Particle Size and Iron Oxide of the Clay on the Colour of the Pigments*; 93rd American Ceramic Society Proceedings, Cincinnati, Ohio, USA, 1991.

Hortling, Airi: *Kivinen maa, Suomalaisen vuolukiven ja dolomiitin käyttö keramiikka- ja lasimateriaaleissa*. Yliopistopaino 1995.

Hortling, Airi & Härmälä, Olli & Kaarna, Kirsi & Sotamaa, Tuuli: The effect of phlogopite mica on the sintering point and colour of a clay body, Conference and Exhibition of the European Ceramic Society. June 22–26, *Euro Ceramics* V, Volume 3, 11: pp. 2156–2159. Versailles, France 1997.

Hortling, Airi: *Kiiltävä lasitepinta*, in *Materiaalin merkitys*, Taideteollisen korkeakoulun julkaisusarja F11, Helsinki 2000.

Hortling, Airi & Jokinen, Eeva : CaO and MgO glaze on cordierite body. Euro Ceramics VII, Bruges, Belgium 2001.

Hortling, Airi & Jokinen, Eeva: Ledless Glazes, *Euro Ceramics VII*, Bruges, Belgium 2001.

Hortling, Airi & Mannonen, Risto & Räsänen, Jaana: Reindeer Bone China of Lapland, The 6th Conference and Exhibition of the European Ceramic Society, June 20–24, Brighton Conference Centre. ECer Proceedings n 60 Vol. 2, England, 1999.

Jokinen, Eeva: *VALO-merkki. Riisiposliinin historia, tekniikka ja materiaalit*, Master's degree dissertation in fine art. University of Art and Design, Helsinki 2002.

Launonen, Krista: Muotoilun nuoret ehdottomat, in the magazine *Gloria*, March-April, 2000.

Latva-Somppi, Riikka: *Lupiininsiemen ja muita kokemuksia*, Master's degree dissertation in fine art. University of Art and Design, Helsinki 1995.

Mikkilä, Timo: *Näkymätön tekijä. Kertomus Bang & Bonsomerin 75-vuotisesta taipaleesta*; PicaScript Oy, Helsinki, 2002.

Sotamaa, Yrjö: *Onko suomalainen muotoilu vain tyhjä myytti?* Speech at the opening of the 26th academic year, 31 August. University of Art and Design, Helsinki 1998.

NOTES AND SOURCES FOR ARTIST PRESENTATIONS
chronologically by year of birth

A. W. FINCH, b. 1854

1 *Alfred William Finch 1854–1930*, pp. 43–46.
2 *Alfred William Finch 1854–1930*, pp. 47–50.
3 Between 1971 and 1974 I carried out several firing experiments with clay from various places in the Porvoo area and concluded that even in the day's modern electrical kilns it was difficult to achieve an even result. The iron content and vitrification points varied. In the early 1970s I used the Atheneum's old wood-burning kiln to fire large sculptures made of Porvoo clay, half of which melted, losing their shape.
4 Rosenberg & Selin, 1995.
5 Saaristo: 'Savenvalanta Keravalla I & II' and Sampola interviews, transcripts 14, 24 and 42. Potter August Ek mentions that Finch's student Aina Eklund trained at his workshop with some kind of 'government grant'. In conjunction with the research for this book it was also found that master potter Gustaf Alexander Franzén (born in Nurmes, 8 February 1867), having worked for a time at Ek's pottery in Kerava in the 1890s, moved to Porvoo to work for Finch at AB Iris. The move is documented in his son Gösta Franzén's family records. G. A. Franzén's sixth child (of ten), potter Gunnar Franzén, told Catharina Kajander (employed at the Franzén pottery in Täkter) in the 1960s that his father had worked at the Iris factory.
6 Saaristo: 'Savenvalanta Keravalla I'.
7 Cf. note 9. At least Gustav Adolf Franzén, son of Iris potter Gustaf Alexander Franzén, studied with Finch (also see the presentation of Johan and Anna Grönroos, elsewhere in this book). Finch appears to have allowed some students to study free of charge; they were only registered in the university's books for short periods, sometimes not at all. On the whole, Finch comes across as a gentleman who would not have turned away those of lesser means.
8 An advertisement published in 1898 mentions that AB Iris's domestic wares were glazed with La Bâte's guaranteed lead-free glazes (Supinen 1993, p. 38). It appears that most Iris pots made for storing foodstuffs used lead-free borax glazes, whereas a great deal of their decorative and unique ceramics show characteristics typical of traditional lead glazes. As with the high-fired celadon glazes used in traditional Chinese ceramics, the iron content in Finnish earthenware clay causes beautiful olive-green hues to appear in transparent lead glazes in a reducing atmosphere (cf. Terminology). Copper oxide generally produces grass-green colours. The factory's pea-green glazes containing chrome oxide are rich and expressive, and form a stark contrast to the usual copper green. Turquoise and blue-green shades, on the other hand, were achieved with borax glazes.
9 Memorandum by A. W. Finch from 1914, microfilm, Archive II of the University of Art and Design Helsinki.
10 In several of the interviews I carried out in 2002 and 2003, Finch's student Valentina Modig-Manuel, aged ninety-six but full of vigour and with a keen memory, mentioned that Finch spoke fluent Swedish. According to Modig-Manuel, he could also write Swedish very well without help from his secretary. She was referring to the 1920s when Finch had been in Finland for a long time.

SOURCES:

Tuusula Museum, Kerava Museum, archive of the University of Art and Design Helsinki, archive of the Design Museum, Helsinki, archive of the National Museum of Finland, Porvoo Museum collection, ceramics collection belonging to Lea Niemi (Johan Grönroos III's daughter-in-law).

Materials from Kerava Museum:
Saaristo, Martti: 'Savenvalanta Keravalla I' and 'Savenvalanta Keravalla II', manuscripts [n.p./n.d.].
Sampola, Olli: Interview with potter August Ek (b. 1888) on 3 September 1966, transcript 42.
Sampola, Olli: Interview with Hilppa Nummela née Grönroos (b. 1915) on 16 May 1979, transcript 24.
Sampola, Olli: Interview with Katri Johanna Kari née Saarela (b. 1899) on 29 May 1979, transcript 14.

Bibliography includes:
Alfred William Finch 1854–1930, exhibition catalogue (Swedish edition), Atheneum Art Museum, Helsinki 2 October–1 December 1991, Musées des Beaux-Arts de Belgique, Brussels, 16 January–31 March 1992; Atheneum Art Museum and Design Museum, Helsinki, 1991.
Franzén, Gösta: 'Hur min far G. A. Franzén blev krukmakaremästare med egen verkstad i Täkter, Ingå och med fem söner, som alla blev krukmakare och fortsatte att arbeta i lergods och keramikbranschen.' [n.p./n.d.].
Gulin, Åke: *Målare*; Söderström & Co Förlags Ab, 1978.
Kajander, Maija: 'Rakkaudesta saveen. Taiteilijayhteisö nosti Tuusulan käsityöläisperinteen kunniaan', *Keski-Uusimaa* newspaper, 17 September 2000.
Kalha, Harri: *Modernin suomalaisen keramiikka-taiteen juurilla Alfred William Finch – opettaja, esikuva, suunnannäyttäjä*; Taidehistoriallisia tutkimuksia 13, Helsinki, 1993.
Kalha, Harri: 'A. W. Finchin aika 1902–1930', in Kalha, Harri and Leppänen, Helena: *Ruukuntekijästä multimediataiteilijaan. Suomalaisen keraamikon ammatillinen ja taiteellinen identiteetti 1902–1995*, Taideteollisen korkeakoulun julkaisusarja B 49, Helsinki, 1996; pp. 19–35.
Kenyon, Richard Allan: *A. W. Finch and the Emergence of Modern Ceramic Design in Finland*; Columbia University Teachers College, USA, 1982.
Laiho, Arja: 'Erkkolan tarinat I', *Keski-Uusimaa*, 26 October 1986.
Mannerheim Sparre, Eva: *Konstnärsliv – Sparreminnen från gamla tider till 1908*; Holger Schildts förlag, Helsinki, 1951.
Priskurant över Aktiebolaget Iris keramiska tillvärkningar; Lilius & Hertzberg, Helsinki, 1901. Porvoo Museum, 1979.
Rosenberg, Antti and Selin, Rauno: *Suur-Tuusulan historia III 1809–1924*; Municipality of Tuusula, City of Kerava and City of Järvenpää, 1995.
Supinen, Marja: *A. B. Iris Suuri Yritys*; Sulkava, 1993.
Supinen, Marja: 'Van de Velde och Finch, profeter i främmande land' in *Henry van de Velde 1863–1957*; Design Museum and Museum of Finnish Architecture, Helsinki, 1986.
Tamminen, Marketta: 'The Dream of the Home as a Total Work of Art' in *Now the Light Comes from the North. Art Nouveau in Finland*; Bröhan Museum, Vammala, 2002; pp. 95–106.

WILLY FINCH'S FIRST STUDENTS

1 Von Essen 1925, p. 171.
2 Saaristo, Martti: 'Savenvalanta Keravalla', in *Myllyjen Kerava. Kotikaupunki Kerava*; Kerava-seura ry:n julkaisuja no. 5, Savio, 1984 (manuscript borrowed from Kerava Museum). This book includes interviews with potter August Ek and Osmo Helenius, son of potter Johan Artturi Helenius. The text illustrates how potters in the Tuusula-Kerava region worked closely with local painters, the Iris factory, Willy Finch and his students (the article erroneously calls Anna Dahlbeck Anna Dahlberg). Cf. the presentation of A. W. Finch in this book.
3 'Naistaiteilijain näyttely Pietarissa', *Suomalainen Kansa* newspaper issue 25, 2 February 1910, and 'En "damernas utställning" i Petersburg', *Hufvudstadsbladet* newspaper, 9 January 1910.
4 *Den finske utställning*, exhibition catalogue, Charlottenburg, November–December 1919; Finnish National Gallery Central Art Archives.

5 *Den fria utställningen – Vapaa näyttely*, exhibition catalogue, Kunsthalle Helsinki, 1930; Finnish National Gallery Central Art Archives.

6 Information on E. Borenius is based on the annual reports of the University of Art and Design Helsinki and on research carried out by Leena Svinhufvud in 2002, found in the archive of the Design Museum, Helsinki. Cf. also von Essen, Werner: *Suomen taideteollisuusydistys ja sen keskuskoulu 1870–1875–1925*; Finnish Society of Crafts and Design, Helsinki, 1925. The archive of the University of Art and Design Helsinki also contains letters by E. Borenius (Brummer file E).

7 According to Sven Eriksson, the Juselius family referred to 'Elin's pots' in a humorous (and slightly disparaging?) tone.

8 Information from Marja Castrén.

9 A. W. Finch wrote in a memorandum of 1914 (point 6): 'A wheel should be made available for students of lesser means to use free of charge at certain times (e.g. 9 a.m. to 12 p.m.), as should pigments and firing equipment.' (Archive of the University of Art and Design Helsinki)

10 Microfilm, Archive II of the University of Art and Design Helsinki.

11 Saaristo, Martti: 'Savenvalanta Keravalla', in *Myllyjen Kerava. Kotikaupunki Kerava.*; Kerava-seura ry:n julkaisuja no. 5, Savio, 1984 (manuscript borrowed from Kerava Museum). Interview with potter August Ek, where he describes Miss Eklund's work at his workshop.

12 Kenyon 1982, p. 259.

13 Johannes Wilskman was an advisor at the Viipuri courts of law, later to become a Member of Parliament resident in Helsinki and Heinola. In 1925 he reassumed his original surname, Wilskman.

14 Surviving letters indicate that Sigrid Wiljomaa suffered ill health. Her life had a tragic undertone, with the dissolution of her marriage in the early 1930s and the death of her only child, Aune, shortly after that.

15 A. W. Finch wrote in a memorandum of 1914: 'A new wheel is needed (at least one!). The old ones must be repaired, though it would be preferable to acquire new wheels, as the old ones are ill constructed – much too heavy, suitable only for use by big, strong men!' (microfilm, Archive II of the University of Art and Design Helsinki).

16 Information from Marja Castrén.

17 'Käsityö ja kulttuuri', *Uusi Suomi* magazine, 3 December 1969.

18 Supinen 1986.

19 Kruskopf 1989, p. 78.

20 The exhibition of prizes in the draw organized by the Finnish Society of Crafts and Design in 1908 aroused great interest in the press. *Nya Pressen* newspaper mentioned on 29 May 1908 ('Konstflitföreningens vinstexposition') and on 3 June 1908 ('Konstflitföreningens lotteri') prizes made by Sigrid Wickström (Siru Wirva),

including a vase costing FIM 40, won by K. M. Vainio from Turku.

21 'Taiteilija Elsa Elenius 70-vuotias', *Helsingin Sanomat* newspaper, 7 September 1954.

22 Information from Anneli Warén-Branders.

SOURCES:
Antti Laakkonen and Carl Fredrik Sandelin participated in the research for this book and contributed significant materials on Finch's first students.

Central Register of Congregations in Finland, archive of the Turku Swedish Congregation, archive of the University of Art and Design Helsinki (student registers, annual reports, documents on the Finnish Society of Crafts and Design's annual prize draws, Arttu Brummer's archive), Brage press archive, Finnish National Gallery Central Art Archives, archive of the Design Museum, Helsinki, Porvoo Museum, archive of the National Museum of Finland, Tuusula Museum, Kerava Museum, Ainola, several private collections.
Telephone interview with Sven Eriksson (Elin Juselius's relative), 2002.
Interview with Marja Castrén (granddaughter of Aili Warén), 2002.
Interview with Marita Wilskman (daughter of Johannes Wilskman by his second wife), 2002.
Interview with Anneli Warén-Branders (daughter of Anni Brandt), 2003.

Bibliography includes (in addition to newspaper articles mentioned in footnotes):
Kenyon, Richard Allan: *A. W. Finch and the Emergence of Modern Ceramic Design in Finland*; Columbia University Teachers College, USA, 1982.
Kruskopf, Erik: *Finlands konstindustri – Den finländska konstflitens historia*; WSOY, Porvoo, 1989.
Supinen, Marja: 'Van de Velde och Finch, profeter i främmande land' in *Henry van de Velde 1863–1957*; Design Museum and Museum of Finnish Architecture, Helsinki, 1986.
Von Essen, Werner: *Suomen taideteollisuusyhdistys ja sen keskuskoulu 1870–1875–1925*; Finnish Society of Crafts and Design, Helsinki, 1925.

VILLE VALLGREN, b. 1855
1 Kava 1993, pp. 239–40.
2 Vallgren, Ville: 'Terracottaföreningens utställning', *Allas Krönika*, 6 December 1924.
3 Söderström 1999, p. 662. Söderström mentions that Vallgren admired the work of the Ostrobothnian potter Karl Hildén.
4 An important source of information was a scrapbook composed by Terracotta member Gregori Tigerstedt with articles, advertisements and exhibition reviews, which his daughter Yvonne Tigerstedt-Suonne kindly made available to me.

5 Vallgren 1931, p. 156.

SOURCES:
Lecture by museum curator Marketta Tamminen on Ville Vallgren, Borgå Medborgarinstitut, 9 September 2003.
Porvoo Museum, Brage press archive.
Gregori Tigerstedt's scrapbook.

Bibliography includes:
Ahtola-Moorhouse, Leena and Green, Selma (ed.): *Ville Vallgren 1855–1940*; Atheneum Art Museum/Finnish National Gallery, Helsinki, 2003.
Ahtola-Moorhouse, Leena: 'A Toast to Ville Vallgren'; *Form Function* magazine 2/2003.
Karvonen-Kannas, Kerttu and Kivimäki, Kati (eds.): *Kosketuskohtia ja kipinäväli*; Gallen-Kallela Museum, 1997.
Kava, Ritva: *Emil Cedercreutz – Satakunnan eurooppalainen*; Finnish Historical Society, Helsinki, 1993.
Kuvataiteilijat Oy; Julk. Suomen taiteilijaseura r.y., K. J. Gummerus, Jyväskylä, 1979.
Söderström, Eugen: *Märkesmän och -kvinnor i karlebynejden*; Fram AB, Vaasa, 1999.
Vallgren, Viivi: *Sydämeni kirja*; Werner Söderström Oy, Porvoo, 1979.
Vallgren, Ville: *Minnen från mitt liv - Hemma och ute*; Mercators tryckeriaktiebolag, Helsinki, 1931.
Vallgren, Ville: *Mat och dryck med roliga gubbar*; Tryckeri- & Tidnings Ab, Porvoo, 1975.
Vallgren, Ville: 'Inhemsk konst till Paris', *Hufvudstadsbladet* newspaper, 12 October 1922.
Vallgren, Ville: 'Finlands dolda skatter', *Hufvudstadsbladet*, 16 October 1922.
Vallgren, Ville: 'Terracottaföreningens utställning', *Allas Krönika*, 6 December 1924.
'Valois' (pseudonym): 'Ville Vallgren bränner', *Hufvudstadsbladet*, 18 March 1923.
'Valois' (pseudonym): 'Vallgrens terrakotta', *Hufvudstadsbladet*, 19 April 1923.

SIGRID AF FORSELLES, b. 1860
1 Written sources and the dates on some of her pieces indicate that Sigrid af Forselles made and fired some of her work abroad and some in Finland.
2 Interview with Marianne Frietsch.
3 Information from Simon Cottle, director of the ceramics and glass department at Sotheby's, London.

SOURCES:
Materials from the Loviisa City Museum.
Interview with Marianne Frietsch (daughter of Sigrid af Forselles's niece). Materials borrowed from Marianne Frietsch.

Bibliography includes:
Hartikainen, Arja: *Sigrid af Forselles ja reliefisarja "Ihmissielun kehitys"*, thesis; University of Jyväskylä, 1994.

Hoffman, Christian: 'Sigrid af Forselles: Uurna'; *Museotiedote Turusta* magazine, Taide 3, 1992.

Westermarck, Helena: *Tre konstnärinnor*; Helsinki, 1937.

JOHAN (b. 1863) AND ANNA GRÖNROOS

1   Rinta-Aho, 1989.
2   A. W. Finch's presentation describes the links between the potters in the Tuusula-Kerava area and AB Iris.
3   Rosenberg & Selin 1995, p. 141. Janne Grönroos manufactured the green tiles for the tiled stove in Jean Sibelius's house Ainola. Carl Edvard Green's pottery was still in operation in Porvoo around the time when AB Iris was established (Supinen 1993); it also made tiled stoves and it is possible that the Iris Room tiles were Green's handiwork.
4   Kajander 2000. Around ten pieces thrown by Janne Grönroos and decorated by his daughter remain in the possession of Anna's children. Some artists' homes on the famed road of Tuusulan rantatie also contain Grönroos ceramics.

SOURCES:
Telephone interview with Lea Niemi (Anna Grönroos's daughter-in-law).

Telephone interview with Erkki Fredriksson, curator of the Museum of Central Finland, 2003.

Photographer Toivo Lumme's slide series from the 1970s featuring the Grönroos family of potters.

Bibliography:
Interview with Hilppa Nummela née Grönroos, b. 1914. Transcript 24, 15 February 1996, Kerava Museum.

Halonen, Antti: *Taiteen juhlaa ja arkea*; Tammi, 1982.

Holma, Sirkka: *Tuusulan rantatie Pekka Halosen aikaan*; Pieksämäki, 1990.

Kajander, Maija: 'Rakkaudesta saveen. Taiteilijayhteisö nosti Tuusulan käsityöläisperinteen kunniaan', *Keski-Uusimaa* newspaper, 17 September 2000.

Laiho, Arja: 'Erkkolan tarinat I', *Keski-Uusimaa*, 26 October 1986.

'Puolustusvoimat kunnostaa savenvalajien rakennuksen', *Keski-Uusimaa*, 17 September 2000.

Rinta-Aho, Johanna: *Halosenniemen rakennushistoria* (Section 5.3.1., 'Halosenniemen uunien rakentaminen'), unprinted study; Tuusula Museum, 1989.

Rosenberg, Antti and Selin, Rauno: *Suur-Tuusulan historia III 1809–1924*; Municipality of Tuusula, City of Kerava and City of Järvenpää, 1995.

Smeds, Kerstin: *Helsingfors – Paris. Finlands utveckling till nation på världsutställningarna 1851–1900*; Society of Swedish Literature in Finland, Finnish Historical Society, 1996.

Supinen, Marja: *A.B. Iris Suuri Yritys*; Kustannusosakeyhtiö Taide, 1993.

SIGRID GRANFELT, b. 1868

1   Sigrid Granfelt donated Husö to Åbo Akademi University in 1940. Today the estate is a biological station that employs some ten researchers each summer. Preserved at the house are not only ceramic pieces but also original furniture and textiles as well as wood-carvings and decorative painting work by Sigrid Granfelt.
2   Milky-white patches where glaze has been applied too thickly suggest borax glazes.
3   Husö contains two large stove tiles stamped 'Turun kaakelitehdas'. They don't belong to any of the stoves at the estate but were apparently used as separate decorations. According to an antique dealer from Porvoo, Sigrid Granfelt may have worked at the Turku tile factory, but this has not been confirmed. The tiles found at Husö may have been designed by Granfelt, as she tended to decorate her home with her own work.

SOURCES:
Archive of the University of Art and Design Helsinki, Åland Art Museum and Åland Museum. Visit to Husö Estate in 2002.

Bibliography:
Konstnärinnan Hantverkaren SIGRID GRANFELT 1868–1942, exhibition at Åland Art Museum 10 December 1988–8 January 1989, organized by the Åland Martha Organization and the Åland Art Museum.

Lindqvist, Viveka: *Sigrid Granfelt – hennes liv och verk*, thesis in art history; Åbo Akademi University, 1985.

Nyman, Valdemar: *Finströms sockenkrönika V Vassrike*; Ålands Folkminnesförbund r.s., 1990.

'Sigrid Granfelt 1868–1942', *Åland* newspaper, 1942 (exact date unknown).

Åländska kvinnoporträtt, exhibition publication; Åland Museum and Åland Art Museum, 2000.

GERDA THESLEFF, b. 1871

1   The Arabia Museum Gallery attracted great critical attention in 1999 with an exhibition of Gerda Thesleff's work.
2   Our pioneer ceramists battled with countless technical problems. Teaching in ceramic chemistry was non-existent and materials were difficult to obtain. This is described in further detail in the article 'The advent of small ceramic workshops in Finland'.

SOURCES:
Archive of the University of Art and Design Helsinki (student registers, prize catalogues of the Finnish Society of Crafts and Design), Brage press archive.

Bibliography:
Bäcksbacka, Leonard: *Ellen Thesleff*; Konstsalongens förlag, Helsinki, 1955.

'Crayon' (pseudonym): 'Inhemsk konstfajans', *Svenska Pressen*, 23 May 1922.

'H j. H' (pseudonym): 'Gerda och Ellen Thesleffs utställning', *Svenska Pressen* newspaper, 24 March 1941.

Hellman, Åsa: 'Hemlighetsfull krukmakare', *Hufvudstadsbladet* newspaper, 8 November 1999.

Kalha, Harri: *Taidekeramiikka Suomessa 1920- ja 1930-luvuilla*, art-historical study; University of Helsinki, 1990.

Kumela, Marjut: *Gerda Thesleff 1871–1939*, exhibition at Arabia Museum Gallery, 1995.

'Nils W' (pseudonym): 'Konstfajanser', *Hufvudstadsbladet*, 25 May 1922.

Petterson, Susanne: *Gerda Thesleff, orientalismen, fauvismen och dess influenser i hennes keramik*, thesis; Åbo Akademi University, 2000.

THURE ÖBERG, b. 1872
Bibliography includes:
Ekholm, Kurt: 'Keramikern Thure Öberg', *Arkkitehti – Arkitekten* journal 3/1956.

Kumela, Marjut: 'Taideosasto' in *Arabia*; Oy Wärtsilä Ab Arabia, Helsinki, 1987.

Maunula, Leena: 'Hundra Arabia-kärl – Arabias brukssortiment sedan 1874' in *Keramik och glas, Arabia 100 år – jubileumsnummer 1973*; Oy Wärtsilä Ab Arabia, Helsinki, 1973.

KARL HILDÉN, b. 1873

1   Information corroborated by Professor Åke Hellman, who visited Hildén's workshop several times in the early 1940s. Hildén's friends included many artists and designers of the time.
2   Söderström 1999, p. 62.
3   Interview with Professor Erik Kråkström, 2002.
4   Interview with K. Hildén, *Seura*, 20 August 1936.

SOURCES:
Study of Hildén's ceramics in the K. H. Renlund Museum, the Ostrobothnian Museum, the collections of Kaarelan kotiseutuyhdistys and several private collections in Pohjanmaa and Uusimaa.

Interview with goldsmith Helge Hildén (grandson of Karl Hildén), 2003.

Interviews with architect Krister Korpela, 2003, and architect Erik Kråkström, 2003.

Bibliography:
Söderström, Eugen: *Märkesmän och -kvinnor i karlebynejden*; Fram Ab, Vaasa, 1999.

Magazine clippings kindly provided by the Kokkola Art Museum, including 'Savenvalaja vuosikymmenen takaa'; *Kokkola* newspaper, 1 July 1982, and 'Hildén teki savikukot joilla ryssäläismieliselle luotsivirkamiehelle Kokkolassa vihellettiin', *Seura* magazine, 20 August 1936.

EMIL CEDERCREUTZ, b. 1879

1 Items thrown by Cedercreutz as a beginner in the craft naturally differ from pieces thrown by professional potters.
2 Photographs of these pieces were published in Cedercreutz's book *Häststudier i skulptur och klippning* (Lilius & Hertzberg, Helsinki, 1902). Cylindrical pots decorated with equestrian silhouettes appear on a pedestal, probably photographed at the University of Art and Design Helsinki.
3 Kava 1993, p. 240, and Lydecken 1927, p. 57. At least a few large, white, relief-decorated vases made by Cedercreutz at Arabia still survive.

SOURCES:
Materials and factual data kindly made available by Ritva Kava, Director of the Emil Cedercreutz Museum and Culture Centre.

Bibliography includes:
Cedercreutz, Emil: *Yksinäisyyttä ja ihmisvilinää*; Harjulan Kilta r.y., 2000.
Kava, Ritva: *Emil Cedercreutz – Satakunnan eurooppalainen*; Finnish Historical Society, Helsinki, 1993.
Lydecken, Arvid: *Suomalaisia taiteilijakoteja ja taiteilijoita*; WSOY, Porvoo, 1927.
Gregori Tigerstedt's scrapbook.

GUNNAR FINNE, b. 1886
Puokka, Jaakko (ed.): *Gunnar Finne, kuvanveistäjä*; Otava, Helsinki, 1947.
Kuvataiteilijat 1979; Artists' Association of Finland, 1979.

GREGORI TIGERSTEDT, b. 1891

1 Yvonne Tigerstedt-Suonne's house still contains some early ceramic pieces by Tapio Wirkkala, fired at no.12 Pohjoisranta, Helsinki.

SOURCES:
Interviews with Yvonne Tigerstedt-Suonne, 2002.
Gregori Tigerstedt's scrapbook with photographs, newspaper clippings, notes, etc.

GUSTI FRANZÉN, b. 1892

1 According to a historical text written by his son Gösta, Gustaf Alexander Franzén worked initially in Kerava in the 1890s and then in Porvoo. Furthermore, Gunnar Franzén told Catharina Kajander that his father had been employed at AB Iris. A turn-of-the-century handled vase, signed 'F.', found in a Porvoo home, could be attributed to him.
2 Memorandum by A. W. Finch from 1914, microfilm, Archive III of the University of Art and Design Helsinki; Finch defends the idea that potters might be permitted to study at the school and use glazes and pigments free of charge.

SOURCES:
Archive of the University of Art and Design Helsinki (student registers, prize catalogues of the Finnish Society of Crafts and Design, Arttu Brummer's archive), archive of the National Museum of Finland.
Interviews with members of the Franzén family, including Bo-Gustaf Franzén, Gunnar Lindholm and Hedvig Järvinen.
Gusti Franzén's study certificate, contract with Kupittaan Savi Oy, letters, photographs and ceramic items preserved by the Franzén family.
Visit to Täkter workshop c. 1972.
Franzén, Gösta: 'Hur min far G. A. Franzén blev krukmakarmästare med egen verkstad i Täkter, Ingå och med fem söner, som alla blev krukmakare och fortsatte att arbeta i lergods och keramikbranschen.' [n.p./n.d.].

WÄINÖ AALTONEN, b. 1894

1 A product catalogue from 1941 shows that Aaltonen's dish was still in production.
2 Verbal information received from Maija Aaltonen, Auli Urrila (niece of Elsa Elenius) and countless students.

SOURCES:
Interviews with Maija Aaltonen, 2002 and 2003.

Bibliography includes:
Kalha, Harri: 'Keramik från Kupittaan Savi Oy' in *ABOA*, Turku Provincial Museum yearbook, 1989–90.
Pfäffli, Heidi (ed.): *Wäinö Aaltonen 1894–1996*; Wäinö Aaltonen Museum publication no. 10, Turku, 1994.

GRETA LISA JÄDERHOLM-SNELLMAN, b. 1894

SOURCES:
Kalha, Harri: *Taidekeramiikka Suomessa 1920- ja 1930-luvulla*, art-historical study; University of Helsinki, 1990.
Kruskopf, Erik: *Finlands konstindustri – Den finländska konstflitens utvecklingshistoria*; WSOY, Porvoo, 1989.
Kumela, Marjut: 'Taideosasto' and 'Koristeesineitä' in *Arabia*; Oy Wärtsilä Ab Arabia, Helsinki, 1987.
Nyman, Hannele: 'Greta Lisa Jäderholm-Snellman', lecture at Thure Öberg Seminar, Arabia, 1996.
Vem och vad; Centraltryckeriet, Helsinki, 1941.

SIIRI HARIOLA, b. 1895

1 Sigrid Högström changed her name to the more Finnish-sounding Siiri Hariola c. 1934.

SOURCES include:
Design Museum, Helsinki, artist archive and ceramics collections.
Kalha, Harri and Leppänen, Helena: *Ruukuntekijästä multimediataiteilijaan. Suomalaisen keraamikon ammatillinen ja taiteellinen identiteetti 1902-1995*; Taideteollisen korkeakou-

lun julkaisusarja B 49, Helsinki, 1996, pp. 33–34, 53–54.
University of Art and Design Helsinki annual reports and student registers.

EMIL REKOLA, b. 1895

1 After Gusti Franzén's death, his wife gave their niece Hedvig Järvinen a large decorated vase signed 'E R −24', saying it had been made by 'Gusti's fellow student'. During my research for this book, Hedvig Järvinen found a photograph in their family album, taken at Kupittaan Savi Oy in the early 1920s. In it her aunt Edith Franzén (later Lindholm) is decorating a vase, accompanied by a young man, against a background of several fired and decorated pots. Edith Franzén herself wrote under the image: 'Here I sit, all day long, painting. As you can see, there is plenty of painting to do. My friend is Rekola, the artist.' Gusti Franzén's and Emil Rekola's friendship is corroborated by a greeting card sent by the former to the latter.
SOURCES:
Facts on the people mentioned in the text were acquired by Carl Fredrik Sandelin, among other places from the Central Register of Congregations in Finland. Antti Laakkonen found information on Emil Rekola's studies in the student registers of the University of Art and Design Helsinki.

ELSA ELENIUS, b. 1897

1 Franck 1982.
2 Urrila-Stenbäck 1983, p. 6.
3 The countless women ceramists who gave up ceramics in their middle age include Kyllikki Salmenhaara, Piippa Tandefelt and Marita Lybeck. Many of those who worked with their husbands, including Valentina Modig-Manuel, continued until their retirement.
4 As a student with Kyllikki Salmenhaara, I heard her say a couple of times: 'I have often thought that I really did have a good teacher!'

SOURCES:
Archive of the Design Museum, Helsinki.
Interview with Auli Urrila-Stenbäck (niece of Elsa Elenius), 2002.

Bibliography:
Franck, Kaj: 'Iriksen jälkeen', lecture at the Design Museum, Helsinki, 21 November 1982.
Kalha, Harri: 'Elsa Eleniuksen aika 1930–1962', in Kalha, Harri and Leppänen, Helena: *Ruukuntekijästä multimediataiteilijaan. Suomalaisen keraamikon ammatillinen ja taiteellinen identiteetti 1902–1995*; Taideteollisen korkeakoulun julkaisusarja B 49, Helsinki, 1996; pp. 40–65.
Kalha, Harri: 'Materiaalin sielua etsimässä. Keramiikan estetiikasta 1930–50-luvuilla', in Leppänen, Helena (ed.): *Ruukun runoutta*

ja materiaalin mystiikkaa; University of Art and Design Helsinki, 2003, pp. 66–81.
Urrila-Stenbäck, Auli: 'Elsa Elenius – keramiikkataiteilija', art-historical study, University of Helsinki, 1983.

TYRA LUNDGREN, b. 1897
SOURCES:
Information from Jan Norrman, curator at Nationalmuseum, Stockholm.

Bibliography includes:
Kalha, Harri: 'Tyra Lundgren och Arabia – en blick på konstnären i industrin' in Nyman, Hannele and Kalha, Harri (eds.): *Keramos – Kirjoituksia keramiikasta – Artiklar om keramik*; Keramos - Keramiikan ystävät ry, 1996.
Kruskopf, Erik: *Finlands konstindustri – Den finländska konstflitens utvecklingshistoria*; WSOY, Porvoo, 1989.
Kumela, Marjut: 'Taideosasto' in *Arabia*; Oy Wärtsilä Ab Arabia, 1987.
Nationalencyklopedin; Bokförlaget Bra Böcker, Höganäs, Sweden, 1993.
Vingedal, S. E.: *Porslinsmärken*; Forum, 2000.

MAIJA GROTELL, b. 1899
1   Verbal information from Rolf Nystén.
2   Electrical kilns were not built in Finland until the 1930s, and only those working in industrial environments such as Arabia could fire in high temperatures. Cf. the article 'The advent of small ceramic workshops in Finland'.
3   Schlanger and Takaezu 1996, p. 9.

SOURCES:
Archives of the Design Museum, Helsinki, and the University of Art and Design Helsinki.
Maija Grotell's photograph album depicting her youth in Finland.
Verbal information received from Rolf Nystén (related to Maija Grotell on his mother's side).
Study of Maija Grotell's ceramics in museums and private collections.

Bibliography:
Schlanger, Jeff and Takaezu, Toshiko: *Maija Grotell: Works Which Grow From Belief*, a Studio Potters Books Monograph, Gerry Williams (ed.); Stinehour Press, Lunenburg, Vermont, USA, 1996.

MICHAEL SCHILKIN, b. 1900
SOURCES:
Notes made at a retrospective exhibition of Schilkin's work organized at the Amos Anderson Art Museum in 1997–98.
Ahtola-Moorhouse, Leena, Kalha, Harri and Tervo, Tuija: *Michael Schilkin 1900–1962*; Förlag W. Hagelstam, 1996.
Arabia; Oy Wärtsilä Ab Arabia, Helsinki, 1987.
Kruskopf, Erik: *Finlands konstindustri – Den finländska konstflitens utvecklingshistoria*; WSOY, Porvoo, 1989.

TOINI MUONA, b. 1904
1   Paul Envalds, who was employed as an assistant to Toini Muona in the 1960s, said that the artist's glazes were prepared by Forsberg, chemist and director of the Arabia laboratory, specifically for Muona. Her famous oxblood glaze consisted of a combination of three different glazes and had such a high frit content that it could easily become runny and lose shape. Envalds threw the basic forms and Muona gave the finishing touches. The largest white plates were made by a professional thrower. Envalds often glazed Muona's pieces with the spray technique.

SOURCES:
Interview with Paul Envalds, 2002.
Hellman, Åsa: 'Dramatiska konstnärsprofiler', *Hufvudstadsbladet* newspaper, 20 June 2002.
Kalha, Harri: *Toini Muona 1904–1907*; Förlag W. Hagelstam, 1998.
Kalha, Harri: *Toini Muona & Gunnel Nyman*, exhibition publication; Retretti Art Centre, 2002.

FRIEDL KJELLBERG, b. 1905
1   During my summer traineeship at Arabia in the early 1970s, my colleague Henrik Gröhn and I often noticed that the famous rice porcelain department seemed rather mysterious. This naturally awakened our curiosity and we often defied the rule against visiting the department....

SOURCES:
Archive of the Design Museum, Helsinki.
Hipeli, Mirja-Kaisa: *Friedl Kjellberg – Keraamikon tie 1924–1970*, exhibition at Vanha Kappalaisentalo gallery in Porvoo, 9 June–27 August 1989; Oy Arabia Ab, 1989.
Kumela, Marjut: 'Taideosasto' in *Arabia*; Oy Wärtsilä Ab Arabia, Helsinki, 1987.

KERTTU SUVANTO-VAAJAKALLIO, b. 1906
1   See Harri Kalha's article 'In the Shadows of the Grand Narrative'. Valentina Modig-Manuel has also expressed great admiration for Suvanto-Vaajakallio's artistry and believes that Suvanto-Vaajakallio's models were extremely profitable for Kupittaa.

SOURCES:
Artist archive of the Design Museum, Helsinki.
Turku Provincial Museum.
Interviews with Valentina Modig-Manuel, 2002 and 2003.
Ornamo yearbook 11/1941.

TAMARA LAURÉN, b. 1906
SOURCES:
Artist archive and ceramics collection of the Design Museum, Helsinki.
Franck, Kaj: 'Iriksen jälkeen', lecture on 14 November 1981, University of Art and Design Helsinki.

Kalha, Harri and Leppänen, Helena: *Ruukuntekijästä multimediataiteilijaan. Suomalaisen keraamikon ammatillinen ja taiteellinen identiteetti 1902–1995*; Taideteollisen korkeakoulun julkaisusarja B 49, Helsinki, 1996, p. 33.

MARITA LYBECK, b. 1906
1   Verbal information from Marita Lybeck.
2   Although Marita Lybeck managed to make a new career, she was frustrated that her models were – as she saw it – copied and mass-produced at Arabia. It is still noteworthy that Emmel stayed in operation for ten years, relying mainly on handmade work.

SOURCES:
Telephone interview with Charlotte Lybeck (daughter of Marita Lybeck), 2002.
Interview with Marita Lybeck at her home in Kauniainen, early 1980s.
Marita Lybeck's handwritten autobiography from the time of her application for an artists' pension from the government.
Kalha, Harri: *Marita Lybeck 1906–1990*, exhibition at Galleria Septaria, Helsinki, 1996.

KURT EKHOLM, b. 1907

SOURCES:
Franck, Kaj: 'Arabias konstavdelning' in *Keramik och Glas. Arabia 100 år – jubileumsnummer 1973*; Oy Wärtsilä Ab Arabia, 1973.
Hellman, Åsa: 'Arabia als Förderer des Keramischen Kunsthandwerks in Finnland' in *Schweizer Heimatwerk*, Switzerland, 1972.
Kruskopf, Erik: *Finlands konstindustri – Den finländska konstflitens utvecklingshistoria*; WSOY, Porvoo, 1989.
Kumela, Marjut: 'Taideosasto' in *Arabia*; Oy Wärtsilä Ab Arabia, Helsinki, 1973.
Nyman, Hannele: 'The Arabia Art Department: A Solid Group of Professionals', *Form Function* magazine 1/2003.
Ornamo yearbooks, 1930s.

VALENTINA MODIG-MANUEL, b. 1907
SOURCES:
Interview with Valentina Modig-Manuel at her home, 11 July 2002, and several telephone interviews.

Bibliography:
Kalha, Harri and Leppänen, Helena: *Ruukuntekijästä multimediataiteilijaan. Suomalaisen keraamikon ammatillinen ja taiteellinen identiteetti 1902–1995*; Taideteollisen korkeakoulun julkaisusarja B 49, Helsinki 1996.
Kalha, Harri: 'Käsityön arkea ja tulen taidetta. Valentina Modig-Manuel – Suomalaisen studiokeraamikon tarina', retrospective exhibition at Galleria Septaria, 3–30 September 1994; Helsinki, 1994.
Modig-Manuel, Valentina: Letter to Arttu Brummer, Turku, 21 November 1939; archive of the University of Art and Design Helsinki.

Suna, Eija: 'Keramikern Valentina Modig-Manuel' in *ABOA*, Turku Provincial Museum yearbook, 1989–90.

RAKEL BÄCK-USVAALA, b. 1908
1 Lauri Kettunen changed his surname to Usvaala in the mid-1950s. In her ceramic work Rakel Bäck used the names Bäck-Kettunen and later Bäck-Usvaala.

SOURCES:
Telephone interview with Lena Serenius (daughter of Rakel Bäck-Usvaala), 2003.

Bibliography:
Chronicle of Rakel Bäck-Usvaala's life on the occasion of her fiftieth birthday, *Österbottningen* newspaper, 28 February 1958.
'Mx' (pseudonym): 'Keramikkonstnär blev antikvitetshandlare', *Vasabladet* newspaper, 14 December 1960.
'Varm familjeidyll i Kronoby: dekorationsmålare böjde sig, tjänar skulpterande Rachel', *Jakobstadstidningen* newspaper, 6 January 1957.

BIRGIT DYHR, b. 1908
1 Her largest order was seven hundred hand-pressed animal figures for Georg Jensen's design shop in New York.

SOURCES:
Several interviews with Birgit Dyhr. She also kindly let me use her artist album with photographs and newspaper clippings.
Aav, Marianne: 'Birgit Dyhr Skulpturer,' exhibition at the Design Museum, Helsinki, 15 October–3 November 1993.
Hellman, Åsa: 'Från sångfågel till keramiker', *Hufvudstadsbladet* newspaper, 14 April 2001.

AUNE SIIMES, b. 1909
1 These kinds of small clay sculptures were very popular in the 1930s. Ornamo's yearbook from 1936 depicts a bison and a sheep made by Aune Siimes.
2 Verbal information from Marjut Kumela, Director of the Arabia Museum.

SOURCES:
Archive of the Design Museum, Helsinki.
'Aune Siimes', *Saviseppo* magazine 3/1948.
Hellman, Åsa: 'Tidlöst porslin', *Hufvudstadsbladet* newspaper, 13 June 2000.
Kumela, Marjut: 'Taideosasto' in *Arabia*; Oy Wärtsilä Ab Arabia, Helsinki, 1987.
Nyman, Hannele: 'Aune Siimes – posliinin mestari,' exhibition at the Arabia Museum Gallery, 2000.
'Taiteilija Aune Siimes kuollut', obituary in *Uusi Suomi* newspaper, 13 November 1964.

HEIDI BLOMSTEDT, b. 1911
1 A visit to Ainola in 2003 revealed that the house contained countless unique ceramic items by Gerda Thesleff, Elin Juselius and Ellen Borenius.
2 For further information on Johan Grönroos the younger, see his presentation in this book.

SOURCES:
Verbal information from Juhana Blomstedt.
Archive of the Design Museum, Helsinki.
Visit to Ainola and study of the ceramics collection in the house.
Anttila, Elina: *Ainola*; National Board of Antiquities, Helsinki, 2003.
Lindqvist, Leena and Ojanen, Norman: *Taiteilijakoteja*; Otava, 1997.
Meri, Veijo: *Tuusulan rantatie*; 5th edition, Otava, 1997.
Rosenberg, Antti and Selin, Rauno: *Suur-Tuusulan historia III 1809–1924*; Municipality of Tuusula, 1995.

ROBERT HANCOCK, b. 1912
SOURCES:
Visits to Robert Hancock's studio in the late 1960s and in 2002.
Interviews with Kaja Hancock, Michael Hancock and Peter Winquist, 2002.
Arentz-Grastvedt, Mia: *Robert Hancock 1912–1993*, catalogue for memorial exhibition; Åland Art Museum, 1998.
Konstnären och hans musa, video; Ålands Videoproduktion, 1995.

MIRJAM STÄUBER, b. 1912
1 Interview with Peter Winquist, *Västra Nyland*, 25 February 1995.

SOURCES:
Study conducted by museum assistant Pirjo Juusela-Sarasmo for exhibition held at Ekenäs Museum, 1995.
Photographs from Ekenäs Museum. Facts and photographs from countless individuals, including Peter Winquist and Magdalena Holm.
'Minnesutställning', *Västra Nyland* newspaper, 10 November 1973.
'Mirjam Stäubers keramik ska nu dokumenteras', *Västra Nyland* newspaper, 25 February 1995.
'Mirjam Stäubers keramik ställs ut i Ekenäs', *Västra Nyland*, 3 October 1973.
'Till glädje för handen och ögat', *Västra Nyland*, 11 May 1995.

ANNIKKI HOVISAARI, b. 1913
1 Kumela 1987, pp. 110–112.
2 Thanks to this prize, Hovisaari was awarded her first solo exhibition at Wärtsilä Shop on Helsinki's Esplanadi. The favourable reviews written by Annikki Toikka-Karvonen in *Helsingin Sanomat* newspaper also had a positive effect.
3 In 2003 Annikki Hovisaari described how Kaj Franck had asked her to stay on at the art department, but she had chosen to retire due to back and shoulder problems. In her last years at Arabia she received help with throwing, but before then she had insisted on doing her own work at the wheel.

SOURCES:
Telephone interviews with Annikki Hovisaari, 2003.
Kumela, Marjut: 'Koriste-esineitä' in *Arabia*; Oy Wärtsilä Ab Arabia, Helsinki, 1987.
Keramik och glas. Arabia 100 år – jubileumsnummer 1973; Oy Wärtsilä Ab Arabia, 1973.
Vingedal, S. E.: *Porslinsmärken*; Forum, 2000.

BIRGER KAIPIAINEN, b. 1915
1 Interview with Professor Åke Hellman, fellow student of Kaipiainen.
2 During my summer traineeship at Arabia in 1972, I was invited to visit Birger Kaipiainen's studio a couple of times. Its creative atmosphere, lush plants and strong smell of various lustre blends remain fresh in my memory.

SOURCES:
Berg, Maria: *Kaipiainen*; Otava, 1986.
Enbom, Carla: 'Birger Kaipiainen – koristetaiturin salaisuus', *Glorian antiikki* magazine, autumn 2002.
Hellman, Åsa: 'Ornamentikens mästare', *Hufvudstadsbladet* newspaper, 16 September 2002.
Nyman, Hannele: 'Birger Kaipiainen – tarinoita astiaston takaa', *Astian tuntija* journal 3/2000.
Nyman, Hannele: 'Welcome to Paradise: the Works of Birger Kaipiainen', *Form Function* magazine 3–4/2000.
Peltonen, Kaarina: 'Birger Kaipiainen', exhibition at Retretti Art Centre and the Design Museum, Helsinki, 1990; Design Museum publication 32.

KYLLIKKI SALMENHAARA, b. 1915
1 Quote from Kyllikki Salmenhaara from the early 1970s, when I was a student of hers at the university's ceramics department.

SOURCES:
Artist archive of the Design Museum, Helsinki.
Kyllikki Salmenhaara's lectures at the University of Art and Design Helsinki from the 1970s.
Kyllikki Salmenhaara 1951–1981; Design Museum publication no. 20.
Parker-Fairbanks, Dixie and Abbott, Helen: *Essential Passions: Fairbanks/Salmenhaara Letters 1959–1986*; University of Washington Press, Seattle and London, 1999.
Salmenhaara Kyllikki: 'Unohdettu Savi', *Kotiteollisuus* magazine, issues 5–6/1971 and 1/1972.

RUT BRYK, b. 1916
1 Verbal information from Professor Åke Hellman.

Bibliography includes:
Kalha, Harri: *Muotopuolen merenneidon pauloissa. Suomen taideteollisuuden kultakausi: mielikuvat, markkinointi, diskurssit*; Finnish Historical Society, Design Museum, Helsinki, 1997.
Kumela, Marjut: *Rut Bryk (1916–1999) – Urval*, exhibition at the Arabia Museum Gallery, 2001.
Pallasmaa, Juhani (ed.): *Rut Bryk*, publication for retrospective exhibition organized at the Amos Anderson Art Museum and the Rovaniemi Art Museum; Frenckellska tryckeri AB, 1986.

TAISTO KAASINEN, b. 1918
SOURCES:
Artist archive of the Design Museum, Helsinki.
Arabia; Oy Wärtsilä Ab Arabia, Helsinki, 1987.
Keramik och glas. Arabia 100 år – jubileumsnummer; Oy Wärtsilä Ab Arabia, 1973.
Vingedal, S. E.: *Porslinsmärken*; Forum, 2000.

KUPITTAA (f. 1918)
1 Hätönen 2003.
2 Cf. Gusti Franzén's presentation in this book.
3 Gusti Franzén's letters to the factory's managing director Kalervo Koponen demonstrate Franzén's key position during the company's first ten years of operation.
4 The Franzén family owns at least two items designed by Gusti Franzén, serially produced in plaster moulds: a small figurine representing a dog, covered in a dark glaze, and a sculptural ashtray. There are also thrown items and a small slip-decorated vase marked 'Åbo 1 juni 1920 G F'.
5 Pfäffli 1994.
6 Kenyon 1982, pp. 253–54.
7 'En ortsindustri med anor och med kvalitetsproduktion', *Åbo Underrättelser*, 18 March 1937.

SOURCES:
Information related to Gusti Franzén's work at Kupittaa was mainly gathered from documents, letters, contracts, family albums, photographs and other items that have survived with some of his numerous nieces and nephews, including Bo-Gustaf Franzén, Gunnar Lindholm and Hedvig Järvinen. They have kindly let me use the materials and participated actively in my research work. I also studied examples of Kupittaa ceramics in several private collections. In addition, I wish to acknowledge the following sources:
Archive of the Helsinki University Library (original Kupittaa product catalogues), Brage press archive, archive of the University of Art and Design Helsinki, archive of the Design Museum, Helsinki.
Interview with Jorma Kivimäki, Salo, 2003.

Bibliography:
'En ortsindustri med anor och med kvalitetsproduktion. Kuppis Lerindustri hade 1936 en årsomsättning på 8 miljoner mark', *Åbo Underrättelser* newspaper, 18 March 1937.
Hätönen, Paula: 'Savesta saatiin leipä. Maalaamon iloiset tytöt loivat esineistä yksilöllisiä', *Turun Sanomat* newspaper weekly supplement, 22 February 2003.
Hyvönen, Heikki: *Suomalaista keramiikkaa*; WSOY, Porvoo, 1983.
Kalha, Harri: 'Keramik från Kupittaan Savi Oy. Huvuddragen i produktionens stilmässiga utveckling' in *ABOA*, Turku Provincial Museum yearbook 53–54/1989–1990.
Kenyon, Richard Allan: *A. W. Finch and the Emergence of Modern Ceramic Design in Finland*; Columbia University Teachers College, USA, 1982.
Martinkari, Jukka: 'Turun saviteollisuus jää nyt historiaan', *Helsingin Sanomat* newspaper (clipping related to bankruptcy of Kupittaan Savi, date unclear); archive of the Design Museum, Helsinki.
Mattson, Ulla: 'Intohimona Kupittaan Savi', *Turun Sanomat* newspaper weekly supplement, 22 February 2003.
Pakkanen, Helena: *Kupittaan Saviosakeyhtiön koriste- ja käyttökeramiikka 1950- ja 1960 luvuilla*, thesis; University of Turku, 2002.
Pfäffli, Heidi (ed.): *Wäinö Aaltonen 1894–1966*; Wäinö Aaltonen Museum publication no. 10/1994, Turku, 1994.

HILKKA-LIISA AHOLA, b. 1920
SOURCES:
Telephone interview with Hilkka-Liisa Ahola, 2003.
Artist archive of the Design Museum, Helsinki.
Arabia; Oy Wärtsilä Ab Arabia, Helsinki, 1987.
Vingedal, S. E.: *Porslinsmärken*; Forum, 2000.

VILJO MÄKINEN, b. 1920
1 Lindgren 1996, p. 137.
SOURCES:
Telephone interview with Sini-Meri Niinikoski (daughter of Viljo Mäkinen), 2003.
Lindgren, Liisa: *Elävä muoto. Traditio ja modernisuus 1940- ja 1950-luvun suomalaisessa kuvanveistossa*; Finnish National Gallery, Helsinki, 1996.
Viljo Mäkinen, catalogue for retrospective exhibition organized at the Turku Art Museum, 1980; Turun taideyhdistys, 1980.

SAKARI VAPAAVUORI, b. 1920
1 Lindgren 1996, pp. 135–139.
2 Kalha 1997, pp. 213–216.

SOURCES:
Artist archive of the Design Museum, Helsinki.

Arabia; Oy Wärtsilä Ab Arabia, Helsinki, 1987.
Lindgren, Liisa: *Elävä muoto. Traditio ja modernisuus 1940- ja 1950-luvun suomalaisessa kuvanveistossa*; Finnish National Gallery, Helsinki, 1996.
Kalha, Harri: *Muotopuolen merenneidon pauloissa*; Finnish Historical Society, Design Museum, 1997.

KARL-HEINZ SCHULTZ-KÖLN, b. 1921
1 *Ilta-Sanomat*, 15 February 1955.
SOURCES:
Artist archive of the Design Museum, Helsinki.
'B. L–der' (pseudonym): 'Schultz-Köln hos Wärtsilä', *Hufvudstadsbladet* newspaper, 20 February 1955.
'Seinäkoristeita, maljakkoja ja tupakkatölkkejä', *Ilta-Sanomat* newspaper, 15 February 1955.

MARJUKKA PÄÄKKÖNEN, b. 1923
1 Information gathered mainly from a telephone interview with Marjukka Pääkkönen, 2003.

SOURCES:
Turku Provincial Museum, artist archive of the Design Museum, Helsinki.
Telephone interview with Marjukka Pääkkönen, 22 October 2003.
Kalha, Harri: interview with Marjukka Pääkkönen, 6 October 1988; artist archive of the Design Museum, Helsinki.
Kalha, Harri: 'Keramik från Kupittaan Savi Oy' in *ABOA*, Turku Provincial Museum yearbook 53–54/1989–90.
'Taiteilija teollisuuden parissa', *Keski-Uusimaa* newspaper, 8 September 1953.

RAIJA TUUMI, b. 1923
1 Nyman, exhibition text, 2002.

SOURCES:
Artist archive of the Design Museum, Helsinki.
Hellman, Åsa: 'Kraftfullt och naturnära', *Hufvudstadsbladet* newspaper, 3 September 1973.
Hellman, Åsa: 'Kraftfulla lergrytor', *Hufvudstadsbladet*, 16 July 2002.
Kumela, Marjut: 'Taideosasto' in *Arabia*; Oy Wärtsilä Ab Arabia, Helsinki, 1987.
Nyman, Hannele: 'Raija Tuumi: Uncompromising Ceramist', *Form Function* magazine 87, 3/2002.
Nyman, Hannele: 'Raija Tuumi 1950–1974 Arabia', exhibition at the Arabia Museum Gallery, 2002.

MAIJA AALTONEN, b. 1924
SOURCES:
Interviews with Maija Aaltonen, 2002 and 2003.

LIISA HALLAMAA-WALDEN, b. 1925
SOURCES:
Telephone interview with Liisa Hallamaa-Walden, 2003.

Alamaan keramiikka ky, illustrated studio catalogue, 1970s.

Henttonen, Veli-Matti: '"Tuntematon" Liisa Hallamaa-Walden. Keraamikkojen aatelia', *Salon Seudun Sanomat* newspaper, 10 January 1991.

'Lera Linne Glas. Konsthantverk från Finland', exhibition at Galerie Plaisiren, 1979; Hässelby Castle, Nordic Culture Centre, Stockholm, 1979.

OKKI LAINE, b. 1925
1 Hätönen 2003.
2 A collection of thrown earthenware items by Okki Laine can be found at Vanhalinna Museum.

SOURCES:
Artist archive of the Design Museum, Helsinki, Turku Provincial Museum, Vanhalinna Museum.

Interview with Jorma Kivimäki and study of his private collection, Salo 2003.

Written introduction to Okki Laine's ceramics at Kupittaan Savi's booth at Turun Messut fair, 4–14 August 1961.

Hätönen, Paula: 'Maalaamon iloiset tytöt loivat esineistä yksilöllisiä', *Turun Sanomat* newspaper, 22 February 2003.

Pakkanen, Helena: *Kupittaan Saviosakeyhtiön koriste- ja käyttökeramiikka 1950- ja 1960-luvuilla*, thesis; University of Turku, 2002.

'Piquant: Okki Laine-Taiton keramiikkaa', *Hämeen Sanomat* newspaper, 19 July 1963.

DORRIT VON FIEANDT, b. 1927
SOURCES:
Interview with Dorrit von Fieandt, 2002.
Enbom, Carla: *Dorrit von Fieandt*; PunaMusta, Helsinki, 1991.

GUNVOR OLIN-GRÖNQVIST, b. 1928
SOURCES:
Kumela, Marjut: 'Taideosasto' and 'Koriste-esineitä' in *Arabia*; Oy Wärtsilä Ab Arabia, Helsinki, 1987.

Nyman, Hannele: 'GOG eli Gunvor-Olin Grönqvist', *Glorian Antiikki* magazine, autumn 2001.

MINNI LUKANDER, b. 1930
SOURCES:
Leppänen, Helena: *Pot Viapori 1972–1997*; Kustannus Pot Viapori ry, Helsinki, 1997.

Runeberg, Tutta: 'Muiston elementit', *Suomen Kuvalehti* magazine, 7 June 1985.

OIVA TOIKKA, b. 1931
SOURCES include:
Artist archive of the Design Museum, Helsinki.
Hellman, Åsa: 'Utmärkt med lera och pensel', *Hufvudstadsbladet* newspaper, 13 June 2001.

FRANCESCA MASCITTI LINDH, b. 1931
SOURCES:
Enbom, Carla: *Francesca Lindh Mascitti. 40 år med lera* [n.p./n.d.].

Hellman, Åsa: 'Rokokograciös keramik', *Hufvudstadsbladet* newspaper, 20 October 1971.

Hellman, Åsa: 'Trädgård i lera', *Hufvudstadsbladet*, 7 November 2001.

Kumela, Marjut: 'Taideosasto' in *Arabia*; Oy Wärtsilä Ab Arabia, Helsinki, 1987.

Nyman, Hannele: 'Francesca Mascitti Lindh and the Ceramic Touch', *Form Function* magazine 4/2001.

ANNA-MARIA OSIPOW, b. 1935
1 The 'En mä tiedä' exhibition at the Amos Anderson Art Museum in 1972 was one of the first cross-disciplinary exhibitions in Finland and showed artwork by Anna-Maria Osipow, Zoltan Popovits, Howard Smith and Olli Tamminen. (Cf. also Hellman, Åsa: 'Konst utan etikett', *Hufvudstadsbladet* newspaper, 5 April 1972.)

LIISA KURKI, b. 1936
SOURCES:
Interview with Eino Kurki, 2003.

HELJÄ LIUKKO-SUNDSTRÖM, b. 1938
Bibliography:
Heikkilä, Ritva and Pauloff, Marjatta: *Heljä Liukko-Sundström – Jalat maassa, pää pilvissä/Fötterna på jorden, huvudet i det blå/Feet on the Ground, Head in the Clouds*; Otava, Helsinki, 1993.

Nyman, Hannele: 'Heljä Liukko-Sundström – Sielujen Sillat', exhibition at the Arabia Museum Gallery, 1998.

PIIPPA TANDEFELT, b. 1939
1 Cf. the article 'The advent of small ceramic workshops in Finland'.
2 Information from telephone interview with Piippa Tandefelt. Her colleagues at Pot Viapori could clearly tell that Tandefelt lost her motivation to work after her period at Arabia. Many other factors contributed to her giving up ceramics altogether.

SOURCES:
Telephone interviews with Piippa Tandefelt, 2002 and 2003.

FUJIWO ISHIMOTO, b. 1941
SOURCES:
Enbom, Carla: *Matkalla Resan On the Road: Fujiwo Ishimoto*; Marimekko Oyj, 2001.

Nyman, Hannele: *Nietos Fujiwo Ishimoto Keramik*, exhibition at the Arabia Museum Gallery, 1999–2000.

RITVA TULONEN, b. 1941
SOURCES:
Hellman, Åsa: 'Lera och rep', *Hufvudstadsbladet* newspaper, 23 December 1971.

Valkonen, Anne: *Ritva Tulonen – maa, savi, hiljaisuus (Earth Clay Silence)*; G-Print, Helsinki, 1999.

LEENA LILJESTRÖM-PUNTANEN, b. 1941
1 In 1972–74, Leena Liljeström-Puntanen, Peter Winquist and Leena Mannila carried out a study of the professional status of ceramists in Finland (*Tutkimus keraamikkojen ammatillisesta asemasta ja keramiikan harrastustoiminnasta Suomessa*). The project was funded by a grant from Ornamo and has become an important source for further studies.

MARGARETA LÅNGHJELM, b. 1942
SOURCES:
Telephone interview with Margareta Långhjelm, 2003.

Artist archive of the Design Museum, Helsinki.

Smolander, Anja: 'Arabialainen Margareta Långhjelm', *Kuvastin* magazine 6/1971.

Steinby, Ann-Gerd: 'Ung keramiker använder äppel och lök som redskap', *Hufvudstadsbladet* newspaper, April 1971.

ELINA SORAINEN, b. 1943
1 Lukić 2002, p. 45.

SOURCES:
Flander, Brita and Sorainen, Elina (eds.): *Brita Flander Elina Sorainen*, exhibition catalogue, Helsinki, 1999.

Lukić, Tuula: 'Suhde Saveen', *Peilikuva – Spegelbild* journal 1/2002, Porvoon Kirjoittajat ry.

AIRI HORTLING, b. 1943
SOURCES:
Hellman Åsa: 'Verkstadskeramiker visar vad de kan', *Hufvudstadsbladet* newspaper, 28 April 1973.

Nyman, Hannele: *Airi Hortling – Kivinen maa*, exhibition in the Arabia Museum Gallery, 1997–98.

Svinhufvud, Leena (ed.): *Airi Hortling taiteilija-tutkija-opettaja. Keraamikon monet kasvot*, exhibition publication, Craft Museum of Finland, Jyväskylä, 1996.

LEA KLEMOLA, b. 1944
1 Cf. the presentation of Terhi Juurinen in this book.

INKERI LEIVO, b. 1944
SOURCES:
Artist archives of the Design Museum and of Arabia.

Telephone interview with Inkeri Leivo, 2003.

PAUL ENVALDS, b. 1945
1 Information gathered mainly from interview with Paul Envalds.
SOURCES:
Interview with Paul Envalds, 18 July 2002.

Kostiainen, Antti: 'Tyylilleen uskolliset Envaldsit', *Saviisi*, KeraPro Oy's customer magazine 1/2003.

Nyman, Hannele: *Paul Envalds. Keraamikko*, illustrated brochure made with Keramiikkastudio Envalds and Sinikka Envalds [n.p./n.d.].

TERHI JUURINEN, b. 1945
1 Cf. the article 'The advent of small ceramic
   workshops in Finland' and the presentations
   of Lea Klemola and Riitta Siira in this book.

SOURCES:
'Keramiikkaa puupoltosta pakkaukseen', exhi-
   bition at Pro Puu gallery, Lahti, 2002.
Strandman, Pia: 'Tea needs a soft shape', Form
   Function magazine 4/1992.

ULLA FOGELHOLM, b. 1945
1 Cf. the article 'The advent of small ceramic
   workshops in Finland'.

KARIN WIDNÄS, b. 1946
SOURCES:
Enbom, Carla: Konstruktio – Karin Widnäs
   Kaakelimuotoja, exhibition at the Arabia
   Museum Gallery, 2000.

KERTTU HORILA, b. 1946
1 Sundell, Dan: 'Notationer vid livets ström-
   fåra', Hufvudstadsbladet newspaper, 24
   August 2002.

ÅSA HELLMAN, b. 1947
1 Enbom, 1997.

SOURCES:
Enbom, Carla: 'Ur den grekiska gudavärlden',
   Hufvudstadsbladet newspaper, 20 February
   1997.
Helkama, Iris: 'Sukellus Välimereen', Helsingin
   Sanomat, 1 March 1997.
Sundell, Dan: 'Gudinnor i flott keramik', Huf-
   vudstadsbladet, 13 October 2001.
Von Knorring, Mirja: Pensselit padassa; Otava,
   2000.

KATI TUOMINEN-NIITTYLÄ, b. 1947
SOURCES:
Nyman, Hannele: 'Reflections on Objects, Form
   and Empty Space', Form Function magazine
   4/1998.
Nyman, Hannele (ed.): Kati Tuominen-Niittylä;
   Helsinki, 2001.

RIITTA SIIRA, b. 1948
1 Seenat is described in more detail in Terhi
   Juurinen's presentation and in the article
   'The advent of small ceramic workshops in
   Finland'.

TAPIO YLI-VIIKARI, b. 1948
1 Verbal information from Tapio Yli-Viikari.
SOURCES:
Leppänen, Helena (ed.): Ruukun runoutta ja
   materiaalin mystiikka; University of Art and
   Design Helsinki, Ilmari Design Publications, 2002.

OUTI LEINONEN, b. 1950
SOURCES:
Leinonen, Outi: Earth, water, fire, secret – Maa,
   vesi, tuli, salaisuus, brochure [n.p./n.d.].

Naumann, Joachim and Peltonen, Kaarina
   & Jarno (eds.): Junge Kunstszene Finnland
   Keramische Skulpturen und Installationen;
   Hetjens-Museum, Deutsches Keramikmu-
   seum Düsseldorf, 12 March–21 May 1995,
   Landesgewerbeamt Baden-Württemberg,
   Karlsruhe 15 September–18 October 1995;
   Düsseldorf, Germany.

ERNA AALTONEN, b. 1951
SOURCES:
Steffa, Tim: Erna Aaltonen; Tammer-Paino Oy,
   Tampere, 1997.

SAVITORPPA (f. 1951)
SOURCES:
Interview with Erkki Stenius, 2003.
Artell, Esko: 'Kullattujen päivien kimallus
   hiipumassa. Dreija pysähtyy Savitorpassa',
   Nurmijärven Extra Uutiset newspaper, 23
   March 1999.
'Klaukkalassa on kappale Suomen taidehistoriaa
   Savitorpan kullattu menestys'; Nurmijärven
   Extra Uutiset, 7 July 1996.
'Savitorpan Saul Nordqvist haikeana: Mikään
   ei voi jatkua ikuisesti', Nurmijärven Extra
   Uutiset, 20 June 1999.
Stenius, Erkki: Keramiikka-Ateljee Savitorppa
   (lyhyt historiikki) [n.p./n.d.].

ANNELI SAINIO, b. 1953
1 Paljakka, 2002.

SOURCES:
Huusko, Anna-Kaisa: 'Anneli Sainio – Bare
   Form, Sensitive Nuances', Form Function
   magazine 2/2002.
Paljakka, Anna: 'Anneli Sainio – Kohti valoa,'
   exhibition at the Arabia Museum Gallery,
   2002.

THE BERGLÖF COMPANY (f. c. 1954)
SOURCES:
Interview with Tor and Ilma Berglöf, 2003.
Berglöf, Tor: 'Lyhyt katsastus Berglöf'n kera-
   miikkaverstaan toiminnasta v. 1955–1985',
   photocopy, Porvoo, 1985.
Blom, Yvonne: Keramikverkstad Berglöfs verk-
   samhet åren 1954–1976 i Borgå, art-historical
   study; Åbo Akademi University, 1976.
Rämö, Marjo: 'Tor ja Ilma Berglöf ovat teh-
   neet keramiikkaa 50 vuotta. Ensimmäisten
   töiden savi nousi omasta pellosta', Uusimaa
   newspaper, 16 August 2003.

JOHANNA RYTKÖLÄ, b. 1956
SOURCES:
Johanna Rytkölä, brochure; Helsinki, 1999.

SRBA LUKIĆ, b. 1957
1 Porvoo was home to the famous ceramics
   factory AB Iris, established in 1897 by the
   Belgian A. W. Finch. For further information see the presentation of A. W. Finch in
   this book.

2 Several ceramics exhibitions were organized
   in conjunction with the Iris seminars; the
   Iris Collection consists of works donated by
   the participants. Plans were afoot to establish a ceramics museum in Porvoo.

ELISA ISONIEMI, b. 1960
SOURCES:
Isoniemi, Eliisa and Mäkelä, Maarit (eds.):
   Kuuma Linja; NewMediaCenter/Taik, Media-
   laboratorio, Helsinki, 1998.

PEKKA PAIKKARI, b. 1960
SOURCES:
Verbal information from Pekka Paikkari.
Römiger-Czako, Ritva: 'Pekka Paikkari, Monu-
   mentales und Serielles/Monumental and
   Serial', exhibition at the Hetjens Museum,
   Düsseldorf, 2001.

PAULA BLÅFIELD, b. 1960
SOURCES:
Telephone interview with Paula Blåfield, 2004.
Blåfield, Paula: Paula Blåfield. Muisti. Minne,
   exhibition catalogue, Vaasa City Art Gallery,
   2001.
Blåfield, Paula: Paula Blåfield Transformation,
   exhibition catalogue, Vaasa, 2000.

KRISTINA RISKA, b. 1960
SOURCES:
Kalin, Kaj: 'Hauras aika', exhibition at the
   Arabia Museum Gallery, 1987.

KIM SIMONSSON, b. 1974
SOURCES:
Interview with Kim Simonsson, 2003.

*Facts about contemporary ceramists are based on
information received from the artists themselves.*

PHOTOGRAPHY CREDITS

Museums, archives and collections
American Craft Museum, New York
Arabia Museum, Helsinki
Arabia Art Department, Helsinki
Emil Cedercreutz Museum, Harjavalta
Helsinki City Art Museum, Helsinki
K. H. Renlund Museum, Kokkola
Kyösti Kakkonen Collection
Otava picture archive, Helsinki
Porvoo Museum, Porvoo
Pot Viapori ry, Helsinki
Collection of the Turku Provincial Museum, Turku
Vanhalinna Museum, Lieto
Yrjö A. Jäntti Collection, Porvoo
Åland Museum, Mariehamn

Private collections
Raili Aaltio, Sigrid af Forselles's estate, Franzén family, Maija Grotell's estate,
Ritva Karpio, Terttu Lemström, Sini-Meri Niinikoski, Lena Serenius,
Yvonne Tigerstedt-Suonne, Auli Urrila-Stenbäck, Wilskman family, Maaru Wirkkala,
other private collections, artists' collections

Other sources
Die Kunst magazine 1910, Ornamo yearbook 1933, Ornamo's 25th anniversary
publication 1936, University of Art and Design annual reports 1939–41

PHOTOGRAPHERS

Project photographer: Johnny Korkman

Other photographers: Terho Aalto, Atelier Apollo, Antti Bengts, Jaap Borgers, Maja Eklöf,
Felix Forsman, Kimmo Friman, Katja Hagelstam, Kari Hakli, Åsa Hellman, Eva Heyd,
Kari Holopainen, Pasi Hornamo, HS-lehtikuva, Malla Hukkanen, Juha Ilvas, Indav,
Mainos-Valokuvaamo Iquistus, Rita Jokiranta, Jukka-Pekka Juvonen, Matti Järvi,
Ilari Järvinen, Jouko Järvinen, Martti Kapanen, Kari-Kuva, Timo Kauppila,
Arto Keskinen, Ilmari Kostiainen, Jan Lindroth, Toivo Lumme, Jorma Marstio,
Augusto Mendes, Museokuva, Gero Mylius, Pertti Nisonen, Ulla Paakkunainen,
Jussi Peltola, Juha Perämäki, Pietinen (studio), Ana Pullinen, Pertti Rikkilä,
Hanna Rikkonen, Seilo Ristimäki, K.-G. Roos, Kristian Runeberg, Nanna Salmi,
Simo Salmi, Raija Siikamäki, Yrjö Sotamaa, Starfoto Oy, Studio Jaakko Ojala,
Osmo Thiel, Jussi Tiainen, Rauno Träskelin, Auli Urrila-Stenbäck, Tapio Väinölä,
Erkki Valli-Jaakola, K. Victorzon, Sakari Viika, Tuomo-Juhani Vuorenmaa,
Lasse Wallenius, Julia Weckman, Ture Westberg, Winfrid Zakowski and the artists.

AUTHORS

Åsa Hellman has a broad background in the arts. Having studied art history at the University of Helsinki, she moved to the ceramics department of the University of Art and Design Helsinki, from which she graduated in 1973. She continued her studies at the University of Belgrade, 1973–74, and the Royal College of Art in London, 1978–79. Alongside her work as a ceramic artist she has been a part-time teacher at the University of Art and Design and has reported on art exhibitions and events for *Hufvudstadsbladet* and other newspapers and magazines. She has a studio in her home town of Porvoo, and her works are included in many renowned international collections.

Ceramist **Airi Hortling** has a Licentiate in Art and Design and is a senior lecturer in the ceramics and glass degree programme of the School of Design at the University of Art and Design Helsinki. Although she has participated in many significant exhibitions, she regards teaching and nurturing a new generation of ceramists as her main occupation. She has also carried out research into new aesthetic applications of ceramic materials and practices, and has presented international conference papers on the innovative use of Finnish raw materials and natural minerals in ceramics.

Harri Kalha, PhD, is a Senior Lecturer at the University of Helsinki, where he is a member of a research collegium in visual culture. He has published extensively in the fields of the history of design, the visual arts and gender theory. His research career nevertheless originated in the field of ceramics. His study *Ruukuntekijästä multimediataiteilijaan* '(The Making of the Modern Finnish Potter'), was published in 1996 and his work on design history includes a PhD dissertation on the post-war Finnish design phenomenon (1997) and books on Toini Muona (1998), Ralf Forsström (1999), Nanny Still (2001) and Eero Aarnio (2003).

Johnny Korkman established his own photographic studio in 1978 and has since then specialized in photographing design products, arts, crafts, architecture and theatre. He has been involved in numerous large-scale book projects, including *Esineitä ympärillämme* ('Objects around us', Otava, 1981) and *Tiloja elämää varten* ('Spaces for life', VVO, 1998). Among his many clients are the Design Museum, the Finnish National Theatre, Grafia ry, the Friends of Finnish Handicraft and the Academy of Finland, as well as many individual artists.

Marjut Kumela has been director of the Arabia Museum since 1984, having previously been head of public relations for the Nuutajärvi glassworks and curator at the Finnish Glass Museum. She was the editor of the notable book *Arabia* about the Arabia company's history and has written numerous magazine articles on Finnish ceramics and glass. She has designed and curated exhibitions on these topics and on the history of cutlery for the Arabia Museum Gallery and other museums. She has also produced exhibition catalogues on the work of Toini Muona and Kurt Ekholm.

Architect **Esa Laaksonen** was appointed the first director of the Alvar Aalto Academy in 1999. With Kimmo Friman and Sari Nieminen, Laaksonen heads the architectural firm Arkkitehdit FLN Oy in Helsinki. He has previously been an assistant in the Department of Architecture at the Helsinki University of Technology, a visiting professor at several institutions in the United States and Australia, editor in chief of *Arkkitehti* magazine, resident artist for the province of Uusimaa and head of the exhibitions office at the Museum of Finnish Architecture. He has written widely on the subject of architecture and has been a regular columnist for *Helsingin Sanomat* newspaper since 2001.

Hannele Nyman is an exhibition curator and expert adviser to the Arabia Museum and Gallery. A prolific writer on the industrial arts, she specializes in ceramics as well as photographic editing. She contributed to *Muovikirja – arkitavaraa ja design-esineitä* ('The Book of Plastics: Everyday Ware and Design Products', WSOY, 2004), was the photographic editor for *Ateneum maskerad – Taideteollisuuden muotoja ja murroksia* ('The Atheneum in Disguise: Forms and Transitions in the Industrial Arts', UIAH, 2000), and has contributed to *Form Function Finland magazine* since 1998.

Jennifer Hawkins Opie is senior curator and head of the Ceramics & Glass Collection at the Victoria and Albert Museum, specializing in the nineteenth and twentieth centuries and in contemporary work. She was sole curator for the exhibition 'Scandinavian Ceramics & Glass in the 20th century', and was responsible for the related publication. She has contributed to many other exhibitions and the accompanying books, most recently *Art Nouveau 1890–1914* and *Art Deco*.